AF615028

World Christianity as Public Religion

World Christianity as Public Religion

RAIMUNDO C. BARRETO JR.,
RONALDO CAVALCANTE, AND
WANDERLEY P. DA ROSA

FORTRESS PRESS
MINNEAPOLIS

WORLD CHRISTIANITY AS PUBLIC RELIGION

Copyright © 2017 Fortress Press. All rights reserved. Except for brief quotations in critical articles or reviews, no part of this book may be reproduced in any manner without prior written permission from the publisher. Email copyright@1517.media or write to Permissions, Fortress Press, PO Box 1209, Minneapolis, MN 55440-1209.

Cover image: Thinkstock 2017 / Crowd of Christians from Ablestock.com.
Cover design: Alisha Lofgren

Print ISBN: 978-1-5064-3371-4
eBook ISBN: 978-1-5064-3372-1

The paper used in this publication meets the minimum requirements of American National Standard for Information Sciences — Permanence of Paper for Printed Library Materials, ANSI Z329.48-1984.

Manufactured in the U.S.A.

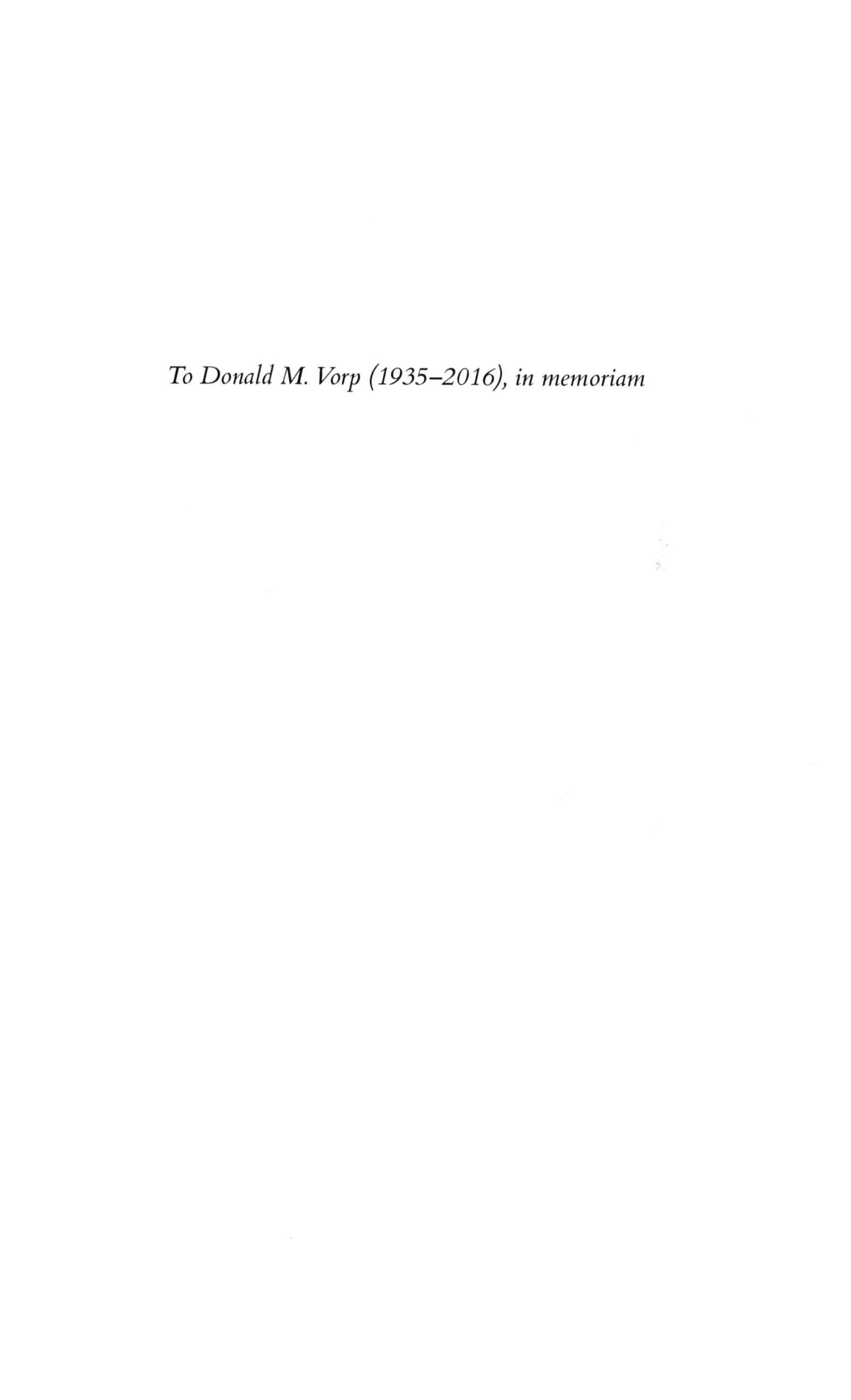

To Donald M. Vorp (1935–2016), in memoriam

Contents

Acknowledgments

As all academic projects, this book, the first volume of the World Christianity and Public Religion series, is the result of the work and collaboration involving a number of people and institutions. We are grateful to the many minds and hands that have made it possible, although we cannot name all of them.

We owe a great debt to Faculdade Unida de Vitoria, through its president, Wanderley Pereira da Rosa, and its publisher, Editora Unida, for the publication of a bilingual version of this book in Brazil (2016), in partnership with Princeton Theological Seminary. Princeton Theological Seminary's president, Craig Barnes, and its dean of academic affairs, James Kay, have unabatingly supported this project from its inception. Because of their firm commitment to it, Princeton Seminary has sponsored its translation. Several chapters of this book were originally written in Portuguese, whereas all contributions made originally in English have also been translated into Portuguese for the version published in Brazil.

We are particularly grateful to our ten authors, named accordingly in their respective chapters, who notwithstanding their busy schedules, made themselves available to participate in this book, providing outstanding contributions in a relatively short time. The result of their dedication to this project can be found in the pages that follow.

Considering the bilingual character of this work and the strenuous effort to translate essays from Portuguese into English and vice versa, on top of painstaking proofreading, we would like to express special thanks to our translator, Saulo Adriano, and to Melissa Martin, editorial assistant to Professor Raimundo Barreto, who read the English manuscript a number of times, offering inestimable suggestions that have enriched its final result.

Last but not least, we are deeply indebted to Will Bergkamp and Jesudas Athyal at Fortress Press. On top of their editorial excellence, their interest in facilitating cross- and intercultural exchange in their publications and their keen understanding of the shifts taking place in world Christianity have been crucial to make this series available to a larger readership in the English-speaking world.

Everyone involved in this project spent dozens of hours to get it done. Our earnest thanks to all of you!

Foreword

Princeton Theological Seminary is honored to join with the Faculdade Unida de Vitoria in supporting the launch of this first volume in the Fortress Press series World Christianity and Global Religion. Historically speaking, it is difficult to imagine either the phenomenon or the emerging academic field of world Christianity without the nineteenth-century missionary movement fueled by such student fervor at the colleges, universities, and seminaries of the early American republic, including Princeton. Out of this movement, ecumenical partnerships across Protestant denominations were forged, and the study of world religions arose in order to translate the Christian message into the idioms and vernaculars of diverse cultures. In 1936, with the coming of missionary educator John Alexander Mackay (1889–1983) as president of Princeton Theological Seminary, missions, ecumenics, and history of religions became recognized as integrally related areas of academic inquiry and were seen as intrinsically interdisciplinary. Taken together, they have been featured in the seminary's curriculum for the better part of a century.

More recently, Dale Irvin reminds us that, "As a field of study World Christianity has its historical roots in the disciplines of missions, ecumenics, and world religions. It continues to pursue a threefold conversation, across borders of culture (historically the domain of mission studies), across borders of confession or communion (historically the domain of ecumenics), and across borders with other religious faiths (historically the domain of world religions)."[1] Significantly, Irvin's metaphor of "conversation" fittingly replaces the

1. Dale Irvin, "World Christianity: An Introduction," *Journal of World Christianity* 1, no. 1 (2008): 2.

language of crusade or conquest, which too often infused Euro-American missionary labors in Africa, Asia, and South America in the heyday of colonialism and imperial expansion. Today, vibrant churches on these continents are reflecting boldly and widely on the Christian message from their distinctive contexts, and today, through immigration, these same churches are planting their communities and networks throughout the world, including Europe and North America. In this way, they are already having an impact on formerly "established" churches and enriching the ecumenical and intercultural scope of theological education and ministerial formation.

What we are all learning in the process, and what the essays in this volume clearly announce, is that Christianity is "not one thing." As genuine partnerships replace patterns of paternalism, Princeton Theological Seminary welcomes the opportunity to join with Faculdade Unida and Fortress Press in amplifying for English-language readers the voices of those on the frontiers of World Christianity. Through them, may we "listen to what the Spirit is saying to the churches." Paradoxically, through these new inflections—which yesterday's missioners could scarcely imagine—we can know and give thanks that in the Lord their labor was not in vain.

James F. Kay

Preface

The World Christianity and Public Religion Series

RAIMUNDO C. BARRETO JR., SERIES EDITOR

During the latter half of the twentieth century, Christianity became truly worldwide, polycentric, and culturally diverse. For the first time in almost a thousand years, there are more Christians living in the Global South than in the Global North. In 1910, 66 percent of all Christians lived in Europe; now 61 percent live in Asia, Africa, and Latin America. Projections suggest this trend will continue and that it will be more pronounced in coming decades.

A number of books have been written in an attempt to offer clues on how these drastic demographic changes affect the shape Christianity will take in the coming decades. Beyond the fascination with the exciting numbers, one might notice that as Christianity rapidly spreads in the Global South and its diaspora, the rise of a new world Christian consciousness brings along deep cultural, social, and economic consequences, which demand further scholarly attention. In regard to the cultural sphere, it is worth stressing that as more people around the world have access to the gospel in their own languages, they are embracing Christianity in their own terms, giving it different cultural flavors. Christianity can no longer be dominantly conceived from a Western perspective. The modern missionary age is behind us. We have stepped across the threshold of a new era. As Lamin Sanneh has highlighted, in the era of world Christianity, the appropriation of faith by different indigenous Christian communities is favored over "external transmission."[1] New and creative

1. Lamin Sanneh, *Whose Religion Is Christianity? The Gospel Beyond the West* (Grand Rapids: Eerdmans, 2003), 10–11.

theological insights are emerging out of those contexts. Conversions to Christianity, especially in former Western colonies, have not coincided with westernization as some missionaries expected. As popular Catholicism in Latin America has shown, the indigenization of Christian images and symbols has created living signs that indigenous cultures and their spiritualities remain alive. Christianity has often changed in the encounter with world cultures and religions, a phenomenon that continues to happen as more and more indigenous cultures in the Global South became the new Christian milieu. Evangelization has never been a one-way process. This series engages some of the voices emerging within indigenous Christianities around the world, paying attention to their theological questions, reflections, and articulations.

While in the past five centuries, Christianity's most immediate surrounding environment was highly influenced by Western dominance and its priorities (like the long debate around secularization), world Christianity exists primarily in a context of religious pluralism, which necessarily puts it in relationship with other world religions. In fact, from its inception, Christianity has always been shaped by its encounter with other religions. No religion is hermetically sealed. Such reality, increasingly common also in the West, due to the way globalization and numerous migration waves have brought different peoples and cultures face-to-face with one another, gives rise to a growing demand for studies that take seriously intercultural communication, intercultural theologies, and interfaith dialogue. Likewise, there has been a growing interest in issues such as hybridity, liminality, border thinking, the search for contact zones, and intercultural interweaving—particularly in the context of formerly colonized cultures and within the Christianities emerging in those places.

Old problems still linger. Scientific and technological advances have not reduced existing injustices. Rather, many of them have worsened. Socioeconomic injustice is as fiercely prevalent as when the first theologies of liberation emerged in the 1960s. According to Indian theologian Felix Wilfred, the demographic shift of world Christianity is not simply a shift "from the West to the South, but a shift of Christianity from the rich and middle classes to the poor." In other words, "those with below $500 as annual income are the ones who will be, if not already, the most numerous Christian disciples in our world."[2]

In a context of such an economic disparity, there is a moral demand on Christians around the world, which cannot be overlooked. Standing in solidarity with the poor is extremely important. Yet it is not enough. Christians emerging in contexts of poverty and injustice in different parts of the world have been asking challenging and complex questions about the reasons for such inequality. The persistence of mass migration, particularly from poorer parts of the world to the most affluent regions, and the grave problems related to the inhuman treatment that many migrants, refugees, asylum seekers, and stateless persons receive when crossing borders are examples of how structural injustices are knocking at every door, requiring renewed moral commitments and creative responses to what is amounting to a global human calamity. Likewise, unjust relations based on race, gender, and sexuality, along with important land-related disputes and environmental concerns, are part of the public agenda Christians are called to engage in both the Global North and South.

World Christianity has a public face, voice, and reason. Christians from the Global South and its diaspora increasingly participate in and have an impact on what has been known in the West as the public square, even if that notion has particular nuances in different contexts. As they do that, they produce new perspectives on the role of religion in public life and an array of approaches on issues related to citizenship, public witness, peace, justice, environmental relations, and contemporary migration.

This series, which stems from a partnership between Princeton Theological Seminary and Faculdade Unida, aims to provide a unique space for sustained dialogue on all those issues. It blends methods and approaches from the emerging field of world Christianity, in conversation with other fields of study, including studies on the public role of religion and on religious reasoning in the public sphere, postcolonial/decolonial theories, intercultural studies, migration studies, social ethics, and globalization theories. The series intentionally brings religious scholars and theologians from varied Christian traditions and countries into conversation with one another. At its birth lie two schools from the Reformed tradition, one in South America

2. Felix Wilfred, "Christianity between Decline and Resurgence," in *Christianity in Crisis?*, ed. Jon Sobrino and Felix Wilfred, *Concilium* 3 (2005): 27–37 (31).

and the other in North America. One is young, and the other has a tradition spanning more than 200 years.

In the first half of the twentieth century, Princeton Seminary appointed John Mackay as president after he lived for years as a missionary in Latin America, a period that deeply influenced him. Mackay himself, by turning ecumenism into a mandatory field of study for the church in the twentieth century (as the founder of the field of ecumenics), anticipated the emergence of the field we know today as world Christianity: "a new reality has come to birth. For the first time in the life of mankind the Community of Christ, the Christian Church, can be found, albeit in nuclear form, in the remotest frontiers of human habitation. This community has thereby become 'ecumenical' in the primitive, geographical meaning of that term. History is thus confronted with a new fact."[3]

In turn, Faculdade Unida has a history marked by a commitment to the retrieval of a particular memory. Such memory is linked to theologians such as Richard Shaull and Rubem Alves. Shaull was a pioneer who encouraged young Latin-American Christians such as Rubem Alves, Jovelino Ramos, João Dias de Araújo, Joaquim Beato, Beatriz Melano, and others to think theologically from their own social and cultural location, that is, as Latin-American Protestants. He also encouraged ecumenical solidarity, and contributed to the rise of liberation theology in Brazil. Shaull's pupil Rubem Alves wrote the first book-length treatise on liberation theology,[4] while living in exile in the United States. He was one of the most creative thinkers of his days, having also contributed to the rising interest in emerging fields such as theopoetics.

This series is, therefore, deeply rooted in a long tradition, which is renewed by the circumstances of a new era. It enables a dialogue that places priority on voices from the Global South but invites participants from the old centers of modern Christianity, in Europe and North America, to engage with their peers from the South. Although it arose in the context of those schools, participants from several schools in Latin America, the Caribbean, Africa, Asia-Pacific, Europe and North America are invited to provide contributions.

3. John Mackay, *Ecumenics: The Science of the Church Universal* (Englewood Cliffs, NJ: Prentice-Hall, 1964), vii.

4. Rubem Alves, "Towards a Theology of Liberation: An Exploration of the Encounter between the Languages of Humanistic Messianism and Messianic Humanism" (PhD diss., Princeton Theological Seminary, 1968).

The series is published in English and Portuguese. Its bilingual nature garners an inclusionary approach. A variety of texts originally produced in Portuguese, which otherwise wouldn't be available to English readers, will now be accessible in the anglophonic world. Similarly, the work of authors known in the English-speaking world who had previously been unexplored in studies on religion and theology among scholars working in Portuguese or Spanish in Latin America, are engaged in this dialogue, becoming more easily available for Latin American readers. Above all, we show that it is possible to promote this type of transnational and transcultural dialogue without placing priority on one language as lingua franca.

The first volume stresses world Christianity as a form of public religion, identifying areas for possible intercultural engagement. The following volumes will focus on more specific topics, which make up a public agenda for world Christianity in the twenty-first century. The subjects of subsequent volumes include: World Christianity and Migration; World Christianity, Urbanization, and Identity; World Christianity and Interfaith Relations; The Environment through the Lenses of World Christianity; and World Christian Perspectives on Race, Ethnic Conflicts, and Gender and Sexuality.

It is our hope that this series will also serve as a new platform to enable an intergenerational dialogue by creating opportunities for greater interaction between established scholars and emerging writers, especially from the Global South and its diaspora.

Introduction

World Christianity as Public Religion

RAIMUNDO C. BARRETO JR.

This is a book about the public nature of religion in world perspective. It is not confined to the emerging field of public theology. Instead, it assumes that there is a public reality where public theology emerges. In an important study of Latin American liberation theology, Brazilian-French scholar Michael Lowy distinguished between liberation theology as a body of literature and the milieu in which it was formed, i.e., the broad network of social movements whose praxis gave birth to liberation theology. He called that broader movement "liberationist Christianity."[1] According to him, liberationist Christianity preexists liberation theology. The latter is the spiritual product of the former. I would like to use a similar analogy to explain our choice for public religion instead of public theology as the focus of this book. In this book, public religion and public theology are intrinsically connected. The qualifier "public" broadly refers to the "inescapable sociality" of both religion and theology.[2] Speaking in terms of a minimalist definition of public theology, Mark L. Taylor calls attention to the fact that all theologizing is inscribed in a field that is social and intersubjective. In that sense, theology and religion are inescapably public.

The need to qualify religion as public emerged in the context of the Western theories of secularization, which in some of its versions

1. Michael Lowy, *The War of Gods: Religion and Politics in Latin America* (London: Verso, 1996), 32–33.

2. Mark L. Taylor, "Duas Palestras Sobre Teologia Publica," in *Religiao e Sociedade (Pos)Secular*, ed. Wanderley Pereira da Rosa and Osvaldo Luiz Ribeiro (Santo Andre, Brazil: Editora Unida, 2014), 149–78 (152).

prescribed a private place and role to religion in modern democratic societies.[3] In contrast to that prescribed private role, Spanish sociologist Jose Casanova, in his classic *Public Religions in the Modern World*,[4] identified the phenomenon of the deprivatization of religion "as a global trend."[5] Since then, that case for the publicness of the diverse religions of the world not only has been confirmed but has also become almost self-evident. In fact, in non-Western contexts, religion has always played an important role in the fabric of society, including its public and political dimensions.

In the Global South, Latin America is probably the most emblematic case, although not the only one, in which secularization was also discussed in terms of the privatization of religion. That was the case particularly in the postcolonial era, as the Latin American modern states sought to affirm their autonomy against the background of the central role the Catholic Church played in Latin American colonial societies. Even in that context, attempts to drive religion to the private sphere repeatedly failed. The *cristero* rebellion in the 1920s in Mexico is one of the many examples of how liberal governments, with very few exceptions, had to reach a compromise to stay in power in a very religious environment. Latin American Catholicism remained influential. It never accepted the private role secular governments tried to prescribe to religion. The most successful form of Protestantism in the region, Pentecostalism, also has proved to have a clear public vocation.

Although public theology is a concern in some chapters of this book, it is mostly understood in the context of that "inescapable sociality" mentioned by Taylor. Such an approach prevents the hegemonic and elitist views of public theology formed in the West and sponsored by Western institutions from taking center stage, leading to the neglect of other forms of public theologizing, especially those labeled "contextual theologies."

As its title indicates, this book focuses particularly on world Christianity. As a new field of studies, world Christianity has uniquely contributed to the understanding of Christianity as a world religion.

3. Jose Casanova, "Rethinking Public Religions," in *Rethinking Religion and World Affairs*, ed. Timothy Samuel Shah, Alfred Stepan, and Monica Duffy Toft (Oxford: Oxford University Press, 2012), 25–35 (25).

4. Jose Casanova, *Public Religions in the Modern World* (Chicago: University of Chicago Press, 1994).

5. Ibid., 25.

In other words, it has reversed a trend that was dominant in the North Atlantic academy to interpret Christianity through Western lenses. Priority is given to emerging Christianities in the Global South, although not to the exclusion of the Christianities of the North, particularly in light of the fact that through migration and globalization, the interaction between North and South, and between East and West, have significantly increased. Whereas one cannot ignore socioeconomic, ethnic, and political divides, the constant movement of peoples, ideas, and cultures has blurred many of the borders in the present world. Some of the most vibrant Christianities in Europe and North America, for instance, have their origins in the South. Today, the flux of Christian missionaries is no longer unidirectional. Lay and ordained missionaries are moving from the South to the North, on top of vivid South-South interactions.

As it pays attention to those multidirectional fluxes and interactions, this book is an exercise in intercultural communication. It brings together culturally different subjects, women and men from four continents and a number of Christian traditions, to reflect on the meaning of world Christianity in the societies where they are inserted. The authors represent different areas of expertise. Some of them are theologians. Others are religious scholars in conversation with theories of communication, history, social theories, migration studies, post-/decolonial theories, human rights, and globalization theories. As representative of intercultural conversations, this book highlights an emerging expression of ecumenical concerns, which understands that the barriers to be overcome in the twenty-first century are not necessarily confessional in nature but increasingly involve socioeconomic, cultural, and ideological motifs. It is in this context that world Christianity emerges as a field, challenging old conventions and offering new language and tools to enlarge the understanding of the diverse Christian expressions in the world and the relationships among them.

In contrast to the way Christianity was predominantly studied in the modern era, world Christianity challenges the habitually silent assumption of a monocentric Christianity, expanding from its heartlands—Europe and more recently North America—to the margins, namely, Asia, Africa, and Latin America. According to that modern worldview, Christian history and mission were split. The growth of Christianity in other parts of the world (the so-called third world or

Global South) tended to be perceived in light of the work of Western missionaries.

The modern ecumenical movement emerged in this context, taking a further step. It recognized that the presence of Christianity on all continents called for an undivided approach, which for some ecumenists demanded the creation of a new discipline. Consequently, the discipline of ecumenics resulted from an attempt to heal that modern dichotomy by placing emphasis on the universal nature of the church.[6] That golden age of ecumenical Christianity, though, did not last long. New crises and splits emerged in the last quarter of the twentieth century.[7] The nature of religious difference and conflict has drastically changed in the past century. In this context, there is a demand for new ecumenical reflections and new ecumenical epistemologies.

Following the tragedy of two world wars, a generalized aspiration for a global order that would prevent such barbaric events from happening again captured the imagination of many thinkers and political leaders. The creation of the United Nations, the adoption of the Universal Declaration of Human Rights (UDHR), and—one could add—the creation of the World Council of Churches symbolized the hope that an era of greater internationalization with renewed attention to human dignity was about to emerge. Such dreams, however, were shattered not only by the shadow of the emerging Cold War but also by the increasing suspicion that the concerns with universal rights, for instance, would be used as a pretext for stronger nations to impose their political and economic interests upon the weaker ones.[8] In the realm of the international human rights movement, the universal claims of the UDHR began to be questioned. Similarly, in the ecumenical movement, also part of the emerging international ethos of the era, questions were raised about whose voices and interests prevailed in ecumenical institutions represented in the ecumenical

6. John Mackay created the first chair of ecumenics in the United States at Princeton Theological Seminary and articulated the rationale of this new discipline in a classic book in 1964. See John Mackay, *Ecumenics: The Science of the Church Universal* (Englewood Cliffs, NJ: Prentice-Hall, 1964).

7. See, for instance, Michael Kinnamon, *Can a Renewal Movement Be Renewed? Questions for the Future of Ecumenism* (Grand Rapids: Eerdmans, 2014); and Wesley Granberg-Michaelson, *From Times Square to Timbuktu: The Post-Christian West Meets the Non-Western Church* (Grand Rapids: Eerdmans, 2013).

8. For a lively narrative of the events leading to the formation and adoption of the Universal Declaration of Human Rights, see Mary Ann Glendon, *A World Made New: Eleanor Roosevelt and the Universal Declaration of Human Rights* (New York: Random House, 2001).

movement and whose voices were missing or overlooked on that universal table.

The suspicion of neocolonialism fueled the liberation and postcolonial movements that emerged in the final decades of the past century. In spite of that justifiable suspicion, ecumenical and intercultural initiatives toward mutual understanding and dialogue persisted amid intensifying awareness of differences and power relations. In such a context, world Christianity emerges as a renewed form of ecumenicity, advancing new language and new forms of dialogue. As such, world Christianity seeks to continue the work that ecumenics and mission studies sought to accomplish in the modern era.

Ecumenics and mission have not provided sufficient epistemological renewal to overcome the split between "the West and the rest."[9] World Christianity takes mission and ecumenics seriously, in addition to challenging some of the modern dualisms. By putting greater emphasis on indigenous Christianities, the field of world Christianity invites new voices and new ways of living and knowing into ecumenical fellowship.

Similarly, Western understandings of public and private are also challenged. Going beyond Casanova's understanding that religion has rebelled against the privatized role attributed to it in the West, non-Western cultures do not always acknowledge such a clear-cut division between public and private. Such a division has commonly legitimized patriarchal and colonial notions of gender and racial superiority. Because of this, it needs to be revisited and in some cases challenged.

This book advances an intercultural conversation on the public nature of world Christianity. The public realm highlighted in most essays is that of the civil society, which both Jose Casanova and Jürgen Harbermas have described as a "free space in which antisystemic and countercultural discourses and organizations can flourish and, under certain circumstances, have an impact upon the political establishment."[10]

9. An expression that conveys the assumption of Western superiority in relation to the rest of the world, as epitomized by Niall Ferguson's bestseller *Civilization: The West and the Rest* (New York: Penguin, 2011).

10. Matthew R. Wood, "Public Religions and Civil Society: The Case of London Methodism," *Fieldwork in Religion* 1, no. 3 (2005): 235–51 (238).

A few common threads run throughout the following chapters:

- In the emerging-world Christian era, all contexts matter, and all narratives and theologies are contextual. Thus, in her contribution from Germany (chapter 7), Uta Andrée expresses her surprise when she was asked to offer a contextual perspective from the Global North, "because usually when we think about contextual research, it is concerning specific topics of theologies from the Global South." This book assumes the contextual nature of all narratives, regardless of possible "global designs."[11]
- We agree with Lamin Sanneh's view that "World Christianity is not one thing, but a variety of indigenous responses through more or less local idioms, but in any case without necessarily the European Enlightenment frame."[12] There is a need to expand the corpus of Christianity by excavating less elaborated-upon expressions of Christianity engendered everywhere in the world. This collection of essays hopes to be a contribution in that direction.
- In spite of the contextual nature of each contribution, the diverse authors of this book also show deep awareness of what Martin Luther King called a "world perspective."[13] At times when globalization, migration, and the rapid development of transportation and communication have brought different cultures and peoples into contact with one another, the appeal to context and the respect for particularity must not lead to tribalism. On a certain level, as King eloquently stated, all lives are interrelated, and the injustice that directly affects a given context has consequences that extend beyond that context. Thus, as neighbors sharing a common world house, we understand that King's ethical appeal remains relevant: "Our loyalties must transcend our race, our tribe, our class, our nation."[14] Starting from the irreducible particularity of one's experience and narrative, one

11. Walter D. Mignolo, *Local Histories/Global Designs: Coloniality, Subaltern Knowledge, and Border Thinking* (Princeton, NJ: Princeton University Press, 2000).

12. Lamin Sanneh, *Whose Religion Is Christianity? The Gospel Beyond the West* (Grand Rapids: Eerdmans, 2003), 22.

13. Martin Luther King Jr., "A Christmas Sermon on Peace," in *A Testament of Hope: The Essential Writings and Speeches of Martin Luther King, Jr.*, ed. James M. Washington (New York: HarperCollins, 1991), 253–58 (253).

14. Ibid.

reaches out to others, based on the understanding that there is a common humanity and a common house, both of which refer to a world or ecumenical consciousness. Allan Boesak uses the term "inclusionary particularity" to speak of this broadly ecumenical exercise of moving from one's particularity to ask questions and seek responses in encounters with others.[15]

- At the same time, as the two final chapters of this book highlight, more than 250 million people today live "on the move," as migrants. Their experience of the world is transnational, and their worldview from the borderlines is increasingly informing religious practice and belief around the world. The multiple dialogues that the reader will see in the following pages bring different cultures, contexts, and languages in conversation with one another. Its editors are not concerned with harmonizing possible tensions. Whereas women's ordination, for instance, is a no-brainer in a number of contexts and traditions, in others, women continue to struggle to have the same recognition as men in their ministries. That does not mean, however, that one reality is necessarily superior to another. In contexts where women's ordination is not an issue, questions might be raised about other aspects of gender equality, such as equal pay and equal opportunities in the executive leadership of larger denominational and ecumenical organizations.
- Finally, this book avoids idealized notions of world Christianity that overlook the colonial experience and memory that inform power relations in the integrated global structures, which Christians from the South and from the North are part of.[16] By giving voice to critical articulations from within different world Christianities, and encouraging honest and sustained conversations among them, this book seeks to contribute to preventing the idealistic trap of the otherization of post-Western Christianities.

The book has five sections, with two chapters each. The first section, on theology, doctrine, and ecumenical dialogue offers two contributions from Latin America. The authors advance proposals

15. Allan A. Boesak, "Theodicy: 'De Lawd Knowed How It Was'; Black Theology and Black Suffering," in *The Cambridge Companion to Black Theology*, ed. Dwight N. Hopkins and Edward P. Antonio (New York: Cambridge University Press, 2012), 156–68 (158).

16. See, for instance, Sathianathan Clarke, "World Christianity and Postcolonial Mission: A Path Forward for the Twenty-First Century," *Theology Today* 71, no. 2 (2014): 192–206 (194).

to rethink Christian faith and ecumenism in creative and liberating ways.

In chapter 1, Ronaldo Cavalcante, a Brazilian Presbyterian theologian and minister, recounts the journey of Christian theology in the West and the early articulations of its conception as *intellectus fidei*. He moves then to show its later enslavement by rationalistic formulas, which turned it into *regula fidei*, making doubt the enemy of faith. Cavalcante aims at liberating theology from this subjugation to legalism by appealing to the human and relational nature of the theologizing task. He does so in conversation with thinkers such as Forte, Ricoeur, Levinas, and Duquoc, among others. As a response to exclusivist doctrinal certainties, he proposes a doctrinal emptying inspired by the gospel imperative of self-denial as the way to healthier ecumenical relations in a conflict-rotten world. In accord with that proposal, biblical narratives become tools for bridge building between the same and the other.

Magali Cunha's contribution is informed by her dual training in theology and social communication, and by years of ecumenical activism. Her approach is balanced and realistic, pondering successes and limits in the international ecumenical movement. Cunha highlights the contributions made by Latin American Christians to the international ecumenical movement, focusing on the obstacles for ecumenism in the region. Some of the main obstacles she identifies for the ecumenical movement today include indifference to ecumenism and anti-ecumenical feelings among Protestants and Catholics (the dominant Christian traditions in her context). Cunha also draws attention to Latin American churches' low participation in the World Council of Churches, in spite of holding the second-largest number of Christians in the world. Additionally, she denounces how a dominant patriarchal and paternal culture limits the expansion of one of the greatest contributions from Latin America to the ecumenical movement: base ecumenism. A final obstacle is the individualism and competitiveness present in a market-oriented religion, which mimics the values of globalized capitalism. In response to these limitations, Cunha challenges the reader to rethink ecumenism, advancing a proposal that frees the word *ecumenical* from common associations with a particular movement and specific ecclesiastical structures, and thus rearticulating it as a mosaic of members and bodies joining to share initiatives in areas such as education, gender, theology, environment, youth, health, human rights, and overcoming violence.

The second section focuses on pluralism, ecumenism, and intercultural communication, gathering contributions from South Africa and Brazil.

In chapter 3, Retief Müller, a senior lecturer in church history at Stellenbosch University in South Africa, offers a sharp narrative about ecumenical collaboration and tensions involving national and international ecumenical organizations in South Africa. Like Cunha in the previous chapter, Müller moves from the ecumenical golden age in South Africa to controversies and conflicts concerning violent or nonviolent resistance to the apartheid regime between different ecumenical bodies. Müller problematizes the tensions involved in the contrast between imperialism and cultural relativism, warning his readers of the risk of turning Andrew Walls's concept of cultural translatability into cultural imperialism. He thoughtfully analyzes the development of two ecumenical traditions in South Africa, one emphasizing cultural translatability and the other highlighting the normativity of the missionary's culture (which he calls imperialist), avoiding easy vilification of the missionary culture but at the same time raising important questions about the risk that the absolutism of pluralism overrides the importance of ecumenicity. Favoring ecumenical perspectives, he highlights the centrality of intercultural communication in that context.

Chapter 4 is written by Korean Brazilian liberation theologian Jung Mo Sung. Noticing the lack of clear definitions in many works addressing the public nature of religion or Christianity, Sung offers a perspective that goes beyond the public-private framework to highlight the importance of religious pluralism for a deeper understanding of the public nature of religious faith in a globalized world. Defining secularization in terms of separation, Sung turns to Latin American theological movements such as liberation theology and *mision integral* and their attempts to overcome the modern relegation of Christianity to the private sphere. Along with black theology, these movements are named as Christianity's prophetic reservoir. In his discussion of religious pluralism, Sung argues that beyond moving from the private to the public sphere, Christians must engage others on the basis of the biblical image of "hearing the cry" of those who suffer, developing the capacity to understand the difference between religion and God's reign and justice.

The third section of the book focuses on Latin American perspectives on ethics and society.

Puerto Rican historian and theologian Luis Rivera-Pagan focuses on the contributions to church and society made by Latin American liberation theology (LALT). Moving beyond common caricatures, Rivera-Pagan shows how LALT reconfigured the interplay between religious studies, ethics, and politics, representing a drastic "epistemological rupture, a radical change in paradigm, a significant shift in both the ecclesial and social role of theology." This chapter summarizes the historical conditions that contributed to the rise of LALT and its continuous development. Its main contribution was to forge a new way of being the church in the world—something exemplified most of all through the base ecclesial communities. Understanding its dynamic nature, Rivera-Pagan's narrative highlights several contributions to the development of LALT as a theological movement, including Catholic and Protestant antecedents, U.S. Latina/o perspectives, and the evolution of its topics and concerns. The chapter also offers some provisional predictions, which, in particular, connect its legacy with other struggles around the world and with the contributions offered by other subordinated subjects, which together work in solidarity to construct the hope for "another possible world."

Chapter 6 highlights the importance of retelling the history of Latin American Christianity from below, repositioning indigenous and Afro-Latin American voices, along with women and other minoritized groups in order to reinvent it. A narrative from below is rooted in particular stories of pain and hope. Barreto argues that just as indigenous Christianities are contextually named, so European and Eurocentric colonial Christianities also must be. The Christianities emerging from indigenous responses to encounters between gospel and culture are the ones that more appropriately can be called Latin American Christianities. Among other things, this chapter shows how much Christian history and experience is enriched, redeemed, and renewed through non-Eurocentric Christian narratives in the region.

The fourth section offers contributions on gender and church from two particular contexts, in Brazil and Germany.

In chapter 7, Uta Andrée, an ordained Lutheran pastor and the director of the Academy of Mission for ecumenism and dialogue at the University of Hamburg, recognizes the atypical nature of an invitation from a Brazilian colleague to offer a contextual perspective from the Global North. Most times, contextual perspectives are quickly associated with theologies and scholarship from the Global South. She starts her chapter by confessing that such a contextual perspective is "a challenging but urgent shift." Another way she departs from convention is evident in her choice to make German men/masculinity her contextual subject. By offering a woman's perspective on men and church in Germany, she signals that she is moving beyond men-centered understandings of themselves.[17] The author seeks to avoid stereotypes and clichés common in essentialist approaches to gender identity by favoring a focus based on the idea of partnership and historical analysis over against an approach based on gender-specific categorization/description. A crucial question the author asks is, Where are the men in German churches? Why aren't they in the churches? Most churchgoers in Germany, as in other parts of the world, are women. In her quest for the absence of men in German churches, Andrée also considers other groups who are absent from church, including people in their twenties and the poor. Such an approach allows her to factor in other aspects of church participation as she seeks to understand the gender imbalance in German churches, including age and socioeconomic affiliation.

Claudete Beise Ulrich is a Brazilian theologian and religious scholar who lived and worked in Germany for some years. In chapter 8, Ulrich reflects on the experience of female students in Faculdade Unida, Vitoria, Brazil. Whereas, in the previous chapter, Andrée shows that an increasing number of women are going into ordained ministry in Germany (she refers to it as the feminization of church ministry), in the context of Ulrich's students in Vitoria, Brazil, many of whom come from Evangelical and Pentecostal churches, the ordination of women is still an issue. Ulrich's chapter, although focusing on the particular context of the school where she is currently the only female professor, collaterally discusses the context of many churches in the state of Espirito Santo, which has the largest percentage of

17. For those interested in the problematization of men/masculinities identity theoretical frameworks, see Chris Beasley, "Problematizing Contemporary Men/Masculinities Theorizing: The Contribution of Raewyn Connell and Conceptual-Terminological Tensions Today," *British Journal of Sociology* 63, no. 4 (2012): 747–65.

Evangelical population in Brazil, over 30 percent. In that context, Ulrich makes the claim that theological education, like education at large, is a human right for girls and women. She backs that claim with a robust discussion blending various feminist theological approaches and the voices of female students at Faculdade Unida, which leads her to the threefold conclusion that (1) women's theological education expands their knowledge and practice of theology itself and thus breaks paradigms of patriarchal church traditions; (2) women's theological education qualifies and enables women theologically to act in an ethical and responsible way in their religious communities or in other societal spaces; and (3) women's theological studies empower them to have their own say in regard to their own experience with the divine. Although radically contextual in method and approach, this chapter offers important contributions to similar contexts in other parts of Latin America and beyond.

The final section of the book focuses on migration, a theme of increasing concern in world Christianity.

In chapter 9, Y. Joy Harris-Smith, a scholar in the field of communication and culture who has spent time in Senegal, West Africa, and in the Dominican Republic, advances the urgency of a migratory epistemology, describing Christianity as a religion constantly moving through cultural contexts. She portrays migration as a new frontier to studies in world Christianity, relating current shifts in migration patterns to the need for greater emphasis on intercultural communication. Harris-Smith speaks from a U.S. perspective, paying particular attention to the need for churches in host cultures to learn more effective ways of intercultural communication. U.S. churches are urged to become more culturally sensitive in order to respond to the increasing presence of immigrants among their parishioners and neighbors. Along with that, "the church must become aware of its assumptions regarding race, class, gender, culture, and theology." Recognizing that in the context of the U.S. churches, Eurocentric perspectives are still held as central, Harris-Smith calls for a migratory epistemology, which unsettles Eurocentric centrality, turning the lived experience of migration into the primary location of meaning.

Afe Adogame, a leading scholar of migration and the African diaspora, writes the closing chapter on the lively subject of the experience of African diaspora Christianities vis-à-vis the ethical politics of unwanted immigration in Europe. Using migration system theory and transnational theory as his analytical frameworks, Adogame offers a vivid and in-depth picture of African irregular and regular migration, which enables him to thoroughly examine the morality of the politics of migration in Europe and the challenges immigration imposes on Western democracies. Adogame's essay begins with the story of sixteen-year-old Senegalese Abdou as he prepared his perilous journey to Europe on May 2015. Adogame quotes the final advice Abdou received from his father before he left: "Throw your passport into the sea. Who you are doesn't matter in Europe." Adogame's investigation unveils the hypocrisy of political and religious institutions and leaders in Europe and Africa in light of the lack of a vigorous outcry in response to what he describes as an "unwarranted waste of human bodies, mostly African immigrants desperate to cross the sea to Europe," and "an unprecedented watershed in the history and politics of ir/regular migration to Europe." The second part of the chapter examines "whether, how, and to what extent African-led churches in Europe are engaging in (or not) the politics of wasting bodies and unwanted migration," and the social relevance of their responses to the ethical dilemma shaping EU immigration policies.

The topics discussed in each of these sections and chapters are relevant to local, regional, and international affairs in the contemporary world. These chapters' varied hermeneutical lenses, locations, and perspectives contribute insights that expand and deepen our perspectives on these public matters, which will remain central to Christian agendas in different parts of the world in the years and decades to come.

This collection of essays reflects the kind of framework Roland Robertson has called "glocalization," or global localization, recognizing that in the globalized contemporary reality, influence moves simultaneously in two paradoxical directions—namely, through the universalization of the particular and the particularization of the universal.[18] For him, there is a valorization of locality, multiculturalism, home, and community, which is globally sustained today. Robertson highlights the density of worldwide social communication in this globalized reality. His multidimensional approach makes room for

18. Roland Robertson, "Globalization and the Future of 'Traditional Religion,'" in *God and Globalization: Theological Ethics and the Spheres of Life*, ed. Max L. Stackhouse and Peter J. Paris (New York: Trinity Press International, 2000), 53–68.

religion to become a proactive force in the shaping of the global reality, meanwhile recognizing the impact of politico-economic factors in the shaping of religious experiences. Conversely, religion and theological ethics can potentially become important forces in the process of giving the global order a more humane face, as Robertson and other globalization theorists have hoped. Regardless of whether that more structural impact will take place, ultimately religion and spirituality will continue to be meaningful to the daily lived experience of people like the young Abdou and the millions of migrants crossing borders and moving among different cultures today.

This volume, thus, opens up an important conversation that will be fine-tuned in the upcoming volumes, as specific areas, which are briefly addressed in the essays of this book, will be teased out.

PART I

Theology, Doctrine, and Ecumenical Dialogue: Perspectives from Latin America

1.

An Essay on Theology, Doctrine, and Ecumenical Dialogue

Protestant Christian Perspectives in Latin America

RONALDO CAVALCANTE

One of the accomplishments of modernity was the openness to a democratic dialogue between social classes and strata previously unmindful of each other. Otherness was neglected because of deeply ingrained prejudices. A dialogue implies a wish for mutual regard between concerned parties. Such accomplishment has finally come into religious culture, theology, and religious studies through an emphasis on knowledge of the other and the other's perspective. Despite its limitations and even some backward steps, Protestantism played an important role in the early moments of this dialogue by fostering the study of comparative religion, thus breaking down Christianity's self-imposed hegemony and absolute character.

To push this dialogue forward, one needs to be prepared, as I see it, in at least three ways. First, one must always keep the "whole house," the whole *oikoumene*, in mind. Even though this chapter specifically deals with Christianity, it is important to be aware of Christianity's vastness, variety, and richness as a religious phenomenon.

Second, one must adopt a relative approach to doctrinal identity by boldly applying the kenotic process of Christ. Such a method holds the Bible as literature built and inspired by God through the early faith communities and interpreted with a surplus of meaning throughout history, during which our presence is just a blip. This recognizes that the whole truth is much bigger than our individual tradition.

Third, theology must be viewed not as doctrinal apologetics but as an enlightening platform for dialogical relationships. This frames theology as communication, bridging numerous Christian islands, depicting the vastness of world Christianity, establishing an open theology—one that is open to the other and no longer an object of domination or imposition but a space for mutual learning.

REVELATION, FAITH, THEOLOGY: LIMITATIONS AND GREATNESS OF THE TASK

Our starting point is the classical definition of theology as the intelligence of faith, or *intellectus fidei*, which is the understanding and assimilation of a given religious experience observed in history. According to this definition, theology is the effort of meditation on the very act of faith itself, a second moment of religious reality. Theology is faith seeking understanding, as Anselm and his predecessor Augustine defined it,[1] in their reading of Isaiah 7:9: *nisi crediteritis, non intelligetis*.[2] In the encounter between faith and reason, *fides et ratio*, Augustine, using the Septuagint for his translation into Latin, assigns "a priority to faith, which delivers *a posteriori* its revealed content to the scrutiny of reason."[3] For Evangelista Vilanova,[4] the Septuagint, a faulty Greek translation of the Hebrew text, negatively influenced the patristics on this issue. For Vilanova, Anselm corrected this error by saying, "Let me seek you in desiring you; let me desire you in seeking you; let me find you in loving you; let me love you in finding

1. Faith as *regula credenti*; *Crede ut, intelligas* by Augustine and their similar expressions in Anselm: *fides quaerens intellectum*, and *credo ut intelligam*, *Proslogium*, chapter I: *ne que enim quaero intelligere ut credam, sed credo ut intelligam* ("For I do not seek to understand that I may believe, but I believe in order to understand. For this also I believe, that unless I believed, I should not understand"). Latin text in E. Gilson, *A filosofia na Idade Média (*São Paulo: Martins Fontes, 1998), 292; and translation into Portuguese in *Os Pensadores*: Santo Anselmo e Abelardo, (São Paulo: Abril Cultural, 1984), 101. Both contributed to the ingenious synthesis produced by Barth: *analogia fidei*, in response to *analogia entis* by Brunner, giving primacy to faith, *initium fidei*.

2. Dario Antiseri and Giovanni Reale, *História da Filosofia: Patrística e Escolástica* (São Paulo: Paulus, 2005), 104.

3. Adolfo G. Montes, *Fundamentación de la fe* (Salamanca: Secretariado Trinitário, 1994), 78. Translation into English from the Spanish version.

4. Evangelista Vilanova, *Para Compreender a Teologia* (São Paulo: Paulinas, 1998), 96.

you."[5] This corrective highlights the fact that for Augustine, the integration of *fides et ratio* is a key manifestation, as it had been for Origen. For Origen, the result was Christ-mysticism as a contemplative form to attain truth, while for Augustine, the axiom *intellige ut credas, criede ut intelligas* (Serm. 43,7,9) makes it clear—as Gonzáles Montes[6] puts it—that "the confluence of the two elements which systematically articulate the use of the constituent principles of theological knowledge."[7] The primacy of faith would then be guided by the integration of *regula scripturae*, as *auctorictas*, and the *ratio*, producing the famous axiom *Philosophia ancilla theologiae* (Philosophy [is] the servant of theology). In this view, *fides et ratio* is a constituent element of theology. Controversies aside, theology self-defines an understanding of not only itself and its "ultimate object" but also the entire reality.

This holistic vision, then, refers to a human understanding, the "human, all too human." This aphorism from Nietzsche (the title of one of his works) may be an echo of what Feuerbach said, "The true sense of theology is anthropology."[8] This statement dispels the idea that "Theology itself should not be construed as a divinely communicated body of knowledge. It is a human discipline, a human effort to understand and express in human terms the nature of God and reality."[9] Thomas Aquinas and Karl Barth, two of the great luminaries in Western theology, recognized such humanity in the nature of the theological task.[10] Toward the end of his life, Aquinas recognizes that

5. Santo Anselmo, *Proslogion seu Alloquium de Dei existentia* (Covilhã-Portugal: Universidade da Beira Interior, 2008), 11. English translation from Anselm of Canterbury, *Proslogion* 1, http://www.vatican.va/spirit/documents/spirit_20000630_anselmo_en.html, accessed on July 27, 2016.

6. Gilson, *A filosofia na Idade Média,* 114.

7. Montes, *Fundamentación de la fe*, 75. Translation into English from the Spanish version.

8. Friedrich W. Nietzsche, *Human, All Too Human: A Book for Free Spirits*, trans. R. J. Hollingdale (New York: Cambridge University Press, 1996).

9. Ludwig Feuerbach, *The Essence of Christianity* (London: Ludgate, 1881).

10. Roger Haight, *A dinâmica da teologia (*São Paulo: Paulinas, 2004), 240. Translation into English from the Portuguese version.

before the mystery of God, all his writing on theology is "straw."[11] In his turn, Barth made that clear more than once:

> Of all the sciences which stir the head and the heart, theology is the fairest. It is closest to human reality, and gives us the clearest view of the truth after which all sciences quest. . . . What a miserable lot of theologians—and what miserable periods there have been in the history of theology—when they have not realized this! But of all the sciences there is none which is so beset with difficulties, none which is so beset with dangers, as theology! In no other science is it so easy to be caught in despair, or, what is worse, to end in arrogant overconfidence. It is the science which is most easily diffused or petrified, and which can become its own worst caricature.[12]

Acknowledging such limitation may be theology's greatest merit. That is, this human effort is part of the assignment imposed on the human banned from the garden. This is that monolithic and inexorable reality: "By the sweat of your face you shall eat bread,"[13] and I add, you shall also make theology! Paradoxically, the theological task as it pertains to the content of faith is an activity that transcends the limits of the ancient exile of human existence. As Bruno Forte has put it, "Theology as history is that the historicity ratifying it is not only the ineluctable reflection of our human condition, but the journey towards the encounter which happened in the mystery of the incarnation of the Word."[14] Theology allows for this because of its *Logos*—"author and finisher of faith"—connecting with the Primal Truth, the revelation of God contained in the sacred writings. That

11. In a General Audience, Pope Benedict XVI comments, "The last months of Thomas' earthly life remain surrounded by a particular, I would say, mysterious atmosphere. In December 1273, he summoned his friend and secretary Reginald to inform him of his decision to discontinue all work because he had realized, during the celebration of Mass subsequent to a supernatural revelation, that everything he had written until then 'was worthless.' This is a mysterious episode that helps us to understand not only Thomas' personal humility, but also the fact that, however lofty and pure it may be, all we manage to think and say about the faith is infinitely exceeded by God's greatness and beauty which will be fully revealed to us in Heaven." Vatican City, June 2, 2010, http://w2.vatican.va/content/benedict-xvi/en/audiences/2010/documents/hf_ben-xvi_aud_20100602.html.

12. Karl Barth, "Revelação, Igreja, Teologia," in *Dádiva e Louvor: Artigos Selecionados*, Portuguese trans. by Walter O. Schlupp, Luís Marcos Sander, and Walter Altmann (São Leopoldo: Sinodal, 1986), 193. This book is a collection of selected articles by Barth translated from German into Portuguese, used in this chapter as the basis for my English translation. Schlupp's Portuguese version translated from Karl Barth, "Offenbarung, Kirche, Theologie," in *Theologische Existenz Heute* (Munich: Christian Kaiser, 1934), 34.

13. Gen 3:19 ESV.

14. Bruno Forte, *Teologia em Diálogo* (São Paulo: Loyola, 2002), 37.

is, faith (the individual or collective act of believing) in its ipseity acts in awareness of its place and viewing itself on its path toward the desired object, and in this action that is historicized and subject to contingency, it provides the raw material for the identity of theology.

Let us make no mistake, notwithstanding our conversation about "science of faith" and "theology as science,"[15] faith itself does not rest on a scientific *episteme*; its platform is the revelation of God. Thus, faith and revelation are the foundational sources of theology; they are distinct, but converge and blend into the dynamic of theology. Faith observed in human reality (individuals and communities) is described in God's revelation presented in the Scriptures: faith "is human response and commitment; revelation is God's Presence to human subjectivity."[16] The interweaving of faith and revelation (scripture) locates its basic formulation in Pauline theology: *Ergo fides ex auditu auditus autem per verbum Christi* ("So faith comes from hearing, and hearing through the word of Christ").[17]

Therefore, because faith is human (although granted by God as a gift), its *depositum fidei,* its locus and habitat, is Scripture itself.[18] The Scriptures, looking to Abraham (Genesis 12), define faith as the reception of that which is absent and the "possession" of invisible realities (see Heb 11:1). In their turn, the Scriptures reenact the mystery of the incarnated *Logos* (*incarnatione Verbi*), which came from within the divine being that has broken into human reality, acting upon it completely. This is the *notitia bona* explicated by early and canonical authors, from Paul the Apostle (Phil 2:5–11) to John the Evangelist (John 1:1–5; 9:14), and the church fathers of the second to fourth centuries (Ignatius of Antioch, Irenaeus of Lyons, Tertulian,

15. It is important again to highlight that the "science of faith" and "theology as science" were a path first laid out by Clement and Origen of Alexandria, based on a platonic framework that enabled the relation between God and the world, and precisely because of that, it enabled the building of a discourse on God. For more, see Montes, *Fundamentación de la fe* 74.

16. Haight, *A dinâmica da teologia,* 239. Translation into English from the Portuguese version.

17. Rom 10:17 ESV.

18. This discussion of the relation between revelation and Scripture is very important. One good approach to the theme is the text by J. L. Segundo in *O Dogma que Liberta* (São Paulo: Paulinas, 1991), 130–45. He starts from the Old Testament as the revelation of God and addresses the Magisterium of the Catholic Church; he questions Xavier León-Dufour's position when he stresses the fact that Vatican II has dropped the use of the term *inerrancy*, and proposes the "divine pedagogy" for the supposed historical errors in the text of Scripture. For that, he uses *Dei Verbum*; according to him, "God is not so much the author of one or several books as the author of an *educational process* whose stages make up the content of those books" (140). In reality, J. L. Segundo holds the endorsement of the church as the highest instance. It is the Scripture, though read and authorized by the church.

the apologists, Athanasius, etc.). And it is this same mystery that, after lengthy discussions throughout the first three ecumenical councils—Nicaea (325), Constantinople (381), and Ephesus (431)—produced the Chalcedonian Symbol (Council of Chalcedon, 451), endorsing the two natures (divine and human) in just one person (Jesus Christ, the incarnated *Logos*), stating, "Following, then, the holy Fathers, we all unanimously teach that our Lord Jesus Christ is to us One and the same Son, the Self-same Perfect in Godhead, the Self-same Perfect in Manhood; truly God and truly Man; the Self-same of a rational soul and body; co-essential with the Father according to the Godhead, the Self-same co-essential with us according to the Manhood."[19]

This hypostatic union of two natures in one person corresponds to aspects of both the Scriptures and the church. On one hand, both reflect divine ancestry, and on the other hand, they both reflect human existence. But because they do not enjoy the same ontic identity of *Logos*, they both suffer in their own way from human vicissitudes and idiosyncrasies as subjects of temporality. Yet this correspondence to the hypostatic union allows them to point to ineffability amid *tempus fugit;* they speak of glory among the wreckages of civilization. This was the case for Augustine in *Civitas Dei*, in the face of the forthcoming fall of the Roman Empire. Similarly, in the Middle Ages, death and destruction from wars and pests stood before enormous, perfect cathedrals and the safety of monastic cloisters and castles. Likewise, the Scriptures reflect the paradox of this unmistakable duality. However, we need to tackle the problem of the receiving process of this mystery in the church, which as a process has become strenuously complex.

Reception of this mystery has become complex as a result of a variety of factors: the need for a standardized faith (*regula fidei*) to eliminate doubt, which is the enemy of faith; the fight against heresy, which is diverging and heterodox interpretation of Christian facts; the preservation of the apostolic doctrine, which is the memory of the eyewitnesses; the settlement of a canon in the face of a plethora of religious literatures contemporary to canonical writings; and pastoral care for the purpose of offering certainties and convictions to

19. Council of Chalcedon, *Symbolum Chalcedonense*: Denz., n. 301. *Apud* Valtemário S. F. Júnior, "Calcedônia Ontem e Hoje" (master's thesis, PUC-Rio Theology Department, 2011), 65, accessed at http://www.maxwell.vrac.puc-rio.br/17827/17827_4.PDF. Quote above is translated from Portuguese.

believers. These factors prompted the church to take up its role as vehicle of truth,[20] responsible for the task of constructing definitions so that "Peter's vessel" could sail safely on the troubled seas of time. This is what patristics did, with the incipient theological drafts stemming from the Scriptures, and this is what occurred later in the Middle Ages, with the great theological syntheses wrapped up in *summae* and sentences and in several ecumenical synods and councils.

Thus, this is the core issue: receiving the revelation of God and its interpretation through the ecclesiastical institution. In the eyes of the church, the "unhewn rock" of revelation should be polished for better catechism, instruction, and evangelization. This polishing brings forth the *sermo de Deo*, completed by *ratio ecclesiae*, so as to produce the perfect discourse about God. As the church assumes this role, an increasingly hegemonic tendency is born, which became paramount to Christian orthodoxy at the end of Middle Ages for both Catholics and Protestants: indoctrination as a form of apology.

THEOLOGY, FREEDOM, AND ECUMENISM: THE FIGHT, DIALOGUE, AND LIBERATION OF THEOLOGY

Up until the focus in the Middle Ages on producing the perfect discourse about God, the principle guiding the church ways was unity.[21] This focus on unity was a result of the convergence of multiple factors: the primacy of Rome as the only true teaching authority, the *corpus legalis* set forth by the canon law and catechism, the standardization of liturgy (albeit mostly unsuccessful), and the correct interpretation of the Scripture by the clergy. In contrast to such religious status, which grew immense and cemented during the Middle Ages, the new winds of modernity blew across Western Christendom in the fifteenth and sixteenth centuries. This shift was particularly

20. The immediate scriptural basis for such conduct was the reading in a confessional and institutional key of John 16:13 about the coming of the Paraclete: "When the Spirit of truth comes, he will guide you into all the truth; for he will not speak on his own, but will speak whatever he hears, and he will declare to you the things that are to come" (ESV). The Reformation generally tends to engage in an individualistic and reductive reading of this text, anchored in the Lutheran doctrine of the universal priesthood of all believers.

21. The idea of *unity* represented in the Latin word *Una* took effect from the Nicene-Constantinopolitan symbol in the fourth century. It was clearly grounded in statements from the Scripture; however, it fit very well with Roman identity, especially from Constantine to Theodosius. Thus, unity gradually took the meaning of standardization of thought and attitudes. Rome needed a sole religion to help push toward monocracy.

evident in discoveries of the Renaissance, especially in the resurgence of humanism, the resurgence of human reason from classical culture, and the outbreak of the Reformation, which featured whistleblowing on abuses by the clergy. Soon the spirit of freedom in investigation reached Scripture itself; no longer an exclusively religious "object," Scripture could be approached through these new available instruments—for example, the New Testament in Greek by Erasmus of Rotterdam,[22] published in 1516, one year before the surge of the Reformation. This shows that a significant change in Western Christianity was already under way during the late fifteenth and early sixteenth centuries. Erasmus himself had published his important *Enchiridion Militis Christiani* (*Handbook of a Christian Soldier*) in 1503, preaching a literate and learned laicization of Christianity, which broke away from the millennium-long cultural hegemony of the clergy and monasticism.

Because of the Renaissance and the Reformation, religious expressions diverging from tradition that were kept in the shadows could be considered. Rather than the concept of unity and exclusiveness of Christian faith or the idea of totality, "the unknown" fueled curiosity and investigation. Bruno Forte, speaking about more open and less ideological theology and philosophy, asserts, "The great category which provokes us all is not identity, but otherness."[23] I do not believe that his concept of otherness is the same as that of the philosophy of Ricoeur, for whom "otherness reaches its apex in mutuality."[24] Perhaps, it identifies more with Levinas's philosophy. In fact, Forte quotes him by saying the thought of the Bible "does not introduce a teleological system into the totality; it does not consist of teaching the orientation of history. . . . There can be no knowledge of God separated from the relationship with men."[25] This relational distance is why Forte stresses that the category of otherness offers up itself as a

22. This *New Testament in Greek* was printed in Basel, Switzerland, based on the compilation of *textus receptus*, using diverse manuscripts and also showing textual variations. This publication later became the main source for subsequent, more refined translations. Despite sparking turmoil among church authorities, the soundness of his translation was later verified. Luther used it as basis for his translation, which was completed in 1522.

23. Bruno Forte, *Teologia em Diálogo* (São Paulo: Loyola, 2002), 66. Translation into English from the Portuguese version.

24. Paul Ricoeur, *Percurso do Reconhecimento* (São Paulo: Loyola, 2006), 262. In Ricoeur, otherness and mutuality mean that the self and the other must be integrated. Translation into English from the Portuguese version.

25. Forte, *Teologia em Diálogo*, 85. Translation into English from the Portuguese version.

meeting place in three forms: "amazement, agony, and ethics."[26] And he adds, "The epistemology of speculative thought, whether theological or philosophical, needs to remain open, otherwise it will lose its foundational relationship to the other." Thus, the category of "infinity" in Levinas,[27] taken up by Bruno Forte, redefines the very concept of "wholly other" (*Das ganz andere*) as articulated by Luther, Otto, and Barth. This marks a split in the idea of synthesis, or medieval totality, conceived under the auspices of the ecclesiastical institution. Infinity is present in the Other; the metaphysical truth is in the Other, in my neighbor, but that does not denote possession, because the Other is untamable, precisely because it is outside the Same. The acquisition of power was an integral part of the programmatic idea of totality, which the ideological shift fought hard to overthrow. As I see it, such a fissure in the frameworks of authority, in the direction of the individual, would theoretically mean the liberation of theology and a manumission from a hermeneutics subservient to a strictly confessional religious element.

The emancipation of the biblical text meant that, despite remaining essentially religious, the Scriptures could no longer be, according to Duquoc, an "exclusive property of the Church; it is a cultural object, albeit religious."[28] Thus, "free examination" gradually became a fact,[29] at least in Erasmus's and Luther's rhetoric (although both caved and went back to ecclesiastical tradition). This diversity of thought is evident in the fact that Erasmus, to try to prove he was a sincere Christian and settle his differences with the Magisterium, reinforced free will in his *Diatribe*,[30] thus incurring semipelagian suspicions. Similarly, Luther soon had to write treatises and things other than catechisms (1529) to give pastoral guidance; and later he exerted a decisive influence on the content of the *Confessio Augustana* (1530),

26. Ibid., 66.

27. Emmanuel Levinas, *Totality and Infinity: An Essay on Exteriority* (Pittsburgh: Duquesne University Press, 1969).

28. Christian Duquoc, *Teologia no Exílio: O Desafio da Sobrevivência da Teologia na Cultura contemporânea* (Petrópolis: Vozes, 2006), 90. Translation into English from the Portuguese version.

29. The principle of "free examination" was made known as a result of the Protestant Reformation. It referred to the Bible text, which should be accessible to any person in the vernacular of each country, but it was also a response to the Index of Forbidden Books of the medieval church, ensuring that the imprimatur was then allowed. In fact, the sixteenth and seventeenth centuries witnessed a wealth of publications of books and versions of the Bible.

30. *De Libero Arbitrio Diatribe Sive Collatio* (1524).

coordinated and presented by Melanchthon to Charles V and the princes in Augsburg.

Although the Reformation created space for diversity of thought, it also exhibited problematic hegemonic tendencies, particularly in the form of religious intolerance. This intolerance often manifested in disciplinary actions. The most glaring cases took place in the Reformed sector of the Calvinist tradition,[31] whose measures were more radical. Let's take a look at the most famous ones. In Geneva, Calvin and Beza acted with excessive rigor. We have from that same period *Les Ordonnances Eclesiastique* and the *Consistoire de Genève*, in 1541, and in the following year the *Catéchisme de l'Église de Genève*—powerful doctrinal tools for discipline. The most notorious case was Michael Servetus's sentence to death by fire in 1553, but there are many other examples of disproportionate measures in the name of the sound doctrine. The Synod of Dortdrecht, held in the Netherlands in 1618–1619, condemned as heretical the theological ideas held by the Arminians and also delivered a sentence of life imprisonment to Hugo Grotius, one of the leading humanists of the seventeenth century, who was regarded as the father of international law and associated with Arminianism. We know today the plot was sponsored by John Maurice of Nassau, who was interested in political control over the region and instrumentalized the church toward that end. In England, the famous Witch Act was passed in 1604, condemning witches to death, a practice lasting until 1735. England also produced the most prevalent doctrinal document, the *Westminster Confession of Faith* (1647), as well as the *Larger Catechism* and *Shorter Catechism*. The *Confession* is a terse amalgamation of Calvinist ideas under a strong puritan influence, defining faith but leaving out those who did not fit the correct orthodox view: Anabaptists, Quakers, Arminians, Anglicans, etc. In the United States, the most poignant case of intolerance concerning ecclesiastical discipline took place in

31. An unsuspected statement was recently made by conservative Reformed theologians in the work *As Doutrinas da Graça*, in which, despite their defense of Calvinism, they recognize a number of harms from Calvinist doctrine. They state, among other things, "Human depravity is a doctrine Calvinists do not just believe in, but also practice it! It was in Calvin's Geneva that Michael Servetus was burned at the stake for heresy. It was also there where the Puritans executed Charles I and presided over the trial of witches in Salem. Also, Edwards was a slave owner, and some Afrikaners used Kuyper's doctrine of sphere sovereignty (explained in chapter 9) to justify the oppressive *apartheid regime*." James Boice and Philip Ryken, *As Doutrinas da Graça* (Rio de Janeiro: Anno Domini), 2015. Translation into English from the Portuguese version.

Massachusetts with the Salem Witch Trials in 1692. Finally, in South Africa, the racial segregation enforced by the apartheid regime drew from ideas of racial superiority, which were taken from isolated Bible passages and elevated to status of doctrines by Dutch Protestant theologians from the NGK (Dutch Reformed Church of South Africa) living there.

These examples show that the adventure of Reformation was too dangerous and the stakes were too high, causing divergence from the hard-earned unity of Christianity. The irony in the dynamics of history is that at the dawn of new times, after the conflict, Protestantism came to find itself fighting for the exact thing it was reacting against: Protestantism, like Rome, fought for the unity of true faith. It did so in the name of individuality and free will, but still those achievements of the Renaissance—under the protection of the church—tore the seamless robe of Christ.[32] This exuded an air of worry about defining truth to defend faith, an imperative discourse for identification and discipline. Thus, the two main Protestant confessions (Augsburg and Westminster) and a variety of smaller, local documents in Protestant countries were developed. All of them featured a deluge of Bible texts extracted from their original narratives to support the creation of doctrinal identity, aimed at providing an all-encompassing view of the mysteries of God and reality, now revealed to the chosen ones.

From then on, the Bible turned out to be a never-ending source of doctrines, a *vade mecum* of doctrinal apologetics, and not an array of literary and narrative fragments.[33] If theology intends to be, on the one hand, "the intelligence of faith" and, on the other hand, indoctrination, which pays no regard to the native habitat of Scripture, theology then becomes the "rationalist narrowing of faith." Nevertheless, the practice of doctrine development grounded on the Bible is a pleasant and rewarding temptation, as it can hastily solve tortuous issues. It does so by using definite syntheses and by using elementary

32. "The robe of Christ" is a metaphor employed to refer to church unity. Such unity was broken in 1054 with the schism between the Western and Eastern churches, and in the sixteenth century with the Protestant Reformation.

33. Concerning this subject, I recommend the article by João Cesário Leonel Ferreira, "A Bíblia como Literatura: Lendo as Narrativas Bíblicas," *Correlatio*, no. 13 (São Paulo: UMESP, 2008); also, some classics on the theme: Robert Alter, *A Arte da Narrativa Bíblica* (São Paulo: Cia. das Letras, 2007); Northrop Frye, *O Código dos Códigos: a Bíblia e a Literatura* (São Paulo: Boitempo, 2004); Cássio Murilo Dias da Silva, *Leia a Bíblia como Literatura* (São Paulo: Loyola, 2007).

logical operations, disregarding the spirit of community life underlying biblical narratives that, after years or centuries of oral or occasional written tradition, finally give rise to the text.[34] With such a doctrinal system, the mystery of the journey of faith comes to an end. What a curious situation this was! One must keep in mind that the Protestant Reformation rose up against this type of simplistic and deceptive approach and against philosophical and academic subtleties of scholastics, which Erasmus and Luther denounced. In its origins, Christianity itself had identified a similar phenomenon in the Jewish legal system.

Then what is the difference? The exegete Osvaldo Ribeiro provides this answer:

> As Protestantism(s) develop—cracking up, crumbling away, and falling apart at the seams—always following the pattern of 'a new Luther rising against an old Luther, a new little Pope against an old little Pope,' the Statements of Doctrine will end up in a relative position, but under the risk of anyone doing unto them what Luther did to Tradition. Right now, as I write this line, as you read it, both you and I know a new church has been born.[35]

As I see it, Protestantism reproduces *mutatis mutandis* the same usurping reality, the same leviathan ravenous for blood of heretics, tearing down bridges of amity in the *oikoumene*, fueling fundamentalist fanaticism for dominion and control of truth. The difference is just semantic and instrumental. Much of Protestantism is a bastard child of rationalism. Like the prodigal son, this kind of bastard Protestantism requested its inheritance in anticipation and slipped all the way back into the worst expressions of the medieval spirit. This kind of Protestantism in a way rewound time and replicated the inquisitorial *modus operandi* of the medieval era. There is no way it would have sided with Saint Francis of Assisi, the Levellers (social leveling), William Wilberforce (abolition of slave trade and slavery), or Walter Rauschenbusch (social gospel), Dietrich Bonhoeffer (resistance to totalitarianism), Martin Luther King (end of segregation),

34. To go deeper into this subject, I recommend John Milbank's *Teologia e Teoria Social* (São Paulo: Loyola, 1995), especially part IV, "Teologia e Diferença," in which chapter 12, "A outra cidade: a teologia como ciência social," he states, "calling us back to narrative as being that alone which can 'identify' God for us" (491).

35. Osvaldo Ribeiro, "Da indefensável posição protestante," *Ouviroevento*, June 20, 2008, http://www.ouviroevento.pro.br/teologicofilosoficos/da_indefensavel.htm. Translation into English from the Portuguese version.

Mother Teresa (dedication to the destitute), Ignacio Ellacuria and Oscar Romero (fight against dictatorship), Dorothy Stang (fight against big landowners and loggers), Nelson Mandela or Desmond Tutu (fight against apartheid). If none of them, then this Protestantism would not have sided either with Alan Kurdi, the three-year-old Syrian refugee boy washed up dead on a Turkish beach, who carried in his young and frail body, which was full of dreams, all the refugees of the world. And this says nothing of the anonymous people throughout history whose voices will not be heard.

Branding doctrine as something absolute, immovable, as an "eternity clause," is unfair in any religious system, but in our case it is unfair and vilifying, particularly in lieu of those Christian maxims, the two greatest commandments which contain the whole law. Branding doctrine in this way ignores the fact that we love God when we love others, for "Religion that is pure and undefined before God, the Father, is this: to visit orphans and widows in their affliction, and to keep oneself unstinted from the world" (James 1:27 ESV). Branding doctrine as absolute is unfair because it disunites; it does not see the Other, and it does not see because it is inward focused, dull, self-absorbed, *in extremis*. It venerates and praises its ready-made discourse, like Narcissus staring at himself at the mirror. As a result, it serves as a bulwark against "foreigners, orphans and widows" and all marginalized people they represent, including Alan Kurdi. One-sided indoctrination, be it legal, economic, ideological, or religious, often neglects basic feelings of existence, but one-sided religious indoctrination is an acute failure, because it overlooks the misery around it, denying Christian charity in God's name—that is, it involves God in a mad manicheistic crusade of the good against the bad, the chosen against the neglected, a priori. What are we to do with this? Where are we to go?

This gargantuan doctrinal system stands between us and the text of Scripture, and it is not just a chasm separating us from the faith of the communities who wrote the text, it also poses as the text itself, in a simulacrum,[36] and because of that, the link with God's people from the past is surely lost, too. Monumental isolation has set in. Duquoc tells us that "Scripture is the echo of human words; believ-

36. In the light of Jean Baudrillard, I wrote about religious simulacrum in *A Cidade e o Gueto* (São Paulo: Fonte Editorial, 2010).

ers can hear it and understand it as the Word of God."[37] This goes to show that words of Scripture do not hold magic, which unfolds when we listen to them, as if inspiration (θεόπνευστος) were something mechanically mystical in the mouths of those speaking in the name of God and in the ears of those who hear. The inspiration of the Scriptures comes from people who believed and wrote, recording their faith; it is in this sense that "All Scripture is breathed out by God and profitable for teaching, for reproof, for correction and for training in righteousness" (2 Tim 3:16 ESV). The Scripture is the memory of faith, and when we examine it, it teaches us, rebukes us, corrects us, and gives us hope (Lam 3:21).

But how can we have hope today if we lack the memory of faith, if the doctrine system described above has driven us away from the text, if the Scripture narrative itself is missing? Theology today is in search not of the historical Jesus or the historical Paul. Instead, it is in search of the historical text, the way it was conceived, the life of faith it holds within, not its form mediated by indoctrination of institutional faith. Duquoc comes to our rescue once again:

> Scripture can be liberating, but it cannot evade the possibility of destruction. . . . The text plays the role as a counter-power, as it is no longer viewed as an advocate of dogma or a flatterer Church's opinions; it turns away from the institution. Presented by the Church as the testimony of its faith, it keeps itself at distance from it; it is an untamable text. In the past, theologians related to the Bible through the ecclesiastical institution; today its belonging to the Church no longer directly defines its reading.[38]

CONCLUSION

My suspicion is that the Bible has been turned into a book of doctrines and rules, lifeless and detached from its literary origins and community of faith; a hermetic pseudo-theological system with no chances for a critical and open dialogue. A prison was created, which guarantees a certain level of comfort; however, for those who can see, they notice the system's artificiality and its withered cracks preventing it from mirroring not only the atmosphere of faith and joy of

37. Christian Duquoc. *A Teologia no Exílio* (Petrópolis: Vozes, 2006), 90. Translation into English from the Portuguese version.

38. Ibid., 91. Translation from the Portuguese version.

Scripture but also from rising to the challenge of the drama of human existence. A surveillance system cannot conceive that complexity; it is a religious *Matrix Reloaded*.

Therefore, I deem it more reasonable to heed Pauline advice:

> Have this mind among yourselves, which is yours in Christ Jesus, who, though he was in the form of God, did not count equality with God a thing to be grasped, but emptied himself, by taking the form of a servant, being born in the likeness of men. And being found in human form, he humbled himself by becoming obedient to the point of death, even death on a cross. (Phil 2:5–8 ESV)

I deem it more reasonable to boldly enter into a kenotic process of doctrinal emptying of our certainties, obeying the gospel imperative of self-denial, renunciation, and—for the greater religious stability of the *oikoumene*—imbue ourselves with the biblical narrative as it is, thus rebuilding bridges and walking on them—the Same and the Other on one bridge![39]

39. I am grateful to CAPES for granting me a senior fellowship for my research at Princeton Theological Seminary in Princeton, NJ, USA.

2.

Limits and Possibilities for the Ecumenical Movement Today

A Latin American View

MAGALI DO NASCIMENTO CUNHA

The marks left on the contemporary history of Christianity by the international ecumenical movement of the twentieth century are undeniable. Among the marks deserving to be remembered and celebrated are, first, the search for an answer to the demands of unity in the missionary movement, striving "so that the world may believe"; second, the articulations around "practical Christianity" that would overcome historical doctrinal divides; third, the doctrinal dialogue in efforts to produce "faith and order"; and fourth, the joint actions of Christian youth and educators from different churches, confessions, and regional Christian associations.

As history unfolds in the wake of the international ecumenical movement, it has brought a number of new demands and many results: the awareness of the challenges arising from the technological revolution; the church participation in the public sphere; the sharing of human and financial resources; actions concerning human rights (including the fight against racism); projects for popular education; the ecological issue; solidarity toward women; overcoming violence; an ecumenical theology on baptism, Eucharist, and ministry, as well as the Church's *raison d'être*; the promotion of an interreligious dialogue; the joint statements on mission and evangelization; and the quest for economic justice in times of globalization and a borderless market. And we could list other results of the rich, centuries-old history of concrete testimony that Christian unity is possible in a theological dialogue that is coupled with cooperative missionary actions of solidarity.

However, one needs to recognize that ecumenism and the ecumenical movement have never enjoyed unanimous acceptance among churches, whether Roman Catholic, Orthodox, or Protestant.[1] Historically, the results listed above have been met with obstacles from the churches and Christian groups, and we will identify these obstacles in the first section of this chapter.

PRELIMINARY THOUGHTS: LISTING OBSTACLES TO ECUMENICAL PRACTICE

Addressing the ecumenical scenario requires paying heed to the obstacles of the practice of unity. The obstacles listed here are a construct based on an earlier study,[2] coupled with my experience of observing and interacting with different confessional and ecumenical expressions over at least thirty years. This experience was garnered through participation in the church, as well as volunteer and employed work in ecumenical bodies.

The obstacles in question mainly arise from ecumenical indifference and anti-ecumenism, ecumenical indifference being the more prominent of the two. Ecumenical indifference corresponds to the tendency toward schism, which has characterized churches throughout history. This indifference has resulted in the peaceful coexistence of Christians despite the divisions, which is now considered something natural for Christianity. In actuality, this understanding breeds indifference and insensitivity to the challenges of the ecumenical cause and the actions undertaken by the ecumenical movement.

Anti-ecumenism is the stance against the ecumenical principle and the practice it entails. The Latin American context shows some of the causes and motivations of anti-ecumenism, which can be linked to the experiences of other regions of the world. These causes and motivations include the following:

1. Julio Santa Ana, *Ecumenismo e Libertação: Reflexão sobre a Relação entre Unidade Cristã e o Reino de Deus* (Petrópolis: Vozes, 1987).

2. Claudio de Oliveira Ribeiro and Magali do Nascimento Cunha, *O Rosto Ecumênico de Deus: Reflexões sobre Ecumenismo e Paz* (São Paulo: Fonte Editorial, 2013).

- The anti-Catholicism cultivated among Protestants, which is part of the history of churches in some Latin American countries. This also includes the exclusivist way North American missionaries who introduced Protestant Christianity into the continent built their ministry featuring anti-Catholic preaching with a conversionist appeal, which regarded Catholics as pagans and idolaters. These pastoral moves left marks, the effects of which can still be felt today. One such effect includes the perspective that the ecumenical cause is nothing but a strategy of the Roman Catholic Church to steer Protestants back into it.
- The exclusivist attitude of the Roman Catholic Church, recorded in documents such as the "Declaration *Dominus Iesus* on the unicity and salvific universality of Jesus Christ and the Church."[3] This text can be understood as a restatement of views that were once overcome but that conjure up the sovereignty of the Roman Catholic Church over other Christian churches. This text bolstered the anti-ecumenical stance of Catholics and Protestants, which ended up shutting down many channels for dialogue and interaction, reinforcing the anti-Catholic position of many Protestant groups.
- The anti-Pentecostalism of the so-called historical churches, both the Roman Catholic and Protestant churches, which took issue with Pentecostal theology and its way of cultivating faith as well as with its ensuing growth that arose from the sharp adherence of believers to this pastoral proposition. This attitude has led them to downgrade Pentecostal groups, labeling them not as churches but as sects.
- The characteristics of Pentecostal groups: a tendency to denominationalism, made up of schisms and divides within the movement itself and in its relationship with other evangelical expressions; theological disputes and tensions around community power and control among leaders, leading to many schisms; Pentecostal withdrawal resulting from the exclusivist theological and pastoral perspective that is typical of this group.

3. Congregation for the Doctrine of Faith, "Declaration *Dominus Iesus* on the Unicity and Salvific Universality of Jesus Christ and the Church," http://www.vatican.va/roman_curia/congregations/cfaith/documents/rc_con_cfaith_doc_20000806_dominus-iesus_en.html.

- The resulting difficulty Christian leaders have in dealing with religious plurality, which results in prejudice and ensuing disengaging attitudes as "self-protection" and in downgrading or underrating expressions different from what is considered "standard."
- The inherent fear of the different and the neglect of otherness, breeding unawareness, ignorance, and prejudice—the roots of anti-ecumenism.
- The derivative crisis of identity in Christian groups. Being aware of one's identity is a factor also built through relating with others; it provides one with assurance, and it does not hamper relationships. Crisis of identity—that is, not being aware of oneself and not knowing that building oneself is achieved by relating with others—breeds insecurity and a sense of threat, withdrawal, and self-preservation.
- The vengeful attitude arising from the experience of intolerance. This is what happens when a group perceives attitudes of religious intolerance, exclusivism, or arrogance from another group and strikes back with other attitudes grounded in the same principles.
- The ideological issues and power disputes within ecclesiastical spaces, which jeopardize internal unity and resonate throughout the relationship with other groups. As ecumenical practice is weakened by the reasons listed above, it is often politically and ideologically used to justify institutional frailties and threats to the ecclesiastical body.
- Such power disputes lead to other anti-ecumenical attitudes, which are stirred up by the prejudice and a feeling of uneasiness between ecclesiastical leaders toward those who "think outside of the box"—that is, those leaders who take part in ecumenical actions that allow them to expand theological outlooks and worldviews, and give them chances to work in other spaces. Prejudice fuels accusations that people engaged in the ecumenical cause are uninvolved with their own group. This creates feelings of discomfort in relation to others with more opportunities for participation, which can be translated as jealousy or even envy.

- Leaders engaged in the ecumenical cause are unconcerned with an appropriate communication pedagogy to reach the church "bases" and to socialize theology and proposals for actions. Because of that, unawareness and prejudice are bolstered.

Any considerations or assessments of the status of the ecumenical movement must take these preliminary thoughts into account. They help spot the sources of tensions and clashes which also pose significant limitations to the history of the movement, especially as it relates to Latin America.

CRISES AND UNCERTAINTIES

For the first time, in Porto Alegre in 2006, an Assembly of the World Council of Churches was held in Latin America. Undeniably, Latin America has contributed to the efforts for dialogue and cooperation since the Missionary Conference in Panama in 1916 and has been pivotal in building the history of the ecumenical movement around the world. Latin America has provided grounds for this discussion, but these efforts for unity include a history of varying crises and uncertainties, such as political issues of nationalism, "pan-Americanism" and "Latin-Americanism," as well as the cultural controversies that arise at the prospect of building a relevant ecclesial presence on the continent, all of which occur in lieu of the ensuing debate on a Latin American theology, actions for human rights, and a project for popular ecumenical education, among other issues.[4] Such memories help us recognize that finding unity in theological dialogue and missionary actions of solidarity and cooperation is possible. However, these are also memories of clashes and divide, still tangible in the present, which pose a number of limits to the ecumenical movement on the continent. The following section of this chapter will address them.

CATHOLICS VS. PROTESTANTS

Since the early missionary actions in the nineteenth century, the ecumenical movement on the continent has been marked by tensions

4. José Miguez Bonino, *Rostos do Protestantismo Latino-Americano* (São Leopoldo: Sinodal, 2003).

with the Roman Catholic Church. Catholic leaders reacted against Protestant presence in Latin America through boycotts and persecution, sometimes backed by governments, and these actions sparked vengeful actions and attitudes as well as resentment from many Protestant leaders. Conversely, the attitudes of missionaries promoting Protestant unity as a response to the hegemonic Catholic presence on the continent ended up instilling an anti-Catholic stance, which has lingered to the present day.

It is true that this situation has undergone changes brought about by the passing of time, such as the opening of the Catholic Church toward perspectives of unity among Christians and a rapprochement with the ecumenical movement as of the 1960s, a result of the Second Vatican Council. This new attitude has burgeoned in Latin America through the Catholic Episcopate Conferences in Medellín (1968) and Puebla (1979). In that spirit, a meeting of the World Student Christian Federation (WSCF) in Bolivia in 1955 pointed out that ecumenical relations in Latin America should include the Catholic Church.[5]

The experience of the church and society in Latin America (ISAL) movement has also shown that Protestants and Catholics have been able to engage in dialogue and joint actions. The ISAL was the result of connections among Latin American Protestants, made real through the Latin American Evangelical Conferences (CELAs) held in 1949 (Buenos Aires), 1961 (Lima), and 1969 (Buenos Aires). At the CELAs, which gathered 200 Protestants from over forty churches and thirty countries, they discussed the social dimension of Protestant theology, the geographical organization of the ecumenical movement, and issues such as underdevelopment, hunger, and agrarian reform on the continent.

ISAL was established at the 1961 CELA and aimed to steer churches to the biblical and theological bases of Christian social and political responsibility. It gave rise to the publication of the *Christianity and Society* journal and books with reflections by Latin American Protestant theologians such as Jose Miguez Bonino, Julio de Santa Ana, and Rubem Alves, who are considered founders of the Latin American theology of liberation. Hugo Assmann and Pablo Richard

5. Dafne Sabanes Plou, *Caminhos de Unidade: Itinerário do Diálogo Ecumênico na América Latina* (São Leopoldo: Sinodal; Quito: Clai, 2002).

were some of the Catholics participating in this space for theological dialogue.[6]

Nevertheless, we need to admit that those attitudes, both for overcoming anti-Catholicism and asserting the ecumenical spirit among Latin Americans, have always been taken up by a minority. As an example, ISAL has faced criticism and rejection from most churches.

WITHDRAWAL FROM DIALOGUE AND COOPERATION

The same difficulty can be seen in regard to the level of adherence to national Latin American and world church councils. The official presence of churches from the continent in those associations is meager if we consider the huge number of Christian churches and associations on the continent. For example, very few Latin American churches are members of the World Council of Churches (WCC)—only twenty-seven from eleven of the twenty Latin American countries. The continent is considered the second in number of Christians in the world, most of whom are members of the Roman Catholic Church, which is experiencing a fall in the number of believers in face of the fast growth of Pentecostalism and Evangelical revivalism. Proportionally, that is the lowest presence of churches per continent in the WCC. In fact, since the first efforts for unity in Latin America, most Protestants have taken up a conservative posture and believe the ecumenical movement poses a risk and a threat to Christian churches and groups, and together with Catholicism, they believe it should be avoided and repelled.[7]

It is important to note here that we cannot address those elements in a simplistic way, without taking into account the political and ideological dimensions involved in the ecumenical movement. Throughout its history, ecumenism in Latin America has proved itself to be a change-making agent, an agent for social transformation and renewal of churches in the theological, pastoral, and liturgical areas. Social and political conservatism coupled with theological and pastoral positions of churches, which hinder prospects of change and inhibit the transforming presence of churches in the public space, have certainly been an influential factor leading to the rejection of the

6. José Bittencourt Filho, "Por Uma Eclesiologia Militante: ISAL Como Nascedouro de Uma Nova Eclesiologia para a América Latina" (master's thesis, Instituto Metodista de Ensino Superior, 1988).

7. Ribeiro and Cunha, *O Rosto Ecumênico de Deus.*

ecumenical movement and its expressions. A historical fact confirming this conclusion would be the cruel persecutions that ecumenical-movement leaders suffered in the Latin American countries under military dictatorships from the 1960s to the 1980s. Those Christians experienced imprisonment, death, forced disappearance, and exile.[8] The period of repression by military dictatorships was also reflected in the internal repression of ecclesiastical institutions, contributing to the growing crises and setbacks in the ecumenical movement, having implications for the present. One example of that is the effort made by church councils such as the Latin American Council of Churches (CLAI) on the continent and national church councils to move toward representativeness and visibility, which ultimately resulted in reflecting the limitations of the churches in regard to ecumenical engagement.

We also need to recognize that many of those negative attitudes stem from a lack of access to proper information about ecumenism and a lack of training on unity in church Christian education. Misinformation and prejudice abound. There are leaders who sometimes speak against ecumenism and the ecumenical movement without knowing the actual positions of the movement. In their turn, those embracing the movement seem not to have found a pedagogy or an effective form of communication. Consequently, these ecumenical leaders lack the language to connect with local communities, and because of that, programs and materials often fail to communicate properly.

Compounding this deficiency in education is the fact that the greatest ecclesial phenomenon of the continent—the growth of Pentecostal churches—has not changed that situation. As previously mentioned, specific features of this Christian group compound this phenomena.

HIERARCHIES VS. "BASES"

It is important to recognize that many of those crises and uncertainties in the ecclesiastical arena owe more to the power of hierarchy and clericalism, which have characterized the life of Latin American Christian communities. This is possibly because of the patriarchal and paternalist culture of the continent. As a result, people hold very

8. Plou, *Caminhos de Unidade.*

different positions concerning everyday experiences, in which confessional tensions and classical divisions are overcome without any planning or structuring, and which promote unity in the fights for life and rights. Joint actions among Latin American Christians in response to community needs are a reality as well as a wish to be together for common prayer and Bible study. The experiences of Protestants, both traditional and Pentecostal, with base ecclesial communities of the Catholic Church are a powerful example. Some call these experiences "base ecumenism."[9] They exist and are a reality in Latin America. Moreover, they are a sign of strength in an ecclesial and ecclesiastical context that shows itself to be unfavorable to ecumenical practice in Latin America because the current church context has assimilated a new religious order: market-based religion.

MARKET-BASED RELIGION: INDIVIDUALISM AND COMPETITION

The advance of globalized capitalism as of the 1990s has brought about a new world order in which technological investment has become a decisive strategy. Information and communication channels have been granted a privileged space. A big share of world economy has turned its focus to information and communication, and in the twenty-first century, the communication and information industry has cemented its position as the biggest in the world. The marriage between market and media has solidified.

In such a social, political, and economical context, the Latin American religious field has been experiencing the phenomenon of the growth of Pentecostal movements. Numerous autonomous churches have sprung up; they are organized around leaders and based on proposals of healing, exorcism, and prosperity; and they do not stress the need of moral or cultural restrictions to reach divine blessing. They are also grounded on the rehashing of traits of popular Latin American religiousness and on valuing the use of symbols and iconic representations. There is also a more recent type of Pentecostalism, which privileges the search for young, middle-class followers and religious music and entertainment as a communication resource.

9. Zwinglio Motta Dias, "O Movimento Ecumênico: História e Significado," *Numen* 1, no. 1 (1998): 127–63.

Such Pentecostal presence can be seen in the life of the continent mainly in two forms: heavy investment in media spaces and participation in political parties or pursuit of public offices. The Pentecostal growth has deeply influenced the state of other Christian churches. It has left Protestants with an uncomfortable feeling regarding an aspect that has marked the historical churches in Brazil: stagnation and a considerable numerical abatement, prompting some sort of motivation for competition and the search for new followers. It has posed a threat to Catholics, for their followers are targeted by the Pentecostal proselytism, and that has led to a numerical decrease among those who profess the Catholic faith. Its influence has especially materialized in the enhancement of the so-called "revivalist" or "charismatic renewal" groups, whose proposals and postures are similar to those of Pentecostalism, and they have taken up important spaces in the religious practice of the historical churches, which are trying to regain some ground or achieve some numerical growth.

Also, there is the growth of the so-called faith-based market. Christians make up a sector of the market. Products and services are specially designed to meet their religious needs, be they consumptive goods or leisure and entertainment activities. There has been a considerable increase of number of products (goods and services) marketed to Christians. We can find a wide variety of products, such as clothes, cosmetics, sweets, and travel packages, with brands using slogans with religious appeal, Bible verses, or simply the name of Jesus. Big commercial events, like Catholic and Evangelical fairs—meant to display products especially geared to those consumers—have enjoyed more and more success.

Simultaneously, big (secular) media agencies have absorbed the energy from this flurry of activity and started to produce shows to compete for Christian audiences: space for contemporary Christian music (gospel music) and its artists, sponsorship of street festivals, mega-events, and broadcasting of religion-based entertainment shows. Such interactions have affected the culture of religious groups, especially their celebration practices (Catholic masses and evangelical cults), which have ended up taking on aspects of broadcast media. That has translated into a high dependency on technology and on the reproduction of performance formats, as well as a surge of interest in content developed around religious media celebrities. Consequently, that results in homogenization (standardization) and a slackening of spontaneity, characteristic features of the cultural industry—religious culture, in this case—which confirms the magnitude of the religion-market-media relation.

Market-based religion has emerged as a religious culture assimilated by Protestants and Catholics on the continent, with the following features: a pursuit of measurable results by leaders (gains in numbers and in properties), a search for visibility in the social space (public offices and media presence), the preaching of an intimate religion characterized by the search for answers to immediate practical problems, the valuing of consumption goods, and the pursuit of social mobility as evidence of God's blessing of the life of the faithful. In this regard, we should not only focus on the practices engaged in by the so-called neo-Pentecostal groups, which is the tendency of a number of analysts in regard to these theological and pastoral forms. A large number of historical churches on the continent, including the Roman Catholic Church, have assimilated those dimensions into their discourses and practices, mainly through the charismatic renewal movement.

A REVISION OF THE UNDERSTANDING OF MISSION

At this point, we can bring up a discussion that has been present in the Latin American ecumenical movement since its inception: the understanding of mission. If in the past, mission was an essential element for promoting Christian unity, "so that the world may believe" (John 17:21 ESV), the religious field on the continent added another idea to it: that we cannot do mission without promoting life, peace, and justice.

At present, Protestant churches are challenged by the prospect of working with "missions" in their different iterations: transcultural, national, indigenous, and window focused, among others. This posture increases the detachment between the church and the general population, its existence and its needs. Instead, what matters is numerical growth and recruiting members for the churches. Here we reach a sensitive point: this push for growth at any cost, for new forms of religious proselytism, and for a revival of anti-Catholicism has resulted in a rise in the number of people withdrawing from any proposals for dialogue and interreligious cooperation, rendering the potential ecumenical relationships even weaker.

In this context of the search for achieving and consolidating "Evangelical visibility" on the continent, social actions take place. In a response to the current political and economic model (globalized capitalism), governments and companies have their stopgap programs to counter the effects of the exclusion (these include "foundations," "charities," and "community projects"), but they have fallen short of consistently and coherently overcoming causes and structures. Likewise, a number of churches have invested in social work, but the lack of critical analysis in regard to the root cause of the social functions they seek to change points to the fact that this investment has just become a source of evangelization or institutional marketing.[10]

As a result, Protestants have garnered self-confidence and started feeling they can have a significant voice in society. Statistics on the growth of some churches, their growing media presence (TV and radio, publications, different spaces on the Internet), and their participation in the political sphere reveal increasing numbers.

Such a description does not imply a homogeneous situation across the Latin American Christian scenario. There are other perspectives that work toward more community-based and contextualized actions. However, the situation described seems to be the hegemonic theological and pastoral panorama which brings about the crises and the uncertainties that plague the ecumenical movement on the continent.

FROM LIMITS TO POSSIBILITIES

The challenge of addressing the limits and possibilities for the ecumenical movement demands a courageous attitude: turning off or shutting down some equations that often curb and hold back ecumenical reflection. We will look into two of them.

One equation is "Ecumenism = Ecumenical movement." If we work with the understanding that "ecumenism" is God's plan, a Christian principle, a missionary assignment, as presented by the biblical text, then it is clear that what we call the "ecumenical movement," with all its strands and expressions, is the result of efforts working toward its materialization in history. Therefore, we cannot equate the soundness of the principle to the paths, advances, failures,

10. Magali do Nascimento Cunha, *A Explosão Gospel: Um olhar das ciências humanas sobre o cenário evangélico contemporâneo no Brasil* (Rio de Janeiro: Mauad, 2007).

and contradictions experienced by the movement. The ecumenical principle is much bigger than the ecumenical movement as we know it.

Ecumenism is, then, a term referring to the biblical and theological principle of unity of the creation of God, which calls us to value others and diversity (Gen 2:18) and results in acceptance, respect, dialogue, responsibility toward creation, partnership, and love for others (Deut 10:19). It is a Christian principle of overcoming divides in the name of the loyalty to the unity of the Father with the Son (John 17:21). The principle stems from the Judeo-Christian heritage, but the terminology is "recent" (according to Julio de Santa Ana,[11] the first record of the term dates back to the seventeenth century). The ecumenical movement is, therefore, the result of the *oikoumene* principle, God's plan, and should be grounded in it and materialize it, and not the other way around. As it is a movement, ecumenism implies characteristics such as diversity of expression, dynamism, and constant transformation.[12]

In Latin America, the ecumenical movement has gone through golden and noteworthy moments, such as the organization of evangelical conferences (the CELAs); the creation of the ISAL, with its important publication, *Christianity and Society*; youth movements; and the embrace of new extensions, especially in the 1950s. The Latin American ecumenical movement went through hard times in the 1980s because of civil and military coups in many countries on the continent and the ensuing repression period. This led to the overt or covert submission of some church leaders to dictatorships, giving them open or cloaked support through silence and omission. That has been left behind during the past thirty years, and the movement has survived through efforts by some devoted people who got together, albeit in a subversive way, to keep up the principle and the ideals, carried forward by organizations that teamed up and challenged the churches. This process was taken up by some of them, who quickly reorganized themselves in local councils and associations, and later under the Latin American Council of Churches (CLAI, in 1982). This council certainly did not possess the same strength as before, but it inherited the effects of the imposed political and ecclesiastical repression.

11. Cunha, *A Explosão Gospel.*
12. Ribeiro and Cunha, *O Rosto Ecumênico de Deus.*

Another equation that sometimes curbs ecumenical reflection is "Ecumenical movement = Churches/World Council of Churches." This limiting equation can be overcome if we stress that the ecumenical movement is, as its name implies, a movement, and it is made up of a diversity of expressions and vocations in the name of unity. Those who sowed the seeds of this movement were groups of lay people, missionaries, pastors, and theologians—people with a vocation for promoting unity, those who, along with groups of confessional families, gathered among themselves and with others. The ecumenical movement leans on churches as one of its main cornerstones and the WCC as its most significant and important expression; however, its dynamism is consolidated whether it is met with support or opposition, regardless of the adherence or the detachment of churches. History has made this evident.

These ideas are important when we reflect on the landscape of the ecumenical movement. When we assess this dimension and focus on the situation of churches and their stances, attitudes, and decisions, we identify many crises and frustrations. For example, as regards the Methodists from the continent, there are cases like what happened in Brazil, where the Methodist Church pulled out of the National Council of Christian Churches (CONIC) and other bodies in which the Catholic Church takes part. This took place in 2006, rendering the ecumenical perspective even more fragile and making more visible the extremely low adherence of Brazilian churches to those and other ecumenical organizations. Other churches from other Latin American countries share the same stance. There is also the case of Cuba, with tensions between the Methodist Church and the Matanzas Theological Seminary, of which that church was a founding member, along with the Reformed Presbyterian Church of Cuba and the Episcopal Church of Cuba (1946). The Methodist Church left the Matanzas Seminary in 2006 and founded its own school of theology. Also, in Brazil, there was the case of the Presbyterian Church, which historically detached from all national ecumenical organizations after the civil and military coup. It still breathed the winds of unity through its participation in the World Alliance of Reformed Churches when it departed from it in 2006—coincidently in the same year as the Methodist crises—blaming their decision on the excessive permissiveness, thus proclaiming an absolute self-exile. Among Roman Catholics, the pontificates of John Paul II and Benedict XVI brought about a disengagement from ecumenical dialogue, especially by the Latin American Episcopal Council (CELAM), which has become more conservative, with the goal of defending Catholic hegemony on the continent. The pontificate of Francis, the first Latin American pope, has been more ecumenically open, but changes are expected in that scenario. These are some narratives of tensions and conflicts in the continent, and there are certainly others involving churches and their ecumenical associations.

Thus, attaching the ecumenical movement to churches and the ecclesiastical world equals attaching it to those and many other positions that either deny the principle of unity which is part of God's plan for creation or make it relative or even change it to promote their own ecclesiastical institutional projects, almost always grounded on the fundamental issue of power and its controversies.

Here it is worth remembering that the ninth Assembly of the World Council of Churches, held in Latin America, in Porto Alegre, Brazil, in 2006,[13] challenged churches and other participants in at least two ways. One was through the "Ecumenical Conversations" program and in their committees, to think up a path to the future of WCC and the ecumenical movement: the quest for a reflection and practice surrounding the ecclesial and ecumenical context. The second way was the experience of the "Mutirão," or collective effort to get something done. The "Changing the Ecclesial and Ecumenical Context" ecumenical conversation put forward the emerging issues of new forms of ecumenism and challenges for unity—seeking an ecumenical response for today.

Those issues were brought into another conversation, named "Reconfiguration of the Ecumenical Movement." We can no longer view the ecumenical movement as the unity of structures, but must see it as a mosaic with many specialized organs, ministries, and members. The churches, protagonists from the past, now share this landscape with many other players. In one of the plenary sessions, the participants came up with a metaphor to understand this process: an ecumenical choreography, in which many take part, each with their own movement, a different expression, but everyone "dances" in harmony to the same music (God's plan). Just like the other church councils, the WCC is, in fact, one of the many elements of this

13. To learn more about the contents and facts of the ninth Assembly of the World Council of Churches, held in Porto Alegre in 2006, visit the event website, http://wcc2006.info/en/theme-issues.html.

complex context, the one whose vocation is to ensure the coherence of the movement as a whole, for it holds the unifying legacy of the processes that originated from the development of what we call "ecumenical movement."

In the midst of political and financial constraints, the institutionalized ecumenical movement has—with difficulty—managed to recognize that its future can be promising only if it centers itself on its vocation of articulating the process of unity, which is at its core. The Assembly of Porto Alegre already showed that if the ecumenical movement succumbs once and for all to the traps of institutionalization, its organisms will be doomed to extinction or to a vegetative state.

The Collective Endeavor, the second highlighted moment of the ninth WCC Assembly, endorses that view. Hundreds of projects, organizations, and ecclesiastical and non-ecclesiastical groups were there to share their actions, bringing visibility to the mosaic of numerous bodies and members. Education, gender, theology, environment, overcoming violence, youth, health, human rights—it is difficult to list in just a few words all the themes and motivations for action and reflection shared by people from over one hundred countries, of different genders, ages, ethnicities, cultures, and faith confessions. It was inspiring and enthralling to experience such great vigor, which reaffirmed that the ecumenical movement is much bigger than the churches. This approach seems to be the "the most excellent way."

PART II

Pluralism, Ecumenism, and Intercultural Communication

3.

Pluralism, Ecumenism, and Intercultural Communication

South African Experiences

RETIEF MÜLLER

Twentieth-century Christian ecumenism was a form of globalization with universalistic ideals. It would be safe to suggest, of course, that it was a benign form of globalization, but it was certainly an attempt to find common ground and unify global Christianity to an extent hitherto unknown in the world of religions. In this process of Christian globalization, the World Council of Churches (WCC) reigned supreme.

In the contexts of the Cold War, neocolonialism, and colonialism of a special type (as apartheid in South Africa had been described),[1] the WCC made important and decisive statements and contributions to actively promote the cause of human rights. In the case of South Africa, local ecumenical bodies also played significant roles in opposition to apartheid. The South African Council of Churches (SACC) and the Christian Institute (CI) are particularly noteworthy.[2] On most issues the SACC and the WCC worked well together, but there were some disagreements and tensions. One example is the WCC's Program to Combat Racism (PCR), launched in 1969, which

1. Mark Rathbone, "The Road to South African Freedom: Programme of the South African Communist Party," *African Communist* 2, no. 2 (January–March 1963), 43–44.

2. See John W. De Gruchy, *The Church Struggle in South Africa* (Minneapolis: Fortress Press, 2005), 101.

somewhat controversially channeled funds to liberation movements that were engaged in an armed struggle against the regime in South Africa. During this period, whether one agreed with the stance of the WCC or whether one remained critical of the option of violent resistance, as tended to be the normative position within the SACC, there was no doubt that the Christian ecumenical movement was at the cutting edge of pro-democratic activism. Increasingly through the rise of people's clergy in the late 1970s and 1980s, such as Desmond Tutu and Allan Boesak in South Africa, the local expression of Christian ecumenism became personalized (humanized) and came to the fore of the struggle against apartheid. That was a golden era for an ecumenical movement, which somewhat inevitably lost steam once many of those battles were won and South Africa entered into the age of a democratic post-1994.

Despite the disagreement between the SACC and the WCC regarding the specific methods of the PCR, the SACC was a pivotal anti-apartheid grouping, successfully lobbying for international economic disenfranchisement in South Africa and utilizing its official anti-violence stance to maximum effect from the mid-1970s onward by agitating in favor of conscientious objection and against enforced military conscription by the South African Defense Force. SACC members were able to support such a consistently nonviolent stance with a great deal of moral high ground in their favor precisely because of the earlier critical stance against the PCR's program of funding the armed struggle.[3]

This type of ecumenism represents the best of the Christian tradition. It seems to affirm Christianity's central role within the development of human rights, as John Witte has persuasively argued regarding the Reformation in particular.[4] However, if one supports this vision of Christianity, then one must also be honest enough to admit that a consistent stance in support of a specific vision of human rights, premised on equality and equalization, has to be intolerant of hierarchical and patriarchal systems of whatever kind. Such a stance simply could not be culturally relativist, in other words. If the reader agrees with this point, the obvious question immediately follows: Is this a stumbling block for intercultural communication, interfaith dialogue, and so forth? One might perhaps simply answer

3. Ibid., 138–47.

4. John Witte, *The Reformation of Rights: Law, Religion and Human Rights in Early Modern Calvinism* (Cambridge: Cambridge University Press, 2007).

this question by stating that the gospel is a stumbling block for all of us. That is its nature. We are felled and birthed anew in the light of God. However, that in a sense avoids the question, because what is really at stake is the question of whether equalization belongs to the essence of the gospel.

Although Andrew Walls and many missiologists since have argued persuasively for the 'cultural translatability' of Christianity,[5] one might legitimately posit that Christianity is not really the gospel if certain rights of egalitarian humanity are not pursued by Christians. Therefore, the relative success of the translatability thesis might be measured against the extent to which Christian communities proceed to adapt and challenge their own societal norms to reflect a real "equality of believers."[6] However, if one uses this as a measuring rod for authentic Christianity, if one even insists on the idea of an authentic Christianity over against presumably false Christianities, has one not then discarded the very idea of cultural translatability in favor of a kind of cultural imperialism? I shall be problematizing this question some more in what follows, although space disallows me to really attempt resolving the issue here.

THE IMPERIALIST AND CULTURIST MISSIONARY TRADITIONS

The theme of cultural diversity has good reasons for being contentious in South Africa. It was employed as a fixed, divinely ordained principle for keeping different groups of people separate and legally segregated at every conceivable level.[7] This is evident in the history of apartheid and the role of the Dutch Reformed Church in its construction. Although that story is well documented elsewhere, it is important to note that it was specifically the DRC's mission policy that

5. Andrew F. Walls, *The Missionary Movement in Christian History: Studies in the Transmission of Faith* (Maryknoll, NY: Orbis, 1996); *The Cross-Cultural Process in Christian History: Studies in the Transmission and Appropriation of Faith* (Maryknoll, NY: Orbis, 2002).

6. Richard Elphick, *The Equality of Believers: Protestant Missionaries and the Racial Politics of South Africa* (Charlottesville: University of Virginia Press, 2012).

7. It is well known that the neo-Calvinist idea of sphere sovereignty as developed by Groen van Pinsterer and adopted by Abraham Kuyper came into (mis)use by Afrikaner Christian nationalists to argue for race as a sovereign sphere. See Mark Rathbone, "Sphere Sovereignty and Irreducibility: The Ambiguous Use of Abraham Kuyper's Ideas during the Time of Apartheid in South Africa," *Koers* 80, no. 1 (January 2015): 1–8, doi:10.4102/koers.v80i1.2208.

lay the foundations for apartheid.[8] It is perhaps worthwhile to zoom in on the specific missionary traditions that were active in South Africa, because although one missionary tradition was employed in the construction of and justification for apartheid, missionary agents from another tradition attempted to counter it and strove within limits for equalization among the South African population, as the historian Richard Elphick thoroughly demonstrates.[9] The crucial point for this essay is that the one tradition emphasized and even absolutized the importance of not only cultural particularity in the mission field, but especially the Other's culture, whereas the other tradition operated from the point of view that there was only one normative culture, that of the missionary, and that this culture and the gospel were part and parcel of the one and only Christian civilization, which was of course narrowly identified with, if not equal to, the British Empire. Surely, if one were ignorant of how these ideas became contextualized in history, would the former approach not seem the more enlightened one? It appears humbler, less ethnocentric, and less likely to demand the priority of its own temporal mores than the apparently chauvinistic, imperialistic view exemplified by David Livingstone, which ironically grouped together Christianity, Commerce, and Civilization as goals of the missionary movement in Africa.[10]

Yet it was the imperialist version of mission that helped to eradicate the slave trade and instituted legislation (e.g., Ordinance 50) in protection of the human rights of indigenous peoples.[11] By stating this, I am not attempting to sanitize this version of missionary engagement or to isolate it from its utter dependence on a deeply exploitative colonial enterprise. Of course, all colonial-era missions were similarly co-opted by wider systems. Yet individual missionaries were not necessarily dupes of the system, and within the purview of British missions, there are a few prime examples in Southern Africa of missionaries challenging the colonial administrations and the racial attitudes of colonists. London Missionary Society representatives such as Johannes van der Kemp and John Phillip were particularly infamous among Dutch settlers at the cape for their insistence that the natives had rights, and these missionaries were later somewhat vilified

8. Elphick, *Equality of Believers*, 222.

9. See Elphick, *Equality of Believers*.

10. See Stephen Tomkins, *David Livingstone: The Unexplored Story* (Oxford: Lion, 2013).

11. Richard Elphick and Rodney Davenport, *Christianity in South Africa: A Political, Social, and Cultural History* (Berkeley: University of California Press, 1997), 38.

in apartheid historiographies that served as apologia for an Afrikaner tradition of white supremacy.[12] A twentieth-century example of a missionary troublemaker in then Rhodesia would be the Anglican missionary activist Arthur Shirley Cripps (1869–1952).[13]

The Lutheran missions also produced some radicals, including Johannes Winter, who broke ranks with the Berlin Mission Society to found the Lutheran Bapedi Church, one of the first African Initiated Churches in South Africa,[14] as well as more recently the anti-apartheid activist Wolfram Kistner.[15] However, the culturist emphasis within these missions with the theoretical foundations derived from Gustav Warneck, Bruno Gutmann, and Siegfried Knak,[16] and which were also adopted by Afrikaner Dutch Reformed mission theorists, had the generally more profound impact on the religious and eventually political landscape. It will suffice to point out that the culturist emphasis resisted the melting-pot notion of equalization, because the melting-pot logic was viewed as anathema to cultural diversity and particularity. Hence, when apartheid apologists such as the Dutch Reformed Church's G. B. A. Gerdener conceptualized what was euphemistically termed separate development, the theory was that this system they were developing was not based on inequality. Rather, it was supposed to be separate but equal.[17]

It might be easy with the benefit of hindsight to evaluate such missionary theorizing as, at worst, a thin disguise that merely served to legitimize racial oppression, and at best as naive social engineering that essentialized culture and tradition. Yet Gerdener, for example, was probably quite sincere in his misguided belief in the justice of this missionary policy converted into a political program. Yet this system, once instituted, was indeed, among other things, an artificial construction of tribalism and racial categories with racially slanted development and educational policies. Separate but equal proved to be a pipe dream.

12. Apartheid historiography drew heavily on the sympathetic depiction of Boers and not very glowing assessments of English missionaries found in George McCall Theal, *History of the Boers in South Africa, Or, The Wanderings and Wars of the Emigrant Farmers: From Their Leaving the Cape Colony to the Acknowledgement of Their Independence by Great Britain* (London: S. Sonnenschein, Lowrey, 1887).

13. See Owen Sheers, *The Dust Diaries* (London: Faber & Faber, 2005).

14. Elphick and Davenport, *Christianity in South Africa,* 213.

15. Wolfram Kistner, *Outside the Camp: A Collection of Writings* (Johannesburg: South African Council of Churches, 1988).

16. Elphick, *Equality of Believers*, 172.

17. Ibid., 234.

THE TWENTIETH-CENTURY VICTORY OF ECUMENISM

When ecumenical Christian formations in South Africa started to oppose apartheid policies, especially from the early 1960s, such opposition initially came from the ranks of the so-called English-speaking churches that first networked together in the Christian Council, which later became the South African Council of Churches. Out of this formation emerged the "Message to the People of South Africa" in 1968, which was an important protest document. "The Cottesloe Declaration" drawn up by the WCC-convened Cottesloe Consultation of 1960 signified the first major crisis moment for the churches.[18] The consultation was convened after the Sharpeville police massacre of fleeing protesters had demonstrated the brutality of the apartheid regime to international audiences. It also exposed the ideological cracks between white Afrikaans churches on the one hand and the English-speaking churches on the other. Cottesloe declared among other things, "We recognize that all racial groups who permanently inhabit our country are a part of our total population, and we regard them as indigenous."[19] Although representatives of the major Afrikaans churches were present and the delegates of the white Dutch Reformed Church even signed the declaration, they were subsequently repudiated by their synods when it was decided to reject Cottesloe and withdraw from the World Council of Churches. For the white DRC, apartheid had become virtually sacrosanct, and the idea of racial distinctiveness as a theological principle was wholly subsumed within its identity. A former mission policy with its enlightened rejection of the normativity of any specific culture had become hardened into a worldview that conflated culture with race and that insisted on the preservation of distinct boundaries.

One way to bring the just-mentioned history directly in line with the theme of this chapter would be to state that the DRC accentuated pluralism at the cost of ecumenism. For the DRC and apartheid ideologues generally, pluralism or diversity was not a challenge to overcome, but rather something to keep intact as much as possible. In the eyes of the supporters of apartheid, their own

18. See De Gruchy, *Church Struggle,* 101.

19. "The Cottesloe Declaration (1960)," NG Church in South Africa's Archives, http://kerkargief.co.za/doks/bely/DF_Cottesloe.pdf, accessed July 5, 2016.

essentialist constructions of human plurality were exactly what justified their system and protected their white-supremacist identity. For the English-speaking churches represented by the SACC, in contrast, ecumenism and the unity of humanity were the foundational principles.

It hardly requires any soul searching to come to the conclusion that the English-speaking churches were right and the Afrikaner churches wrong. That is how history has already judged them in any case, and that is also how I judge this history. However, this history should still be further problematized for it to be of use to inform current and future challenges facing the church, not only in South Africa but worldwide.

If one states that ecumenicity won at least temporarily the ideological argument and also historical battle against the absolutism of diversity or pluralism, then one should not neglect to remind oneself of the fact that unity in spite of its universalistic pretentions is never neutral. Unity and ecumenicity are based on principles with ideological and cultural foundations. Are these foundations, at least within the South African context perhaps, not the very imperial missionary foundations exemplified in an earlier era by Philip, van der Kemp, et al.? Of course, there were other influences over time, but it is my basic contention that just as the apartheid theology tradition of the DRC and other white Afrikaner churches lay in a continuous line with missionary ideas that accentuated diversity, so the ecumenical Protestant tradition with its insistence on equal rights and the unity of humanity should not be cut off from its missionary roots, which in South Africa at least are roots that are firmly anchored in imperial missionary soil.

NEW CHALLENGES FOR ECUMENISM AND INTERCULTURAL DISCOURSE

With these somewhat contradictory themes in mind, I would now like to move on and discuss more recent situations where the ecumenical movement and other Christian bodies have played an increasingly interesting public role in South Africa. Generally, in global perspective, it would be no exaggeration to argue that the world has seen an increase in intercultural/interreligious tension in recent times. The recent referendum in the United Kingdom that decided in favor of Britain leaving the European Union was to an extent driven by increased xenophobia and Islamophobia as a result of the refugee crisis in Europe. This culture of intolerance seemed to gain momentum in the days after the vote.[20] South Africa has seen less interreligious conflict than other parts of the African continent, but a resurfacing of tensions on the cultural/racial level has regrettably come to the fore after the post-democratic honeymoon era had come to an end. Incidents of xenophobic violence against migrants from other African countries occur increasingly. The ideal of the rainbow nation, so hopefully envisioned by Archbishop Desmond Tutu and other ecumenical Christian leaders and once embraced by most political formations has more recently lost some of its shine. "Rainbowism" is now more likely to be derided as a naive idea or as the subject of apologia for some.[21] Essentialist and binary constructions of whiteness and blackness are increasingly pitted against one another in the media and in debates on university campuses, where the term *decolonization* has gained much traction.

Christianity as a public religion in South Africa has also seen much diversification since the advent of democracy there in the late twentieth century. As one could expect, the ecumenical movement, as particularly represented by the SACC, initially found its role somewhat diminished. As it had been closely identified with the struggle against apartheid for much of its existence, there was initially some ambiguity regarding its proper stance toward the democratically elected government. One early vision regarding its role was that there should be a relationship of "critical solidarity" with the ruling party,[22] an idea that was heavily indebted to a historical legacy of close relationship between the SACC and the ANC as an underground movement. The idea of critical solidarity was, of course, oxymoronic and devoid of real meaning. After all, could you really be critical if you are in solidarity, and vice versa? As Dirkie Smit explains, it was jettisoned in 2001 in favor of the less problematic "critical engagement."[23] Nevertheless, in the early years of democracy, the churches generally

20. See Homa Khaleeli, "'A Frenzy of Hatred': How to Understand Brexit Racism," *Guardian*, June 29, 2016, http://www.theguardian.com/politics/2016/jun/29/frenzy-hatred-brexit-racism-abuse-referendum-celebratory-lasting-damage.

21. Douglas Gibson, "In Defiant Support of Rainbowism," *Independent Online*, accessed July 5, 2016, http://www.iol.co.za/the-star/in-defiant-support-of-rainbowism-1969925.

22. See Dirkie Smit, *Essays in Public Theology: Collected Essays* 1 (Stellenbosch, South Africa: African Sun Media, 2007), 67.

23. Ibid.

maintained an upbeat perspective regarding the societal trajectory in South Africa.

More recently, the relationship between the SACC and the South African government has cooled down. The presidency of Jacob Zuma and the many scandals and allegations connected to his name have been particularly influential in spurring this changed relationship. Part of the tension is that Zuma has preferred to lend his ear to a socially more conservative grouping of religious leaders, the recently formed National Interfaith Council of South Africa.[24] As the name indicates, this grouping is more pluralistic than the mainline Christian SACC. The NICSA theoretically includes representatives from all faith formations in South Africa, including Hindus and Muslims, but the numerical and ideological weight centers in the sizable proportion of Pentecostal and African Initiated Churches, which combined constitute the majority of South Africa's religious population. Jacob Zuma was even ordained as "honorary pastor" at a meeting of "independent charismatic churches," back when he was still deputy president of the ANC in 2007. This event took place in a facility belonging to the Full Gospel Church.[25] However, subsequently, the FGC quickly distanced itself from the controversial "ordination."

Matters came to a head on March 31, 2016, when the Constitutional Court of South Africa found that the president of South Africa had contravened the law of the land by his refusal to repay a substantial sum of public money he had been found to have improperly utilized for renovations at his private rural homestead at Nkandla, Kwazulu-Natal.[26] From the perspective of ecumenism and Christianity as a public religion, there are several points of interest regarding the ruling and its fallout.

The first point of interest concerns the official who delivered the damning judgment regarding Nkandla, Chief Justice Mogoeng Mogoeng. Mogoeng is a devout Pentecostal member of the Nigerian-originated Winner's Chapel International Church. He was appointed to his current position by none other than Zuma, and

24. Ntlantla Kgatlhane, "National Interfaith Council Welcomes President Zuma's Apology," *SABC News*, April 11, 2016, http://www.sabc.co.za/news/a/da582a804c5dac8d866ff79ffda8f5e4/National-Interfaith-Council-welcomes-President-Zumas-apology-20160411.

25. Chris Makhaye, "Church Lauds Zuma as Honorary Pastor," *Independent Online*, May 6, 2007, http://www.iol.co.za/news/politics/church-lauds-zuma-as-honorary-pastor-351656.

26. Stephen Grootes, "Analysis: The Judgment at the End of the Nkandla Road," *Daily Maverick*, March 31, 2016, http://www.dailymaverick.co.za/article/2016-03-31-analysis-the-judgment-at-the-end-of-the-nkandla-road/#.V3y3AKLQPZN.

skeptics pointing to this fact and the shared Pentecostal adherence of the two men had originally thought Mogoeng would simply be a yes-man, as other Zuma appointees in high-profile positions had apparently become. The fear was that his appointment would effectively compromise the independence of the Constitutional Court. Such fears had seemed well founded when the chief justice made some remarks regarding the way he understood the relation between religion and law at a conference in 2014, which made many commentators extremely anxious about what seemed to be an increasing religious encroachment on the public arena in South Africa.[27] Yet, when Mogoeng made his Nkandla judgment that in many respects rebuked the President quite severely, many skeptics became convinced at least of the judge's judicial integrity. In a sense, the case of Mogoeng and his pivotal position in the country's public system is testimony to a growing politicization of certain streams of Pentecostalism in South Africa. Although Mogoeng's judgment—or "sermon," if you will—was, of course, a special case and it would be unwarranted to extrapolate wider trends from individual judgments, it might possibly suggest the emergence of a significant and effective counterpoint to traditional ecumenism in South African religious and social affairs. Of course, individual high-level Pentecostal involvement in the South African struggle for justice is not at all a new trend, as the name of ANC stalwart Frank Chikane would serve to remind, but by and large, Pentecostalism has eschewed the SACC and abstained from making political statements. This was so during apartheid and remains so to a large extent today, but one might imagine with contemporary examples such as Mogoeng in evidence that things are changing.[28]

The SACC, spearheaded by the moral authority of the archbishop of Cape Town, Thabo Makgoba, has steadily become more critical of the government and especially President Jacob Zuma.[29] Therefore, it was not surprising that the SACC would issue a statement demanding Zuma's resignation after the Constitutional Court ruling by Mogo-

27. Pierre de Vos, "Chief Justice on 'Fornication' and 'Sanctity of the Family,'" *Constitutionally Speaking*, May 28, 2014, http://constitutionallyspeaking.co.za/chief-justice-on-fornication-and-sanctity-of-the-family/.

28. See, for example, Maria Frahm-Arp, "The Political Rhetoric in Sermons and Select Social Media in Three Pentecostal Charismatic Evangelical Churches Leading up to the 2014 South African Election," *Journal for the Study of Religion* 28, no. 1 (January 2015): 114–41.

29. Thabo Makgoba, "Mr Prez, Please Step Aside," *CityPress*, March 27, 2016, http://city-press.news24.com/Voices/mr-prez-please-step-aside-20160325.

eng, which found that he failed to "respect, uphold, and defend" the Constitution. What is perhaps somewhat surprising was the fact that the chorus of voices calling for Zuma's head also now includes the interfaith yet socially conservative National Religious Leaders Council (NRLC), which has Muslim, Hindu, Jewish, and Charismatic Christian representation.[30] Although these are extraordinary circumstances and it is unclear what the future might hold, the apparent convergence of opinion on this matter between the SACC and NRLC is significant and might be another signal of a new trajectory in South African ecumenical relations.

If there is reason to think Pentecostals are becoming more politically involved and if there is some optimism for the possibility of ecumenism becoming possibly more expansive and inclusive of a greater diversity of Christianity than the mainline churches that currently make up the SACC, then that optimism must immediately be tempered by another factor, which made itself apparent in the aftermath of the previously mentioned media briefing. That is the fact that South Africa's largest church, the Zion Christian Church, stolidly maintains its historical tradition of political quietism, at least at the official level of the church leadership. This was made clear by a rather extraordinary statement issued by the church leadership, which basically was a statement to the effect that they did not want to make a statement regarding whether or not Zuma should resign. This statement, or non-statement if you will, was prompted by the fact that the Rev. Senamo Molisiwa, a ZCC member but not among their top leadership, was included in the group of clergy who issued the media statement calling for Zuma's resignation. In the ZCC statement, Molisiwa, "who paraded himself wearing the ZCC insignia," was strongly rebuked by his church leadership, because "he was not mandated nor appointed by the ZCC to represent it in that forum."[31]

Molisiwa subsequently explained that in spite of wearing his ZCC insignia, which all ZCC members do as a rule anyway, he was in fact representing the Council of African Instituted Churches (CAIC), of which he is the general secretary. According to Molisiwa, Bishop Barnabas Lekganyane, head of the ZCC, was aware of his involvement in CAIC and approved of it, although Molisiwa had not

30. See "Religious Leaders Say President Zuma Has Lost All Morality to Govern," *Cii Broadcasting,* April 7, 2016, http://www.ciibroadcasting.com/2016/04/07/religious-leaders-say-president-zuma-has-lost-all-morality-to-govern/.

31. "ZCC_Response_Constitutional_Judgement.pdf," Google Docs, accessed July 6, 2016.

been deputized to represent the ZCC there.[32] Of course, the public perception could not have been aware of the finer intricacies of how one could be the head of an ecumenical body, in this case the CAIC, without being placed in that role specifically by one's church of affiliation. It is this public perception, which the ZCC no doubt sought to counter with their official declaration of neutrality on the question of whether Zuma should stay or go.

This situation does, however, serve to expose an interesting underlying tension in the South African religious landscape, regarding the extent to which the ecumenical movement represents grassroots Christianity or not. The ZCC might in a sense be taken as representative of African-Initiated Christianity in South Africa. Not only is it the largest AIC in the country, it is also the largest church. These types of churches with their typically rural loci tend to remain conservative politically. If they are going to express themselves in this arena, which they generally do not do, this will most likely be in support of, rather than opposition to, the status quo. A careful look at the ZCC statement is revealing. Dated April 11, 2016, the statement claims among other things that the ZCC has been brought into disrepute by the fact that Molisiwa (who is only described as a male individual) wore ZCC insignia at an anti-Zuma gathering. A revealing line reads as follows: "We would like to reiterate our long-standing and inelastic policy that THE ZCC IS ABOVE POLITICS." And in the next paragraph: "We urge our members to refrain from any actions and behavior that may harm the good name of the ZCC by aligning it to a particular political view."[33] Hence, the repudiation of Molisiwa does not mean that they are officially in favor of Zuma as president. It means that the arena of politics belongs to a world that is alien to and beneath their vision of church. The ZCC is in some respects a country in its own right, as I have argued elsewhere.[34]

The statement by the ZCC exposes the pluralism within South African Christianity. It points to a deep rift between at least two visions of how a church should relate to politics. On the one hand, there is the unifying, ecumenical vision of church and society where religion and politics are intermeshed. Then there is what I prefer to

32. Vicky Abraham, "ZCC Neutral on Zuma," *Citizen*, April 13, 2016, http://citizen.co.za/1073195/zcc-neutral-on-zuma/.

33. "ZCC_Response."

34. Retief Müller, *African Pilgrimage: Ritual Travel in South Africa's Christianity of Zion* (Burlington, VT: Ashgate, 2011).

call the culturist vision, where the church itself forms a self-sufficient society that imagines itself as free from the tumultuousness of political machinations. Significantly, a large proportion of South African Christians evidently self-identify with the latter perspective, with the ZCC and other Zionist-type churches continuing to attract a large following.

CONCLUSION

The contradistinction between the positions of ecumenical leaders on the one hand, and the official ZCC on the other, might be further generalized as a contrast between right-aligned Christianity and popular culturist Christianity. This contrast, although by no means the same or even historically connected, reminds one of that earlier colonial missionary-era contrast between imperial missionaries, with their specific ideas of the equalizing trajectories that Christian civilization entailed for both "European" and "Native," versus the German Lutheran and Dutch Reformed culturist notions that rejected unifying theories in relation to the demands of the gospel in favor of culturally/racially particularistic visions. In both historical contexts, there is a clear divergence regarding the role of religion in society as a whole. Should churches and individuals have a public voice speaking out for justice and against oppression, corruption, and other excesses committed by those in political authority?

Clearly, the answer to this question is yes, and hence my stance in this essay is that the more universalistic and ecumenical perspectives have been the more authentically Christian, to use a rather blunt term. The culturist perspectives—whether those that insisted on the near-sacral distinctiveness of cultures in colonial and apartheid South Africa or those that insist on the particularity of a specific church as a unique culture in and of itself—are not without hope. Indeed, a kind of intercultural communication is occurring between the two perspectives, as had been the case also in earlier eras. I have mentioned some names of individuals from the German mission societies who rebelled against the dominant paradigm, and I could also refer to the names of twentieth-century Dutch Reformed clergy and missionaries such as Nico Smith and Beyers Naudé, for example, who came to reject apartheid and strongly identified with ecumenical views in spite of their own culturist and nationalist backgrounds.

In a contemporary culturist Christian setting, although very different from those earlier colonialist types, the ZCC remains underwhelming in terms of its political edge. This church's position to wider society is highly complex, but the fact that they have someone like Senamo Molisiwa among their ranks is a sign of hope in spite of the official denunciation of him. The fact that he is there means there could be others with similar views within his church. Through such individuals, a kind of intercultural communication between different visions of Christian culture is already taking place, even if it is at present a highly contentious communication bordering on the excommunication of the intercultural agent in chief.

4.

Christianity as a Public Religion

Pluralism and Dialogue

JUNG MO SUNG

Faced with situations of injustice and human suffering, people with genuine faith cannot remain indifferent. They must take a stand and engage in movements or struggles for justice and for overcoming oppressive situations and suffering. Such engagement breaks away from the divide established by the modern world between public and private spheres, the latter being the one where religion should play its role. That is why Christian groups engaging in those struggles feel the need for theologies that are not restrained by the modern relegation of religion to the private sphere and eternal life; they search for reasons for their struggle in the Bible, in the great Christian authors from the past, and in "engaged" theologies.

The articulation between the practical demands of faith today and the theological teachings from the past works well in a markedly Christian society, such as the Western societies, or when discourse is addressed only to the religious group the activists belong to. However, after the fast-paced globalization process started in the 1980s, the increase of immigration, and the spread of information around the world, religious pluralism has become a new, fundamental, and challenging element in this equation. Furthermore, the biblical and theological texts from the past, which help create a basis for social and political participation of Christians, were written in times different from ours.

Because of that, the participation of Christians in the struggle for a fairer, more humane, and ecologically sustainable society requires more than just overcoming the relegation of faith to the private sphere. Along with the public-versus-private debate, we also need to face the issue of religious pluralism, not only in the sense of acknowledging this fact as unavoidable in the horizon of Christian mission, but also of figuring out whether pluralism is a value to be defended or something to be overcome in the name of a universal religion, be it one considered the true religion or one capable of including in itself all existing religions today.

The theme of public religion or, more specifically, Christianity as a public religion or a public dimension of Christianity, and public theology has been increasingly present in publications and debates within theology and Christian churches. However, we do not always see conceptual clarity or the implications of the adopted senses. Therefore, this chapter puts forward some reflections on concepts encompassed under this theme and seeks to understand better the challenge of the dialogue that emerges when a religion takes up its public dimension in a globalized world, marked by religious and cultural pluralism.

RELIGION, THE PUBLIC, AND THE PRIVATE

I would like to start by quoting a text by Jürgen Moltmann:

> For me, theology is not an inner-church or post-modern dogmatics, designed only for one's own community of faith. . . . Theology springs out of a passion for God's kingdom and its justice, and this passion grows up in the community of Christ. . . . As a kingdom-of-God theology, it needs to be a missionary theology, linking the church with society, and the people of God with the peoples of the Earth. It becomes a public theology, which participates in the "sufferings of this present time," and formulates its hopes for God at the places where contemporaries are and exist. *Kingdom-of-God theology intervenes critically and prophetically in public affairs of a given society*, and draws public attention, not to the church's own interest but to God's kingdom.[1]

1. Jürgen Moltmann, *Experiences in Theology: Ways and Forms of Christian Theology* (Minneapolis: Fortress Press, 2000), xx. Italics added.

In this quotation, Moltmann uses the term "public theology," and not public religion, but he hints at his understanding of public and of Christianity as a public religion. The first thing we can notice is that this idea of public theology opposes the idea of a theology strictly concerned with the internal affairs of the church, and of the Christian church and religions in general being restricted to the sphere of private life. Thus, he links the idea of public theology to God's kingdom and draws attention to the fact that theology should intervene "critically and prophetically in public affairs of a given society," to respond to the sufferings of this time.

In this regard, the idea of public is associated with the idea of social, a term including the economic and political dimensions of life in society. It is a proposal for overcoming the restriction of Christian religion and theology to the sphere of private life and matters regarding the ultimate meaning of existence and the afterlife. It is a proposal for taking up the social and public dimension of religious faith and religious institutions.

As our goal here is not to study Moltmann's thoughts, we are not going to discuss other possible aspects of the idea of public theology he might have addressed. His quotation is used here as an example of how many understand the public dimension of Christianity and Christian theology.

We can say that this broad concept of "public theology" can encompass a diversity of forms of theology previously classified as "political theologies," the various theologies of liberation and also others, which do not stress the strictly political, but work on the social dimension of Christian mission, such as the theology of integral mission in Latin America.

However, this idea of "public" in the expression "public religion/theology"—as the social and political dimension of religion, opposing and complementing the personal dimension—is not enough, and it may not be the most appropriate, for in this public-private, social-personal dimension, the issue of religious pluralism as an undeniable social fact of our times is not necessarily present. When we discuss the social and political dimension of Christianity in a predominantly Christian social context, the issue of religious pluralism does not necessarily come up in the discussion and may not even be seen as relevant. More likely, issues such as different Christian denominations or the legitimacy or not of ecumenical dialogue will be discussed, but not necessarily the issue of religious pluralism. And when the religious diversity of our globalized world is taken into account, people and churches defending the public dimension of Christianity and its mission in the social and political domains do not necessarily defend religious pluralism as something positive to be respected in the mission.

Well-intentioned Christian groups and churches might believe that the only way to solve the serious social and political problems plaguing our world is the way shown by the Bible or their church's social teaching, and they may try to impose—coercively or by convincing—their religious worldview upon the whole society. That often happens when Christians (just like people from other religions) participate in political activities and do not accept the separation of state and religion, which is typical of the modern secularized Western society.

Therefore, the discussion about "public religion" or the public dimension of a religious faith without engaging in a discussion on the issue of secularization and religious pluralism might make us tempted to go back to a type of theocracy or the use of the coercive forces of the state to impose upon the whole society the worldview and system of moral values of a given religious group.

If it is true that we need to overcome this restriction of religion to private life and the issue of afterlife, a typical move of modern societies, it is also true that active participation of religious institutions and groups in the public and political sphere, in the name of their faith or belief, may give rise to serious social problems.

Religious faith tends to claim absolute values and truths, while the domain of politics and the public sphere are spaces for ideological debates and disputes, which cannot assume absolute or definite ideas. I find it important here to distinguish between political, state, and public spheres. The political struggle for power is a dispute for controlling the state, which holds the monopoly of legitimate violence and coercion and the power to lay down upon the whole society laws setting limits for actions, rights, and liabilities. The public sphere, as shown by Habermas,[2] started to emerge in the eighteenth century and has developed as a social space distinct from the state, market,

2. Jürgen Habermas, *The Structural Transformation of the Public Sphere: An Inquiry into a Category of Bourgeois Society* (Cambridge: Polity, 1989).

and family, in which individuals can engage as citizens in the public debate on common good.

When a debate is undertaken between individuals from different cultural and religious backgrounds, we cannot apply debate rules and use a language that is specific to a given group. For example, when a Christian Catholic, a Christian Lutheran Protestant, and an agnostic gather for this debate, a common ground is necessary to make the dialogue possible. The only way to achieve this is through the language of rational and reasonable argumentation, in the sense that anyone of sound mind can understand and follow the argument of others. In other words, it is a place where arguments based on authorities (other than reason)—be they religions or philosophical—have no value.

Such separations between the public and private spheres, between state and church, and an idea of religion limited to private life and eternal salvation are all fruits or fabrications of modernity, through its secularization process. The Bible, for example, does not feature that separation, and religion is related to all aspects of social and personal life. Therefore, we need to revisit this issue of secularization in the modern world.

SECULARIZATION, RELIGIOUS WARS, AND PLURALISM

As seen above, the idea of "public religion" or "public theology" entails the division between the public and private, which did not exist in the ancient world and is still not accepted by theocratic societies such as Iran. The use or creation of the expression "public religion" is an attempt to describe what, in fact, still happens in many societies seen as secularized and, in many cases, to justify the introduction of religion into the public space and in social matters. This expression implies the separation—at least in theory—between state, which should be concerned with social and public issues, and church, which should restrict itself to issues classified as religious, of private nature, such as the belief in the afterlife, the ultimate meaning of life, and personal and intracommunity moral values.

In the late 1960s and early 1970s, when base communities and Latin American liberation theology (LALT) started to relate Christian faith to the issue of poverty and oppression, they were accused—by both church people and state and society at large—of mixing religion and politics, and of meddling in inappropriate affairs. The underlying problem was that this "meddling" was watering down the divide established by the modern world, which was the foundation of a "pact" between church and state. Concomitantly to the emergence of base communities and the LALT, and sparked by the same situation of blatant social injustice, some Evangelical sectors in Latin America put forward the idea of "integral mission," through their Integral Mission Theology (IMT). This concept of "integral" has been an attempt to overcome the relegation of Christianity to the personal sphere, advocating that the churches should take up both the personal and social dimensions of human beings and of the mission.

Although the LALT and IMT did not use the term *public* to refer to social and political dimensions, the meaning ascribed to them is not different from that used by Moltmann when he talked about "public theology" and mission. Theologies advocating the participation of Christian churches in fights for social, ethnic, racial, gender-related, or environmental justice call for overcoming the restriction of religion to the private sphere, and therefore, they challenge, one way or another, the radical separation between state and church.

For us to understand better this complex relationship between the separation between state and church, secularization, and the participation of religions in the public and social domain, I believe it is important to point out that this separation involves two issues: wars in the name of God, and religious and cultural pluralism.

SECULARIZATION AND WARS IN THE NAME OF GOD

It is known that one of the chief causes leading to the separation between church and state, one of the key characteristics of the secularization process of the Western world, was the issue of religious wars. The Protestant Reformation not only broke down the monopoly of religion held by the church that today we call the Roman Catholic Church, but also gave rise to a very serious situation of political and military conflict: the endless wars in the name of God or the in the name of a "true religion." When a war is waged in the name of God, there are only two options: win and wipe out the "heretics" and heresy, or die in the name of God and achieve eternal salvation. Reaching peace through negotiations is out of question, as that would mean entering into a pact with the devil, God's enemy. Because of that, in situations in which military and economic powers are at the same level, wars linger on for an indefinite length of time, until one side is decimated.

When it is impossible to definitely overthrow all enemies of God, as it happened in a Europe divided by the Reformation, the only possible solution to bring religious wars to an end is by secularizing war—that is, eliminating the religious nature of war. War can no longer be seen as fought in the name of God, but in the interests of the state or nation.

The separation between state and church, the distinction between earthly political interests and religious issues, now restricted to the private sphere and related to eternal salvation, is a necessary condition to reach peace through negotiations. In this sense, modern secularization is an advance of the civilizing process of humankind.

For us to have an idea of how important this solution is, we can mention here the example of the Israeli-Palestinian conflict. Without discussing in detail its historical origin or geopolitical interests, we can say that as long as this conflict is viewed by both sides as a war fought in the name of God, negotiating peace will be virtually impossible. That is why it is the more secularized society sectors from both sides of the conflict which seek a negotiated solution, while religious people who refuse to accept the modern secularized idea of the relation between state/politics and religion are the ones opposing and boycotting processes of negotiations for peace. The expression "state and church" originated in a Christian context and cannot be applied to cultural and historical contexts in which the idea of church does not exist.

SECULARIZATION AND RELIGIOUS AND CULTURAL PLURALISM

To understand better the challenge of resuming or strengthening the public dimension of Christianity, we need to understand another aspect of the secularization of the modern world, which is linked to the cause of religious wars: the issue of religious pluralism. For us today, it is difficult to understand how a reformation within a religion or church could lead to so many conflicts and wars. We are children of a culture in which religion does not have the same role or hold the same position as it did in the society at the end of the feudal world in Europe and in the beginning of the modern world.

In premodern Europe, religious homogeneity—the entire nation and whole universe under the same God with the only and true church as God's representative in the world—was a key feature of the worldview and collective identity. Social groups need a device for creating a collective identity that makes individuals feel like they belong to a group and for that group to identify as one. In the past, religion fulfilled that role, either through totems, in tribal groups in varied parts of the world, or through the idea of a unique and transcendental God in medieval Europe.

The Protestant Reformation did not only imply a division within the Christian church but a fissure in the backbone of society and its worldview. People and state, used here in their broadest meaning, could not tolerate religious pluralism, two or more versions of God, God's will, and God's church. Of course, those societies had long been aware of cultural diversity or pluralism because of trade, immigrants, and refugees. However, the presence or awareness of such cultural diversity did not jeopardize or threaten the ruling worldview and the religion underlying and organizing it. Those were minorities aware of their lesser and marginal character, and they adapted to that situation. One example of that was the Jewish communities who, in more intolerant times, practiced their religious rites inside their houses or synagogues, hidden from the public eye.

The Reformation meant something much different in terms of religious diversity. It was not a religious movement that saw itself as marginal or minority inside the medieval Christian world. Rather, it was a breach that challenged the foundations of an established social and religious order and aimed to become the foundation and guiding principle of a new social and religious order. In other words, the Reformation was not a movement for cultural and religious pluralism, but it was a reformation of a social and religious nature to reestablish social order the way "it should be." The religious wars were precisely the fruits of the conflict between two incompatible worldviews and orderings, two orders that did not accept pluralism as a social value or something God desired.

Therefore, secularization meant more than merely separating state from church/religion to bring religious wars to an end. It also meant reordering or repositioning society in relation to religious pluralism.

In this article, I am addressing only religious pluralism and not others, such as cultural, economic, or political pluralism. An important issue, which is beyond the intended scope of this book, would be capitalism and economic pluralism.

Here we have a very interesting situation. The solution to religious wars requires recognizing religious pluralism within the European continent and within the same religion, Christianity, as an insurmountable social fact. But at the same time, it was normative to think that a society or a social order needs one and only one guiding and homogenizing principle. To overcome this paradox, the path adopted was to move religion from its central place in the social order to the margins of society. With that, religion was also stripped of its important social function as the ultimate legitimizing source of the unequal distribution of power and wealth in society.

In regard to urban and cultural geography, over time, cathedrals or big churches in the cities ceased being their geographical mark or the city's epicenter, to be seen instead as the city's historical center, where people go sightseeing to get an idea of what life was like in the past. At the same time, rulers were no longer crowned in the name of God, but elected by people.

In that process, religion was relegated to private life, where pluralism is accepted and even valued as evidence of the civilizing process, but in the public sphere, pluralism is still controlled and tolerated as long it does not threaten the established social order. Moving religion from the center and foundation of social order to the margins does not mean that that order does not need a new foundation and ultimate basis for its decisions on what can or cannot be tolerated, or that religion has completely lost its capacity to act in the social sphere. A number of theologies, such as black theology in the United States and LALT, have served as this prophetic reservoir, a Christian tradition that challenges unfair social orders. When confronted by this type of Christianity or religion, the system does not display an accepting or tolerating attitude toward pluralism. One example of that is the famous Santa Fe Committee document, prepared by Ronald Reagan's advisers in 1980. That document, titled *A New Inter-American Policy for the Eighties*,[3] openly criticizes the LALT for taking a stand against "private property and productive capitalism." This theology

3. L. Francis Bouchey and Lewis A. Tambs, *A New Inter-American Policy for the Eighties*, Committee of Santa Fe (Washington, DC: Council for Inter-American Security, 1981).

was criticized, not for breaking away from Christian tradition or biblical truth, but for abandoning fundamental principles of the social order.

In sum, religious pluralism came to be tolerated, accepted, and valued when religion ceased to be the ideological basis of the social order, was no longer important for keeping and reproducing the social order, and ceased posing risks to the ruling social order.

PUBLIC RELIGION IN SOCIETIES WITH CHRISTIAN TRADITION AND IN NON-CHRISTIAN SOCIETIES

When we talk about world Christianity and religious pluralism in our globalized world, it is important to recognize there is more than one single type of Christianity. It does not suffice to recognize Christianity exists in a variety of forms: Roman Catholic, historical Protestant churches, Evangelical, and Pentecostal. What we are concerned with here is that we need to recognize the diverse social and historical contexts in which concrete Christianities take place, thus creating different conformations of Christianity.

Put simply, we can identify two types of social context in which Christianity is called to or wishes to be present in the public sphere. The first one refers to the societies marked by Christian tradition, called Western Christian society, whose population is made up mostly of Christians—although not all of them are practicing Christians—and most importantly, where Christian symbols are part of the everyday cultural life. The second type refers to societies where Christianity is not part of the cultural tradition, and Christians make up a minority population. This second type can be subdivided into three groups: countries where Christianity or its dissemination is illegal or strictly controlled by the government, such as, for example, fundamentalist Muslim countries, China, and North Korea; countries where Christianity is accepted but Christians make up a small minority, which suffer cultural discrimination from the majority; and countries in which Christianity is deeply associated with past colonizing countries, such as countries in Africa and Asia.

Even when we do not discuss those types of contexts in detail, we can easily notice their big differences when we talk about the public presence of Christianity in those societies. It is one thing to struggle for social justice or a family model in the United States or in Latin

America. In these places, most people understand a proposal, even if they do not agree with what is being proposed or with the participation of religious people in the social and political domain. Another thing, totally distinct, is to talk about social justice in the name of the Christian faith in a Buddhist or Muslim country, where arguments from Christian and biblical tradition are not understood or accepted.

In predominantly Christian countries, Christian churches can either accept religious pluralism or not, and decide whether or not they want to participate in the interreligious dialogue by being present in the public sphere or in the political sphere. However, in societies where Christians are reduced to a minority, Christian churches are the ones taking the responsibility of convincing the majority religions to accept dialogue with Christians. Whereas in the former case, dialogue is an option, and in a certain way a consent granted by Christian churches, in the latter, dialogue is the only possibility for participating in the public sphere.

The perception and experience of Christian churches in situations in which they make up a minority and are marginalized could be very useful for Christian churches in a majority situation to understand the perspective of minority religions and the importance of dialoguing with them—not as a consent but as a value and an important element in mission.

To make this point clear, I think it would help us in our reflection if we distinguished three types of reasons for Christian churches to step beyond the private life of religion, going beyond its walls to the public sphere.

One reason for Christian sectors to break through their community walls is for the purpose of proselytism, which occurs out in the open, in the public arena. Such experience is more common among Evangelical and Pentecostal churches, but it is not unusual to see Christians in many parts of the world preaching in public spaces or knocking on house doors to proclaim the gospel or the name of Jesus. This movement toward the out and open is aimed at preaching, offering a testimony of faith, for the purpose of bringing more followers into one's church or into Christianity. Thus, the geographical division between the church and the public arena is overcome, but that does not necessarily undo the modern division between the public and religious private spheres.

The second reason Christian sectors break through their community walls is for the purpose of going toward society in the public domain to save the world from its social and moral decay. Here it makes no difference what spurs on this effort—be it a more personal moral motivation, especially as regards sexuality and family issues, or social ethics in the face of a social crisis and the growth of poverty and inequality. What joins those two groups is a view that church or Christianity holds the truth that can extricate society from its crisis. In this view of mission, it makes no sense to enter into a dialogue with other religions, unless it is part of a strategy or to be politically correct in the face of religious pluralism. There is no dialogue together to seek a solution to common problems when each religion is based on the assumption that they hold the truth, revealed by God to them.

Those two groups have the church and its mission as a starting point. There is a clear division between "us," the ones with the mission given by God, and the "others," recipients of our proclamation and solution. Even when churches take up the social dimension of mission and engage in causes for social justice, the starting point is Christianity, and they basically make use of Christian arguments and languages, because they believe deep inside Christianity holds the truth and salvation. That works in a portion of Christian societies—albeit less and less—but not in societies where Christianity is a minority religion. Even in the case of those churches that take up the social and political dimension of mission, they neglect something important in this discussion: the social reality of religious pluralism and the specificity of the public sphere, where different religious and cultural traditions exist and participate in the debate around the common good.

The third motivation for going to the public sphere is that in which the wish to surpass limits ascribed by the modern world is born from "hearing the cry" of those who suffer (Exodus 3). The primary and main motivation is not aimed at extending one's church or Christianity as a religion, but at responding to the cry by seeing in this cry a call from God to walk together with the suffering people, thus offering a testimony of God's presence among us.

Here it is important to distinguish between the church as an institution and Christianity as a religion, on the one hand, and the kingdom of God, on the other. I would like to quote Moltmann one more time here, as I did in the beginning of this chapter: "Kingdom-of-God theology intervenes critically and prophetically in public affairs of a given society, and draws public attention, not to the church's own interest but to God's kingdom." The church's mission is not expanding Christianity or itself; it is announcing and testifying to the kingdom of God and its justice among us. As Jesus said, we should "seek first the kingdom of God and his righteousness" (Matt 6:33), and all the other things will be granted to us as well.

This difference between the kingdom of God and church/Christianity is a fundamental issue for the dialogue with other religions and nonreligious cultures. Such dialogue, however, cannot be a you-and-I type of conversation, without a third element—a common problem or challenge to be overcome. If it is like that, the dialogue will end up being a dispute to know who has the better theology or the truer religion, or the dialogue will end up a mere exchange of experiences in which each party politely listens to the other but continues to hold the same convictions he or she started the dialogue with. As Paulo Freire has taught us, dialogue is an encounter between the "other"/you and the "I," in which both parts express their views of the world which are to be transformed, a common problem to be solved.[4]

In a Christian language, the dialogue between Christianity and other religions must be about the kingdom of God and not about ourselves, our religions, and their differences. That is the only way we can honestly and positively acknowledge religious pluralism without denying mission and the identity of Christianity.

THE CRY AND THE DIALOGUE

In this last part, I would like to present a brief reflection on "hearing the cry," which must be the source of motivation for going to the public sphere. The Bible teaches us the great revelation that gave way to the origin of the people of Israel and took place in the encounter of Moses and Yahweh through the burning bush (Exod 3:7–9). God introduces God's self to Moses by saying that he has seen the misery of the enslaved people in Egypt and has heard their cry. As a response to that cry, he decides to come down from heaven, come into our history, and liberate the people through Moses and other leaders.

4. Paulo Freire, *Pedagogia do oprimido*, 7th ed. (Rio de Janeiro: Paz e Terra, 1979), 93–98. Translation from Portuguese into English.

I would like to point out just one fundamental aspect of that revelation: God responds to a cry, not to a discourse-like request. A cry is a shout or a pre-linguistic expression, before discursive language is formulated, of those who suffer deeply and cannot find a discursive form to express that suffering. Language is the expression of a given culture, and discourse is the use of language in a given specific context. The origin of God's movement—that which made God leave God's world and come into our world, lies in hearing the cry of the suffering people, irrespective of cultural or religious differences. The response to that cry, however, must be historical and with available cultural instruments.

The responsive movement of churches and Christians toward the social and public sphere, in the name of their faith, must stem from "hearing the cry," which instills in us compassion and requires a cultural answer. Our religious culture, the viewpoint from which we grasp our spiritual experience, is Christian, but on our path we meet people and groups who respond to the same cry from religious cultures and traditions different from ours. Provided that we share the same original experience, which is "hearing the cry," and the same wish to provide an answer, dialogue emerges as a natural necessity. In such cases, cultural and religious differences are relegated to a secondary status. Dialogue makes us see the richness of the manifestations of God's kingdom among us and understand religious pluralism as an ambiguous social reality, like all the others.

There are cases in which the social fact of religious pluralism breeds conflicts and violence, and others in which it enables a wealth of perception of human reality and solutions to serious social and human problems. The big difference between those two types is located in the capacity of each of them to either hear or not the cry of those who suffer and the ensuing appeal from God. In other words, it lies in the capacity of seeing the difference between religion and God's kingdom and God's justice. That does not mean that Christianity as a religion is not important. It is quite the contrary: it was through Christianity that we have learned to distinguish between religion and God's kingdom, and we have learned that it is not possible to take part in the richness of dialogue in a religiously plural world without having our own religious identity.

PART III

Ethics and Society: Latin America

5.

Theology, Ethics, and Society

Latin American Liberation Theologies

LUIS N. RIVERA-PAGÁN

> The Bible . . . unlike the books of other ancient peoples, was . . . the literature of a minor, remote people—and not the literature of its rulers, but of its critics. The scribes and the prophets of Jerusalem refused to accept the world as it was. They invented the literature of political dissent and, with it, the literature of hope.
>
> —Amos Elon, *Jerusalem: Battlegrounds of Memory*

A THEOLOGICAL ENFANT TERRIBLE

Latin American liberation theology was the unforeseen enfant terrible in the academic and ecclesial realms of theological production during the last decades of the twentieth century. It brought to the conversation not only a new theme—liberation—but also a new perspective on doing theology and a novel way of referring to God's being and action in history. Its project to reconfigure the interplay between religious studies, ethics, and politics became a meaningful topic of analysis and dialogue in the general theological discourse. Many scholars perceive in its emergence a drastic epistemological rupture, a radical change in paradigm, a significant shift in both the ecclesial and social role of theology.

Its origins are diverse and not only native to theological and ecclesiastical horizons. One important source, neglected by some clerical accounts, was the complex constellation of liberation struggles during the sixties and early seventies. It was a time of social turmoil, when many things seemed out of joint: a strong antiwar movement protest, mainly directed against American military intervention in Vietnam and the global nuclear threat; a spread of decolonization movements all over the third world; the feminist struggle against masculine patriarchy; a robust challenge to racial bigotry; the Stonewall rebellion (June 1969) against homophobia and gay discrimination; student protests in Paris, Prague, Mexico, and New York in opposition to repressive states of all stripes; and guerilla insurgencies and social unrest in many Latin American nations. Many of these agents of social protest adopted the title of "liberation movement" as their public card of presentation. "Fronts of national liberation" flourished all over the third world.[1]

Another significant factor was the development of a nondogmatic Marxism that read Marx's texts as an ethical critique on human oppression and as a projection of a utopian non-oppressive future. This heterodox way of reading Marx, by authors like the German philosopher Ernst Bloch, made possible something up to then considered unthinkable—a constructive and affirmative dialogue between theology and Marxism, at the margins of church and party hierarchies' rigid orthodoxies. Influential in this intellectual milieu was Bloch's 1968 *Atheismus im Christentum*,[2] whose hermeneutical performance diagnoses inside the biblical texts a struggle between the voices of the oppressors and those of the oppressed and provocatively asserts that whoever wants to be a good Marxist should constantly read the Bible (and vice versa: whoever wants to be a good Christian should have Marx as bedside reading).

Other iconoclast authors, including Herbert Marcuse and Franz Fanon, were passionately read from Buenos Aires to Berlin, from

1. The most famous of them, and a model for many, were the Algerian Front of National Liberation, established in 1954, which led the revolt against French colonial domination (brilliantly depicted in Gillo Pontocorvo's 1966 film *Battle of Algiers*); the National Liberation Front for South Vietnam, created in December 1960, which successfully fought against the division of Vietnam and the military invasion of the United States; and the Palestine Liberation Organization, founded in 1964 to organize the struggle for Palestinian statehood. See Alistair Horne, *A Savage War of Peace: Algeria 1954–1962* (New York: Penguin, 1987); Frances FitzGerald, "The National Liberation Front," chap. 4 in *Fire in the Lake: The Vietnamese and the Americans in Vietnam* (Boston: Little, Brown, 1972); and Helena Cobban, *The Palestinian Liberation Organisation: People, Power and Politics* (Cambridge: Cambridge University Press, 1984).

2. Frankfurt am Main: Suhrkamp, 1968.

Bogotá to Nairobi, with intentionalities not limited to academia.[3] Exiled from Brazil, Paulo Freire delivered scathing critiques of traditional educational systems and promoted a pedagogy for the liberation of the oppressed.[4] Martin Luther King Jr. and Ernesto "Che" Guevara are probably the main emblematic icons and martyrs of those turbulent times. Paul Éluard's poem "Liberté," recited and sang in many languages, became its poetic hymn.

Within the churches, important processes were taking place. Pope John XIII summoned, to the surprise of many, the Second Vatican Council. Progressive Roman Catholic theologians consider Vatican II an important turning point in the modern history of their church.[5] According to their interpretation, the council had three main objectives:

1. To change the attitude of the Roman Catholic Church toward the modern post-Enlightenment intellectual world from censure and condemnation to openness and dialogue. The Italian word *aggiornamento* became the watchword of the attempts to update the church.
2. To heal the fragmentation of Christianity by inserting the Roman Catholic Church in the emerging ecumenical movement. Delegates from Protestant and Orthodox churches were invited to observe the proceedings of the council. A series of bilateral and multilateral dialogues began between Rome and other Christian denominations.
3. To face with honesty and compassion the plight of a world suffering violence, oppression, and injustice. The council took place in a world sundered by national liberation struggles, civil wars, and the painful gap between the haves and the have-nots of the globe. The quest for peace and justice was conceived as an essential dimension of the being in the world of the church.

John XXIII's 1963 encyclical *Pacem in terris*, published in the context of that conciliar process, seemed to be another sign of renewal,

3. Herbert Marcuse, *An Essay on Liberation* (Boston, Beacon, 1969); Franz Fanon, *The Wretched of the Earth* (New York, Grove, 1965).

4. Paulo Freire, *Educação como prática da liberdade* (Rio de Janeiro: Paz e Terra, 1967); Paulo Freire, *Pedagogía del oprimido* (Montevideo: Tierra Nueva, 1970).

5. See Austin P. Flannery, ed., *Vatican Council II: The Basic Sixteen Documents; Constitutions, Decrees, Declarations* (Northport, NY: Costello, 1996).

from an attitude of anathema to a spirit of dialogue and solidarity. This ecclesiastical openness was accompanied by several theological projects that seemed to shape an alternative way to look at social conflicts.[6] An attempt was made to configure a "political theology," as a way to design a creative dialogue with Marxism and post-Enlightenment secular ideologies.[7]

LATIN AMERICAN LIBERATION THEOLOGIES

Vatican II was followed by regional synods of bishops. The most famous of them was the general meeting of Latin American Roman Catholic bishops that took place August 26 to September 6, 1968, in Medellín, Colombia. To the amazement of many observers, the Roman Catholic Church, which the radical intelligentsia in the continent had considered the ideological bulwark of prevailing social inequities, was promulgating, as a decisive pastoral challenge, solidarity with the poor and destitute.

If Vatican II opened the theological dialogue with modern rationality, Medellín was perceived as a prophetic convocation against poverty, inequality, and oppression. If Vatican II was mainly concerned with the gap between the church and secular modernity, Medellín, according to this reading, was more concerned with the scandal of social injustice in a Christian continent. In a crucial section of their final resolutions, the Latin American bishops linked the Christian faith with historical and social liberation:

> The Latin American bishops cannot remain indifferent in the face of the tremendous social injustices existent in Latin America, which keep the majority of our peoples in dismal poverty that in many cases becomes inhuman wretchedness. A deafening cry pours from the throats of millions of men and women asking their pastors for a liberation that reaches them from nowhere. . . .
>
> Christ, our savior, not only loved the poor . . . but also centered his mission in announcing liberation to the poor.[8]

6. Jürgen Moltmann, *Theologie der Hoffnung* (Munich: Kaiser, 1966); Johannes Baptist Metz, *Zur Theologie der Welt* (Mainz: Matthias-Grúnewald, 1968).

7. See Dorothee Sölle, *Politische Theologie: Auseinandersetzung mit Rudolf Bultmann* (Stuttgart: Kreuz, 1971).

8. Alfred T. Hennelly, *Liberation Theology: A Documentary History* (Maryknoll, NY: Orbis, 1992), 114, 116, English translation somewhat amended.

Certainly, the Medellín conference was a meeting of bishops, not of theologians. But several Roman Catholic theologians perceived the final documents and the general tone prevailing in the conference as allowing the possibility of rethinking the theological enterprise from the perspective of the liberation of the poor and downtrodden.[9] Prior to the Medellín meeting, on July 1968, Gustavo Gutiérrez had given a lecture at Chimbote, Peru, significantly titled "Toward a Theology of Liberation,"[10] which coupled closely spiritual salvation and human liberation. It proved to be a pioneer text for Latin American liberation theology. It also inaugurated Gutiérrez's more than five decades of fertile theological production.

In 1971, the first edition of his most famous book, *Theology of Liberation*, was published, a landmark in Latin American theological writing. His triadic understanding of human liberation—liberation from social and economic oppression, history as a process of self-determined humanization, and redemption from sinfulness—became classic.[11] That same year, Hugo Assmann's book *Opresión–Liberación: Desafío a los cristianos* was also published. Assmann placed the emerging liberation theology in the wider context of the third world: "The contextual starting point of a 'theology of liberation' is the historical situation of domination experienced by the peoples of the Third World."[12] Gutiérrez and Assmann were followed by a spate of other theologians (Leonardo Boff, José Porfirio Miranda, Juan Luis Segundo, Jon Sobrino, Pablo Richard, and Jorge Pixley, among others) whose writings were conceived as expressions of a new intellectual understanding of the faith: liberation theology.[13]

Among the many texts that rocked the placid realm of theological production during those early years of Latin American liberation

9. See Gustavo Gutiérrez, "The Meaning and Scope of Medellín," in *The Density of the Present: Selected Writings* (Maryknoll, NY: Orbis, 1999), 59–101.

10. It is translated and reproduced in Hennelly, *Liberation Theology*, 62–76.

11. Gustavo Gutiérrez, *Teología de la liberación: Perspectivas* (Salamanca: Sígueme, 1973), 67–69.

12. Hugo Assmann, *Opresión–Liberación: Desafío a los cristianos* (Montevideo: Tierra Nueva, 1971), 50.

13. See Samuel Silva Gotay's important book on the origins of Latin American liberation theology, *El pensamiento cristiano revolucionario en América Latina: Implicaciones de la teología de la liberación para la sociología de la religión* (Salamanca: Ediciones Sígueme, 1981), translated into Portuguese as *O pensamento cristão revolucionãrio na América Latina e no Caribe (1960–1973)* (São Paulo: Edições Paulinas, 1985) and into German as *Christentum und Revolution in Lateinamerika und der Karibik: Die Bedeutung der Theologie der Befreiung für eine Soziologie der Religion,* Würzburger Studien zur Fundamentaltheologie 17 (Frankfurt am Main: Peter Lang, 1995).

theology were José Porfirio Miranda's *Marx y la Biblia*,[14] an important contribution to a liberationist hermeneutics, a sort of theological companion to Bloch's *Atheismus im Christentum* and Juan Luis Segundo's *Liberación de la teología*,[15] with its frontal challenge to traditional scholastic ways of doing theology.

What could be considered to be the main tenets of this theological movement?

- The retrieval of the subversive memories inscribed in the sacred scriptures, hidden below layers of cultic regulations and doctrinal orthodoxies but never totally effaced. This featured a specific hermeneutical and exegetical concentration on the Exodus story as a paradigm of the liberating character of God's actions,[16] the prophetic denunciations of injustice and oppression,[17] the confrontations of the historical Jesus against the Judean religious authorities and Roman political powers, and his solidarity with the nobodies of Judea and Galilee.[18]
- A historical understanding of Jesus's proclamation of God's kingdom. The kingdom is conceived as referring not to some otherworldly postmortem realm, but to the unceasing hope of a social configuration characterized by justice, solidarity, and freedom. Leonardo Boff and Jon Sobrino perceive Jesus as the Liberator, going back to the semantic roots of the term *redemption* (the deliverance of a captive or slave).[19]
- The divine preferential option for the poor, the excluded, and the destitute of this world. The church has to become the church of the poor, sharing their sorrows, hopes, and struggles. Initially, the accent was mainly socioeconomic, but it was gradually widened to include other categories of social exclusion (indigenous communities, racial and ethnic minorities, and women).[20]

14. José Porfirio Miranda, *Marx y la Biblia* (Salamanca: Ediciones Sígueme, 1972).

15. Juan Luis Segundo, *Liberación de la teología* (Buenos Aires: Ediciones Carlos Lohlé, 1975).

16. José Severino Croatto, *Exodus, a Hermeneutics of Freedom* (Maryknoll, NY: Orbis, 1981); Jorge V. Pixley, *Exodo, una lectura evangélica y popular* (Mexico City: Casa Unida de Publicaciones, 1983).

17. Walter J. Houston, *Contending for Justice: Ideologies and Theologies of Social Justice in the Old Testament* (London: T & T Clark, 2006).

18. Jon Sobrino, *La fe en Jesucristo: ensayo desde las víctimas* (San Salvador: UCA, 1999).

19. Leonardo Boff, *Jesus Cristo libertador: Ensaio de cristologia crítica para o nosso tempo* (Petrópolis, Brazil: Editôra Vozes, 1972); Jon Sobrino, *Jesucristo liberador: Lectura histórico teológica de Jesús de Nazaret* (San Salvador: UCA, 1991).

- The impossibility of reducing theology to an intellectual understanding of the faith. It must also be a practical commitment for historical transformation. The category of praxis, partly borrowed from Paulo Freire's pedagogy of liberation, partly an adaptation of Marx's eleventh thesis on Feuerbach ("Philosophers have hitherto only interpreted the world in various ways; the point is to change it"), acquired normative status. History, therefore, as the realm of the perennial struggle against oppressions and exclusions, emerged as the locus for Christian praxis.[21]
- The reconceiving of God as not an immutable and impassible entelechy but, according to the biblical narratives, as a compassionate Eternal Spirit that hears and pays close attention to the cry of the oppressed and whose action in human history has the redemption of the downtrodden and excluded as its ultimate telos. Herein might be located liberation theology's main theoretical epistemological rupture and reconfiguration:[22] a novel way of thinking about God's being and action in history. Instead of contriving arcane scholastic definitions of divine essence, God is referred to as Liberator.

Latin American liberation theology strove to forge a new kind of being the church in the world: the base ecclesial communities as seeds for reconfiguring the church as "the people of God." These congregations were considered expressions of the church's solidarity with the poor and oppressed in their aspirations for liberation and human promotion. An impressive wealth of liturgical, musical, exegetical, homiletical, ethical, and literary resources was produced to promote social and human emancipation. Historical transformation was their key theme. Leonardo Boff even advocated a new genesis of the church.[23]

However, many in the hierarchical church, including some members of the Roman Curia apex, viewed with marked distrust their potential disruptions of episcopal authority and moved to restrict

20. Leonardo Boff, *Igreja, carisma e poder: Ensaios de eclesiologia militante* (Petrópolis, Brazil: Vozes, 1981).

21. Jorge V. Pixley and Jean-Pierre Bastian, eds., *Praxis cristiana y producción teológica* (Salamanca: Ediciones Sígueme, 1979).

22. Jonathan Pimentel Chacón, *Modelos de Dios en las teologías latinoamericanas* (Heredia, Costa Rica: Universidad Nacional de Costa Rica, 2008).

23. See Leonardo Boff, *Eclesiogênese: As comunidades eclesiais de base reinventam a Igreja* (Petrópolis, Brazil: Editora Vozes, 1977).

their autonomy. Rome was also concerned about the consequences for dogmatic orthodoxy of this new theological perspective. A long protracted confrontation ensued that still goes on.

Political power matters. Since their colonial inception, an official linkage between the state and the Roman Catholic Church characterized Latin American nations. The royal patronage exercised by the Iberian crown entailed the acknowledgment by the church of the sovereignty and authority of the metropolitan state, but also the state's recognition of the Roman Catholic Church's primacy in religious affairs. It was sometimes the source of acute conflicts, whenever the ethical conscience of bishops, priests, missionaries, and theologians clashed with the severe exploitation of the native communities.

Bartolomé de las Casas, to whose historical significance Gustavo Gutiérrez devoted a magnificent book,[24] is the most famous protagonist of such conflicts. Yet it was a convenient arrangement for both partners, for it conferred a sacred aura to the metropolitan sovereignty and conversely provided the church with state protection. The governments of the new states that emerged after the nineteenth-century wars of independence promptly recognized the advantages of the royal patronage and tried to preserve it. This heritage forged a particular brand of Latin American Christendom closely linking the state and the Roman Catholic Church, a condition juridically inscribed in several national constitutions and Vatican concordats.

This official connection between church and state was venerable but also vulnerable. The prophetic and evangelical subversive memories inscribed in the Christian scriptures and traditions surfaced powerfully during the somber and violent times of Latin American military dictatorships (1964–1989) to shake the alliance between the political powers and church authorities. The most famous of the ensuing conflicts took place in the midst of the violent civil war in El Salvador, a place where nuns, priests, lay workers, and even the primate of the Roman Catholic Church, Archbishop Oscar Arnulfo Romero, were assassinated by the military or their right-wing allies.

Archbishop Romero tried to steer his church to become a defender of the poor and the persecuted. He recognized that the forbearance of the ruling clans was as limited as their economic interests were great. Two weeks before his assassination, in an interview with a Mexican newspaper, he foreshadowed his death and gave a theological and

24. Gustavo Gutiérrez, *Las Casas: In Search of the Poor of Jesus Christ* (Maryknoll, NY: Orbis, 1993).

pastoral interpretation of his personal destiny: "I have frequently been threatened with death. . . . If God accepts the sacrifice of my life, then may my blood be the seed of liberty, and a sign of the hope that will soon become a reality. . . . May my death, if it is accepted by God, be for the liberation of my people, and as a witness of hope in what is to come."[25] His assassination convinced many church authorities that liberation theology was risking seriously the social well-being of the Roman Catholic Church and that a convenient long-standing church-state covenant was endangered by the radical political interventions of some members of the clergy. And they moved decisively to suppress it.

Ecclesiastical and social-political considerations were not the only issues of concern for Vatican authorities. Doctrinal orthodoxy matters for the Roman Catholic Church. Under the prefecture of Cardinal Joseph Ratzinger, the Sacred Congregation for the Doctrine of the Faith strongly criticized what it considered liberation theology's ominous doctrinal deviations. On August 6, 1984, it issued, with the approval of Pope John Paul II, the admonishing "Instruction on Certain Aspects of the 'Theology of Liberation,'" followed by an admonition to Leonardo Boff, and another general critique, "Instruction on Christian Freedom and Liberation" (March 22, 1986). Liberation theology was indicted for borrowing improperly from Marxist thought, emphasizing historical and social liberation to the detriment of spiritual salvation, promoting class struggle instead of reconciliation, disdaining the church's social doctrine, and politicizing biblical hermeneutics, Christology, and the church. The goal of the authoritative reprimands was

> to draw attention . . . to the deviations and risks of deviation, damaging to the faith and to Christian living, that are brought by certain forms of liberation theology. . . . The 'theologies of liberation' tend to misunderstand or to eliminate . . . the transcendence and gratuity of liberation in Jesus Christ, true God and true man. . . . One needs to be on guard against the politicization of existence, which, misunderstanding the entire meaning of the kingdom of God and the transcendence of the person, begins to sacralize politics and betray the religion of the people in favor of the projects of revolution.[26]

25. Oscar Romero, *Voice of the Voiceless: The Four Pastoral Letters and Other Statements*, introductory essays by Ignacio Martín-Baró and Jon Sobrino (Maryknoll, NY: Orbis, 1998), 50–51.

26. Reproduced in Hennelly, *Liberation Theology*, 394, 411–12.

Traditionally, indictments like these were able to silence the accused theologians. Not this time. Prompt reactions by Gustavo Gutiérrez, Leonardo Boff, and Juan Luis Segundo were evident signs that Rome had lost the capability to repress the new theological movement.[27] A letter sent by John Paul II to the Brazilian bishops, dated April 9, 1986,[28] has been understood by several scholars as a truce of the growing dispute to avoid a sharp rupture in the Latin American church but also as a validation of the concept of social and political liberation as an important dimension of the church's pastoral mission. Several Roman Catholic theologians have sustained an effort to convince Rome that liberation theology is a valid and legitimate rethinking of the apostolic tradition that does not constitute a threat to the church's orthodoxy or integrity.[29] However, some influential sectors of the Roman curia still look askance at liberation theology, as evidenced by the Sacred Congregation for the Doctrine of the Faith's recent scathing critique of Jon Sobrino's Christology ("Notification on the works of Father Jon Sobrino, SJ," November 26, 2006).[30]

Many Roman Catholic narratives disregard other sources that contributed to the birth of liberation theology. In the sixties, several Latin American Protestant churches were undergoing similar processes of rethinking the relationship between salvation, history as the sphere of divine-human encounter, and liberation.[31] In fact, the first extensive monograph that focused on historical and social liberation as the central hermeneutical key to conceptualize the Christian faith was the doctoral dissertation of Rubem Alves, a Brazilian Presbyterian. In May 1968, Alves defended successfully his dissertation at Princeton Theological Seminary. Its title was "Towards a Theology of Human Liberation."[32] Alves wrote it under the direction of Richard Shaull,

27. See the strong response of Juan Luis Segundo, *Teología de la liberación: Respuesta al Cardenal Ratzinger* (Madrid: Ediciones Cristiandad, 1985).

28. Reproduced in Hennelly, *Liberation Theology*, 498–506.

29. See Ignacio Ellacuría and Jon Sobrino, eds., *Mysterium liberationis: Conceptos fundamentales de la Teología de la Liberación* (Madrid: Editorial Trotta, 1990). On November 16, 1989, Ellacuría, then rector of El Salvador's Central American University, five other Jesuit priests, and two domestic servants were assassinated by a group of soldiers.

30. See the defense of Sobrino by almost forty theologians in José María Vigil, ed., *Bajar de la Cruz a los Pobres: Cristología de la Liberación* (Mexico City: Ediciones Dabar, 2007).

31. See Alan P. Neely, "Protestant Antecedents of the Latin American Theology of Liberation" (PhD diss., American University, 1977).

32. Rubem Alves, "Towards a Theology of Liberation: An Exploration of the Encounter between the Languages of Humanistic Messianism and Messianic Humanism" (PhD diss., Princeton Theological Seminary, May 1968).

who for a good number of years had been working in theological education in Latin America, first in Colombia and later in Brazil, and who was crucial for the development of a liberationist theology in Protestant Latin American circles.[33] Shaull had also been instrumental in the 1970 English publication of Paulo Freire's *Pedagogy of the Oppressed*, a key text in the development of Latin American liberation theology.

Alves's dissertation is a powerful text, written in a splendid literary style. It was published as a book in 1969, two years before Gutiérrez's, but with a significant change in the title: *A Theology of Human Hope*. Apparently, the publishers believed that the concept of "hope," with its obvious connotations to the writings of Jürgen Moltmann, would be more commercially attractive or relevant than "liberation." Yet, despite the change of title, Alves conceptualizes the temporal dialectics proper to theological language in terms of a historical politics of liberation: "The acts of remembering and hoping that determine the language of the community of faith, therefore, do not have any reality in themselves but in the engagement in the ongoing politics of liberation which is the situation and condition of theological intelligibility."[34]

Possibly the most exciting, intriguing, and controversial contribution to the spreading rainbow of different Latin American liberation theologies are the writings of the late Marcella Althaus-Reid, an Argentinean Protestant theologian teaching and writing in Edinburgh, Scotland. In the heartland of conservative Scottish Calvinism, Althaus-Reid transgressed all the frontiers that have traditionally marked theology as a "decent" and "proper" endeavor. In 2000, she published *Indecent Theology: Theological Perversions in Sex, Gender and Politics*,[35] and in 2003, *The Queer God*.[36] *Indecent Theology* claims to free liberation theology from its prudish inhibitions, resituating it in the perspective of oppressed sexualities, of concrete bodies in love at

33. Richard Shaull, *Hombre, ideología y revolución en América Latina* (Montevideo: ISAL, 1965). See Neely, *Protestant Antecedents*, 253: "It is doubtful if any theologian has more consistently and directly contributed to the shaping of the contemporary Protestant theologians of liberation than Richard Shaull."

34. Rubem Alves, *A Theology of Human Hope* (Washington, DC: Corpus, 1969), 163. On the theological trajectory of Alves, see Leopoldo Cervantes-Ortiz, *Serie de sueños: La teología ludo-erótico-poética de Rubem Alves* (Quito, Ecuador: Consejo Latinoamericano de Iglesias, 2003).

35. Marcella Althaus-Reid, *Indecent Theology: Theological Perversions in Sex, Gender and Politics* (London: Routledge, 2000).

36. Marcella Althaus-Reid, *The Queer God* (London: Routledge, 2003).

the margins of "decency," of sexual dissidence. *Queer God* attempts something even more daring: to rescue God from the monotonous, mono-loving closet where the deity has been relegated. God is subjugated by its forced enclosure in the restrictive role of patriarchal purveyor of a repressive code of thinking and acting. God, not only destitute human beings, needs to be freed and redeemed. Althaus-Reid conceives queer theology as going even further than gay liberation theologies, for it is grounded upon libertine subversions of both oppressive sexual and political heteronomy. Her queer hermeneutics is a methodology of permutations: a fascinating intertextual reading of the sacred scriptures with transgressive and marginal literature to free biblical exegesis from centuries of patriarchal and homophobic exegeses.

A LATINO/HISPANIC CONTRIBUTION

Even in the midst of the new American Empire, within the "entrails of the monster," as José Martí phrased it,[37] recent Latino/Hispanic theological productions bring to the fore a vibrant concept of God as Liberator. Mayra Rivera's *The Touch of Transcendence* is a readable and intelligent tome comprising a complex array of topics:[38] a deconstructive analysis of how a number of contemporary theologies construe God's transcendence, being, and actions in history; a critical discussion of the possible relevance to theology of the texts of several cultural-studies writers (Emmanuel Levinas, Jacques Derrida, Luce Irigaray) and postcolonial authors (Gayatri Spivak, Homi Bhabha, Walter Mignolo); and an examination of the implications of some strands of liberation theology (Latin American, feminist) for the doctrine of God.

It concludes with a very suggestive and seductive proposal to rethink divine transcendence. "Divine transcendence," according to Rivera, "has acquired the reputation of being a tool of patriarchal and

37. José Martí, "Carta a Manuel Mercado," *Obras escogidas* (Havana: Editora Política, 1982), 3:576: "Viví en el monstruo, y le conozco las entrañas: – y mi honda es la de David" ("I lived inside the monster, I know its entrails—and I have David's sling." See José Martí, *Inside the Monster: Writings on the United States and American Imperialism* (New York: Monthly Review Press, 1975).

38. Mayra Rivera, *The Touch of Transcendence: A Postcolonial Theology of God* (Louisville, KY: Westminster John Knox, 2007).

imperial self-legitimation."[39] There has been a multisecular collusion between dualistic metaphysical views of transcendence with multiple entwined projects intending to control and dominate subaltern communities. The critique of those dualistic views and colonizing projects is followed by a complex and rigorous attempt to elaborate a model of divine "relational transcendence" that allows a conception of God as constantly embracing and touching human and cosmic reality, while providing for an endless process of human liberation and for an ethic of solidarity with those "others" whose singularities (national, ethnic, cultural, racial, gender, sexual orientation) are socially signified as emblems of disdain, marginalization, or exploitation: "We will seek a model of transcendence that is attentive to the concrete sociopolitical significance of otherness. . . . Our aim to open ourselves to transcendence in the face of the Other leads us to give special attention to our relationships with those who are marginalized in our communities or simply excluded from them."[40] The touch of divine transcendence is ethically fulfilled in the embracing touch of the pariahs and untouchables.[41]

This is a coherent and impressive theological venture to overcome the dominant dualistic schemes (transcendence/immanence, spirit/body, sacred/profane) that have served as ideological matrices of human subordination and subjugation. Simultaneously, a manner of God-talk is forged that might be faithful both to the biblical witness about the Creator and Sustainer and to the contemporary challenges for social emancipation: "This model of relational transcendence refuses the 'hard boundary' between the divine and the created. Instead it affirms that the beginning, sustenance, and transformation of the cosmos are intrinsically divine. . . . Intracosmic and intercreaturely transcendence are thus inherently linked; both are theologically grounded in an assertion of the beginning of creation in God. . . . We aspire to give and receive that which may open for us new paths for continuous liberation."[42]

39. Ibid., 1.

40. Ibid., 82.

41. Here Rivera quotes one of Althaus-Reid's transgressive texts: "God is to be found in the presence of the untouchables. . . . [Transcendence] is God touching its own limits in the untouchables." Marcella Althaus-Reid, "El Tocado (Le Toucher): Sexual Irregularities in the Translation of God (the Word) in Jesus," in *Derrida and Religion: Other Testaments,* ed. Yvonne Sherwood and Kevin Hart (New York: Routledge, 2004), 394.

42. Mayra Rivera, *The Touch of Transcendence*, 133, 140.

Rivera is well aware that in these times of ours, when new forms of imperial domination are devised, the cross-dialogue between polychromic liberation theologies and postcolonial critical studies acquires theoretical relevance and political urgency.[43] Joerg Rieger has well expressed the challenge that this transdisciplinary exchange poises for the concept of God: "What happens when God-talk is turned loose from the powers that be, when it comes from those who bear the marks of colonialism and neocolonialism in their flesh?"[44] From my Latin American and Caribbean context, however, this requires overcoming the narrow historical vista of most postcolonial authors, who tend to focus their critical gaze on post-Enlightenment imperial formations.[45] After all, modern Western imperial domination began with the sixteenth-century Iberian conquest of the Caribbean archipelago and the Latin American territories.[46]

PROVISIONAL PREDICTIONS

Although several observers have predicted the demise of liberation theology, a better way to describe its actual condition is its proliferation by means of the fragmentation of subversive identities. What is striking is its ability to morph from its antecedents into a plethora of new movements. The original intuition of "preferential option for the poor" has been widened to the "excluded," the "marginalized," "victims," the "disdained," and the "downtrodden." There are even

43. Catherine Keller, Michael Nausner, and Mayra Rivera, *Postcolonial Theologies: Divinity and Empire* (St. Louis, MO: Chalice, 2004); Kwok Pui-lan, *Postcolonial Imagination and Feminist Theology* (Louisville, KY: Westminster John Knox, 2005); Wonhee Anne Joh, *Heart of the Cross: A Postcolonial Christology* (Louisville, KY: Westminster John Knox, 2006); Joerg Rieger, *Christ and Empire: From Paul to Postcolonial Times* (Minneapolis: Fortress Press, 2007); Kwok Pui-lan, Don H. Compier, and Joerg Rieger, eds., *Empire: The Christian Tradition; New Readings of Classical Theologians* (Minneapolis: Fortress Press, 2007).

44. Joerg Rieger, "Liberating God-Talk: Postcolonialism and the Challenge of the Margins," in Keller, Nausner, and Rivera, *Postcolonial Theologies: Divinity and Empire*, 220.

45. See Fernando Segovia's sharp and critical exposition of the theoretical convergences between postcolonial studies and anti-imperial biblical hermeneutics: "Mapping the Postcolonial Optic in Biblical Criticism: Meaning and Scope," in *Postcolonial Biblical Criticism: Interdisciplinary Intersections*, ed. Stephen D. Moore and Fernando Segovia (London: T & T Clark, 2005), 23–78.

46. Enrique Dussel, *1492: El encubrimiento del otro (Hacia el origen del "mito de la modernidad")* (Bogotá: Ediciones Antropos, 1992); Walter Mignolo, *The Darker Side of the Renaissance: Literacy, Territoriality, and Colonization* (Ann Arbor: University of Michigan Press, 1995); Luis N. Rivera-Pagán, "Doing Pastoral Theology in a Post-Colonial Context: Some Observations from the Caribbean," *Journal of Pastoral Theology* 17, no. 2 (Fall 2007): 1–28.

signs of a vigorous reawakening of liberation theology, for its main sources are still with us:

- The worldwide growing social and economic inequities entailed by the global hegemony of a neoliberal capitalist system of free market that validates profit as the hallmark of success. Poverty and injustice still prevail, tragically distorting the fate of millions of human beings all over our planet. Transnational corporations play lucrative chess games with their lives and labors, aborting illusions and shattering dreams.
- But also everywhere, the "wretched of the earth," as Franz Fanon called them, demanding a different and alternative social order and forging innovative models of protest and resistance. Their particular struggles might be different but not incompatible or incommensurable. Some resist poverty and economic misery; others demand full recognition for their racial, ethnic, or cultural identity; others assert the integrity and dignity of their gender or sexual orientation. These diverse perspectives complicate but also widen significantly the horizons of today's struggles for liberation.
- The constant retrieval, by many Christians, of the rebel and subversive memories hidden in the biblical texts and Christian traditions. It is impossible to silence or repress completely the rebellious tones of the Exodus narrative, the denunciatory voice of the prophets, Jesus's disturbing proclamation of good news for the poor and the captives, the attempts by the early Christian movement to shape a participatory and sharing community, or the anti-imperial tone of Revelation. Those memories, which constitute the core of the sacred scriptures, precipitate in the mind and heart of many readers the commitment for liberation. They lead to multiple and diverse meaningful efforts to shape for theology a public emancipatory role.[47]
- The fact that God matters. Even in these postmodernist and cybernetic times, people care about God. In the midst of present disturbances and conflicts, the "battle for God," as Karen Armstrong so aptly has named it,[48] rages ferociously. In the

47. See Benjamin Valentin, *Mapping Public Theology: Beyond Culture, Identity, and Difference* (Harrisburg, PA: Trinity Press International, 2002).
48. Karen Armstrong, *The Battle for God* (New York: Knopf, 2000).

> fascinating and perplexing kaleidoscope of human social existence, God is reimagined as the ultimate source of hope for the oppressed and downtrodden. When the social miseries that afflict so many communities become unbearable, beyond and besides the tiresome quarrels of religious fundamentalism and dogmatic secularism, the memory of God the Liberator erupts again and again: "When the Egyptians treated us harshly and afflicted us . . . we cried to the Lord, the God of our ancestors; the Lord heard our voice and saw our affliction, our toil, and our oppression. The Lord brought us out of Egypt with a mighty hand and an outstretched arm" (Deut 26:6–8 NRSV).

These are the factors that counter and resist the ruling imperial project of controlling and policing the frontiers of human imagination. Deeply felt fears and hopes, as the astute David Hume noted more than two centuries ago,[49] are able to agitate hearts and spirits and to move minds to think the otherwise unthinkable. Suddenly, at the end of the epoch so aptly named the "Age of Extremes" by Eric Hobsbawm,[50] two tendencies clash: The first announces with glib satisfaction "the end of history," the obliteration of transformative social utopias.[51] The second, from the entrails of the subordinated subjects,[52] proclaims a new insurrection of human hopes for "another possible world."[53]

The essential imperative might be to remember and radicalize the prophetic words written by the imprisoned Dietrich Bonhöffer, in a note surreptitiously preserved by his friend Eberhard Bethge: "We have for once learnt to see the great events of world history from below, from the perspective of the outcast, the suspects, the maltreated, the powerless, the oppressed, the reviled—in short, from the perspective of those who suffer."[54]

49. David Hume, *The Natural History of Religion* (London: A. & C. Black, 1956).

50. Eric Hobsbawm, *Age of Extremes: The Short Twentieth Century, 1914–1991* (London: Michael Joseph, 1994).

51. Francis Fukuyama, *The End of History and the Last Man* (New York: Free Press, 1992).

52. Franz Hinkelammert, *El grito del sujeto: Del teatro-mundo del evangelio de Juan al perro-mundo de la globalización* (San José, Costa Rica: DEI, 1998).

53. Jorge Pixley et al., *Por un mundo otro: Alternativas al mercado global* (Quito, Ecuador: Consejo Latinoamericano de Iglesias, 2003).

54. Dietrich Bonhöffer, *Letters and Papers from Prison*, ed. Eberhard Bethge (London: Folio Society, 2000), 16.

6.

Beyond Contextualization

Gospel, Culture, and the Rise of a Latin American Christianity

RAIMUNDO C. BARRETO JR.

Religion played a crucial role in European expansionism. Toward the end of the Middle Ages, the rise of the Spanish Empire, fostered by the myth of the Reconquista, blended nationalist and religious motives. According to that myth, "Spain was born as a nation convinced that God had entrusted it with the defense of the Catholic faith against all Muslims, Jews, heretics, and other unbelievers."[1] Under that banner, the Spaniards invaded and explored the "New World . . . convinced that this was a sacred trust so that they could bring their religion to the benighted people in these lands."[2]

Accordingly, modern colonialism was aimed at eradicating what the *colonizadores* (colonizers) perceived as indigenous superstitions, the religious practices of the people they met. At the end of the day, dominating, civilizing, and converting the indigenous peoples

1. Justo L. González and Ondina E. González, *Christianity in Latin America: A History* (New York: Cambridge University Press, 2008), Kindle edition, 2.

2. Ibid., 3. Walter Mignolo goes even further to establish that both the Reconquista and the "discovery" served as landmarks for modern colonialism. In his words, "The historical coexistence between the expulsion of the Jews and the Moors from Spain and the 'discovery' of America was at the same time a landmark for both modern colonialism and colonial modernities—that is, of modernity/coloniality." Walter D. Mignolo, *Local Histories/Global Designs: Coloniality, Subaltern Knowledges, and Border Thinking*, Princeton Studies in Culture/Power/History (Princeton, NJ: Princeton University Press, 2000), Kindle edition, Kindle Locations 1515–1517.

in the Americas represented different aspects of the colonial enterprise. The way such a project was implemented varied from place to place. Its implementation, though, was often flawed. The *colonizadores* miscalculated the extent to which they would succeed in having an impact on indigenous worldviews. Furthermore, they could not anticipate all political problems and conflicts involving the Catholic hierarchy, the Catholic orders, and the Spanish and Portuguese crowns, which would give birth to conflictive projects, thus preventing the implementation of a hegemonic religion or a hegemonic identity in the region.

On top of that, the deficit of priests to enforce doctrinal acquiescence contributed to Latin American Christianity taking on the face of the laity. In the absence of rigid vigilance, different forms of popular religion among indigenous, mixed-blood populations and enslaved Africans began to take form. Among others, the long-term result of that situation was a widespread, lay-led popular Catholicism. That mestizo religiosity blended elements traditionally identified as Christian with symbols, meanings, and narratives coming from both indigenous and African traditional religions. This chapter examines the rise of Latin American Christianity in light of the formation of peculiar Christian identities that resulted from a violent encounter between European colonial Christianity and the indigenous and African spiritualities in Latin America.

These are some of the working assumptions guiding this essay:

- Christianity is a traveling religion. It takes particular shapes and forms in every culture where it emerges. In other words, Christianity always develops contextually, as a result of concrete encounters between Gospel and culture. Regardless of how it gets started, sooner or later it takes indigenous forms.
- The continuous and dynamic encounters between indigenous cultures and the gospel in Latin America have produced particular Christian expressions in the course of several centuries. What makes a particular Christianity Latin American is not a hegemonic category or identity. Instead, what makes a particular Christianity Latin American is a shared Latin American history and background. This collective memory of a violent invasion and colonization unites the peoples living in Latin America and

at the same time acknowledges their distinctive identities and pre-Colombian histories.

- Latin American Christianity must be studied through non-Eurocentric lenses, even though the opposite is most commonly the case.

I suggest that methodological approaches developed in the emerging field of world Christianity in conjunction with insights from Latin American decolonial theory may contribute to the development of a "decolonizing countermovement to Euro-American glorifications" of the conquest, making room for noncolonial forms of Christianity to come to the forefront.[3] This combined approach prioritizes indigenous Christianities whose voices have been overlooked, pays particular attention to "the indigenous roots of *mestizaje*,"[4] and reclaims indigenous agency in the process of reinscribing indigenous and African imageries as key to the formation of Latin American heritage.

3. George Hartley, "The Curandeira of the Conquest: Gloria Anzaldúa's Decolonial Remedy," *Aztlán: A Journal of Chicano Studies* 35, no. 1 (2010): 135.

4. Ibid. See also Gloria Anzaldúa, *Borderlands/La Frontera* (San Francisco: Aunt Lute, 1987). The word *mestizaje* has been used among Latino/a scholars since the 1970s to describe a particular understanding of cultural identity, which highlights the racial mixing characteristic of most Latino/a experiences in response to ethnocentric racial theories, seeking to move conversations about race beyond the black-and-white binary. In that sense, *mestizaje is* a paradigm for the recognition of Latino/as as a people in the United States. *Mestizage* thus refers not only to racial miscegenation, but also to Latino/a religion and other aspects of Latino/a culture in contrast to dominant assimilationist tendencies. That usage contrasts manipulations of the term by dominant groups in Latin America to "silence difference" and obscure racial and socioeconomic disparities. For more on this topic, see Manuel Vasquez, "Rethinking Mestizaje," in *Rethinking Latino(a) Religion and Identity*, ed. Miguel De La Torre and Gaston Espinosa (Cleveland: Pilgrim, 2006), 129–57. For the use of *mestizage* as a *locus theologicus*, see Nestor Medina, *Mestizaje: (Re) Mapping Race, Culture and Faith in Latina/o Catholicism* (Maryknoll, NY: Orbis, 2009). In Brazil, Gilberto Freyre used the corresponding word *mestiçagem to speak of the singularity of Brazil's multicultural and multiracial experiment, which in his view brought together* three different peoples and cultures, intermingling their traditions, beliefs, and idiosyncrasies. He was likewise criticized for speaking from the perspective of the oppressor and consequently overlooking both the circumstances in which the encounter among those peoples and cultures happened, and the distinctiveness of their histories and perspectives. For a brief text with his argument and a critique of it by Darcy Ribeiro, see Gilberto Freyre, *Casa-Grande y Senzala: Introducción a la Historia de la Sociedad Patriarcal en el Brasil,* Prólogo y Cronologia Darcy Ribeiro (Caracas: Biblioteca Ayacucho, 1977). In this chapter, I side with those proposing a move beyond understandings of this and other terms, like *syncretism*, which emphasize amalgamation, toward definitions that can account for both mixture and difference.

World Christianity is an emerging subfield of Christian studies, with its own methods and theory.[5] Lamin Sanneh, one of the pioneers in this field, emphasizes its preferential option for indigenous narratives: "I have decided to give priority to indigenous response and local appropriation over against missionary transmission and direction, and accordingly have reversed the argument by speaking of the indigenous discovery of Christianity rather than the Christian discovery of indigenous societies."[6] Along those lines, this chapter examines how ethnically and racially marginalized groups in Latin America have appropriated Christianity as their own,[7] and what implications might come out of that process for contemporary understandings of religion, culture, and society in the region.

Throughout its history, Christianity has changed as it travels across cultures. New Christian expressions continue to emerge as people living in different cultures encounter the Jesus story, embrace it, and respond to it. Through renewed and renewing threads formed as a result of multicultural and intercultural efforts of transmission, translation, and indigenization, Christianity moves forward in fulfilling its outward vocation. It repeatedly recreates itself in multiple forms through an urge to move toward the other and through an emphasis on "the world beyond the boundaries of the Church."[8] As a consequence, Christianity feels at home in most cultures it encounters.

The idea of a religion that moves across borders can lend itself to ideals of solidarity and global conviviality. Nevertheless, this border crossing can also take totalizing and hegemonic forms. Unfortunately, Christian border crossing has been too often associated with expansionist and imperialistic agendas. Latin American Christianity has crossed many borders over the span of five centuries. On one hand, Christian border crossing in Latin America has resulted in

5. For some of the perspectives this emerging field offers, see Jonathan Y. Tan and Anh Q Tran, eds., *World Christianity: Perspectives and Insights* (Maryknoll, NY: Orbis, 2016).

6. Lamin Sanneh, *Whose Religion Is Christianity?* (Grand Rapids: Eerdmans, 2003), 10. As he puts it, "It is difficult to overestimate the implications of this indigenous change for the future shape of the religion," 11.

7. "The gospel" is always understood and enunciated from the particular cultural location of whoever reads the Scripture. But it is also always related to the proclamation of God's salvation in Jesus, in accord with the Christian Holy Scriptures. The interpretations of "the gospel" may vary from a cultural context to another. What keeps it "Christian," though, is the centrality of the biblical narrative as its "primary and essential source for theological development." See John W. Kinney, "The Theology of John Mbiti: His Sources, Norms, and Methods," *Occasional Bulletin of Missionary Research* 3, no. 2 (1979): 65–67 (65).

8. Paulus Y. Pham, *Towards an Ecumenical Paradigm for Christian Mission: David Bosch's Missionary Vision* (Rome: Gregorian and Biblical Press, 2010), 315.

multiple indigenous Christianities. On the other, one must not forget that the first encounter with Christianity in the Americas took place in the context of a violent and expansionist project whose outcome was the eclipsing of the brown and black other in the region.[9]

In his discussion about the conversion of the Maya people, William Hanks states:

> The Spanish conquest of Yucatan rested on two major columns, military subjugation and the so-called *conquista pacifica* 'peaceful conquest'. The military conquest was carried out by a relatively small number of soldiers, armed with swords, armour, muskets, horses, and dogs, and assisted by their indigenous allies. After decades of advances, setbacks, and regroupings, it came to an end, at least officially, in 1547. The peaceful conquest, by contrast, was carried out by an even smaller number of missionaries and their recruits, armed with monumental built spaces, the cross, religious vestments, the Bible and doctrine, the Host, wine and oil, and speech.[10]

Narratives that seek to decolonize Latin American Christianity and challenge hegemonic colonial and neocolonial histories must uncover such motivations and reveal alternative or hidden transcripts that have informed Christian and non-Christian responses by oppressed and marginalized peoples in the region to the colonial enterprise.[11] It is the surge of these hidden expressions and narratives among mostly brown and black Latin American Christians that I call the rise of a Latin American Christianity.

9. Enrique Dussel, *The Invention of the Americas: Eclipse of "the Other" and the Myth of Modernity* (New York: Continuum, 1995). Dussel describes the origin of "the myth of modernity," which justifies European expansionist violence. He holds that although the gestation of modernity took place within Europe itself, it only came to birth in the confrontation of Europe with the Other. "By controlling, conquering, and violating the Other, Europe defined itself as the discoverer, conquistador and colonizer of an alterity likewise constitutive of modernity. Europe never discovered this Other as Other but covered over the Other as part of the Same." In other words, "modernity dawned in 1492 and with it the myth of a special kind of sacrificial violence which eventually eclipsed whatever was non-European," 12.

10. William F. Hanks, *Converting Words: Maya in the Age of the Cross* (Berkeley: University of California Press, 2010), Kindle Edition, Kindle Locations 217–21.

11. See James C. Scott, *Domination and the Arts of Resistance: Hidden Transcripts* (Ann Arbor, MI: Yale University Press, 1990).

BEYOND CONTEXTUALIZATION

Contemporary theologians and missiologists have increasingly turned their attention to the contextual nature of theology, particularly when dealing with theologies emerging in the Global South and its diaspora. Unfortunately, though, most theologies of Euro-American origin do not receive the same treatment.

In reaction to such unchecked Eurocentrism, Stephen Bevans made an important contribution to the understanding of the contextual nature of all theology. As he stated, "There is no such thing as 'theology'; there is only contextual theology: feminist theology, black theology, liberation theology, Filipino theology, Asian-American theology, African theology, and so forth. Doing theology contextually is not an option. . . . The contextualization of theology—the attempt to understand Christian faith in terms of a particular context—is really a theological imperative. As we have come to understand theology today, it is a process that is part of the very nature of theology itself."[12] I refer to the nature of Christianity in similar terms. It is an intrinsic paradox to talk about Christianity in abstract and universalistic terms. As a religion made possible through a narrative centered on the idea of incarnation—through which God is revealed in the life of a marginal Jew—Christianity has always existed in contextual, cultured, concrete forms.

If Christianity always exists in contextual forms, how important is the idea of contextualization? According to Darrell Whiteman, contextualization is part of "a stream of thought that relates the Gospel and church to a local context."[13] He relates it to words such as "'adaptation,' 'accommodation,' 'indigenization,' and 'inculturation.'"[14] For Whiteman, "Contextualization attempts to communicate the Gospel in word and deed and to establish the church in ways that make sense to people within their local cultural context, presenting Christianity in such a way that it meets people's deepest needs and penetrates their worldview, thus allowing them to follow Christ and remain within their own culture."[15] Descriptions of contextualization such as this

12. Stephen B. Bevans, *Models of Contextual Theology*, rev. and expanded ed. (Maryknoll, NY: Orbis, 2002), 3.

13. Darrell L. Whiteman, "Contextualization: The Theory, the Gap, and the Challenge," *International Bulletin of Missionary Research* 21, no. 1 (1997): 2–7 (2).

14. Ibid.

15. Ibid.

one seem to understand Christianity as a ready-made commodity in the hands of an outsider who, in spite of being culturally sensitive, is still in control, having the clairvoyance of discerning and penetrating someone else's worldview.

In accord with this understanding of contextualization, agency remains primarily in the hands of the outsider; it is the missionary who takes the initiative to contextualize their message. Evangelization is accordingly understood in terms of transmission, not of indigenous agency. The local culture is still on the recipient end. The universalistic assumption in regard to the "sending" culture/community is manifest in the fact that it is not even necessary to identify who that is. As the supposed default position, the sending culture does not need to be known or challenged. World Christianity as a field of study challenges such assumptions.

Furthermore, such an understanding of contextualization reinforces the grand narrative of Christianity as a universal religion spreading around the world.[16] Conversely, this chapter follows a historiographical approach, which, as Paulson Pulikottil has described it, focuses on locality and historical particularity. From such a perspective, the history of Latin American Christianity must be told again, this time as "history from below," giving priority to the "voices from the edges."[17]

In Catholic writings, inculturation is the dominant concept, equivalent to contextualization among Protestants. Peter Phan affirms that inculturation has been "the *modus operandi* of the church since it moved out of its Jewish matrix into the Greco-Roman, then the Franco-Germanic worlds."[18] He stresses that since Vatican II, the church has been "moving away from a predominantly Hellenistic-Latin (Eurocentric) worldview and transforming itself into a world church characterized by cultural and religious pluralism and consequently facing a host of new theological and pastoral issues

16. There are more nuanced ways to think about contextualization. Samuel Escobar, for instance, speaks about mission as the carrying of the gospel from everywhere to everyone. Samuel Escobar, *The New Global Mission: The Gospel from Everywhere to Everyone* (Downers Grove, IL: InterVarsity, 2003). But the understanding of a universal but contextualizable Christianity remains dominant.

17. Paulson Pulikottil, "One God, One Spirit, Two Memories: A Postcolonial Reading of the Encounter between Western Pentecostalism and Native Pentecostalism in Kerala," in *The Spirit in the World: Emerging Pentecostal Theologies in Global Contexts*, ed. Veli-Matti Karkkainen (Grand Rapids: Eerdmans, 2009), 70.

18. Peter C. Phan, *In Our Own Tongues: Perspectives from Asia on Mission and Inculturation* (Maryknoll, NY: Orbis, 2003), Kindle edition, Kindle Locations 151, 155.

unprecedented in Christian history."[19] Yet Phan's starting point is "the world church," which spreads and incarnates in a multitude of cultures.

Moving beyond that, I suggest, in line with John Mbiti, that Christianity is always indigenous.[20] This radical emphasis on indigeneity sees the encounter between gospel and culture as generative of indigenous Christianities wherever it takes place.

THE FIRST EVANGELIZATION AND THE BREAK WITH ONE'S PAST

The First Consultation on Black Culture and Theology in Latin America, in 1985, drew attention to the fact that the evangelization of Afro-Latin Americans completely ignored the values present in their traditional religions.[21] Under the colonial paradigm, European and Anglo-American missionaries related to non-European nations not only as ambassadors of a superior religion, but also as representatives of an ideal of cultural and racial superiority. The transmission of the Christian faith—evangelization—sacralized and masked, at the same time, that ideal. Duncan Forrester refers to Thomas Barker's painting *The Secret of England's Greatness* to illustrate how theological and religious justifications were used to convey that imperialist sentiment. In that painting, he highlights a young Queen Victoria delivering a Bible to an African chief, who humbly kneels at her feet. For Forrester, the idea the painting communicates is clear:

> Christian mission is an element of the imperial project; colonialism and evangelism belong together; and the expansion of empire is providential, part of God's plan, the fulfillment of which has been delegated to the imperial power. The chieftain who kneels and cowers before the

19. Ibid., Kindle Locations 157–59.

20. In this chapter, I follow John Mbiti's view on the indigenization or contextualization of Christianity, as he says: "I do not think that we need to or can 'indigenize Christianity.' Christianity results from the encounter of the Gospel with any given local or regional community/society. To speak of 'indigenizing Christianity' is to give the impression that Christianity is a ready-made commodity, which has to be transplanted to a local area. Of course this has been the assumption followed by many missionaries and local theologians. I do not accept it anymore. The Gospel is God-given." See John Mbiti's response to John W. Kinney's paper "The Contribution of John Mbiti to the Development of Christian Theology in Africa: An Overview and a Critique," quoted in John W. Kinney, "The Theology of John Mbiti: His Sources, Norms, and Methods," *Occasional Bulletin of Missionary Research* 3, no. 2 (1979): 65–67 (66).

21. CEDI, *Identidade Negra e Religiao* (Rio de Janeiro: Edicoes Liberdade, 1986), 22.

> queen apparently receives the Bible from her hand in awe, reverence and gratitude. That striking picture captures something of the complex and important interweaving of imperialism and Christianity, which, for long, was considered by many as essential to both.[22]

Implicit in the painting is also the idea of subservience. An African leader kneels before a white queen to receive from her a sacred book containing directions for the salvation and subsequent progress of dark-skinned Africa. Such salvation resides in the adoption of core elements of the British civilization.

Vitalino Similox Salazar, a K'aqchiquel Maya Protestant minister from Guatemala, similarly refers to the encounter of his Maya people with European Christianity as "the invasion of Christianity into the world of the Mayas."[23] Guillermo Cook called it a cultural genocide, based on an underlying racism and cultural superiority, thus connecting Christian evangelization with the attempt to eliminate indigenous ways of life considered superstitious and idolatrous.[24]

In other words, European evangelization in Latin America demanded a break with one's indigenous past and the adoption of the superior way of life exemplified by the missionaries. Referring to the missionary work in colonial Yucatan, Hanks says, "For the missionaries . . . the focal object of conversion clearly was Indian behavior and beliefs, as is evident from their actions and from the standard definition of *convertir(se)* as "convince, be convinced or repentant (Covarrubias 1995 [1611], 350). . . . By combining conviction with repentance, conversion designates a voluntary turning away from past and current ways, to take on different, better ways."[25]

In short, there was a consistent attempt on the part of the white colonizer to separate enslaved Africans from their cultural and religious roots. The Africans transported to Brazil, for instance, experienced that kind of oppression. On top of being uprooted from their homes and lands, turned into a commodity, tortured, raped, and killed in the trade process, they were supposed to leave their culture,

22. Duncan B. Forrester, preface to *Decolonizing the Body of Christ: Theology and Theory after Empire?*, ed. David Joy and Joseph Duggan (New York: Palgrave Macmillan, 2012), xi.

23. Vitalino Similox Salazar, "The Invasion of Christianity into the World of the Mayas," in *Crosscurrents in Indigenous Spirituality: Interface of Maya, Catholic and Protestant Worldviews*, ed. Guillermo Cook (Leiden: Brill, 1997), 35.

24. Guillermo Cook, "Introduction: Brief History of the Maya Peoples," in Cook, *Crosscurrents in Indigenous Spirituality*, 15. Cook connects what he defines as cultural genocide with the missionary aim of eradicating all non-Christian religion and beliefs.

25. Hanks, *Converting Words*, Kindle Locations 285–89.

their ways of life, and their religion behind. As Moacir Rodrigo de Costa Maia shows,

> The entrance of the enslaved Africans in the . . . Portuguese territories was made, then, through evangelization and the reception of baptism. They received a new name, the water of baptism and salt as a sign of liberation from original sin, while the baptismal minutes recorded their condition as captives and the name of their owner. . . . The process of making the new slave included the individual's desocialization. . . . In this long process of enslavement of Africans, baptism was a central criterion in the making of a new slave.[26]

This sort of evangelization culturally uprooted Africans and indigenous so that they could adopt the ways of their conquerors. Its implementation failed, though, because the colonizers did not take seriously enough the agency of non-European peoples. Africans and the original peoples in Latin America were not *tabulae rasae*. As Peter Paris says, "Africans brought their worldviews with them into the diaspora, and as a result of their interaction with their new environments, their African worldviews were gradually altered into a new-African consciousness."[27] The persistence of these indigenous and African worldviews is in large measure responsible for the rise of postcolonial Christianities in Latin America and in other formerly colonized regions of the world.

Most native people in Latin America, as well as most enslaved Africans transported to the region, did not have a choice when it came to embracing the new faith. Most of them were forced to convert. Even those who apparently embraced the religion of the conquerors by choice experienced some form of coercion. However, even under coercive circumstances, a significant number of African descendants and indigenous peoples ended up embracing Christianity as their own faith. They were not merely Christianized. In fact, they made Christianity their own. Whereas forced to

26. Moacir Rodrigo de Castro Maia, "Uma Nova Interpretação da Chegada de Escravos Africanos à América Portuguesa (Minas Gerais, século XVIII)," *Anais do XXVI Simpósio Nacional de História (ANPUH)*, São Paulo, July 2011, http://www.snh2011.anpuh.org/resources/anais/14/1308192610_ARQUIVO_TextocompletoANPUHjunho2011.pdf (translation is mine). Such a description of the process of "making a slave" follows the instructions of the *Ordenações Filipinas* promulgated in 1603. See Silvia Hunold Lara, ed., *Ordenações Filipinas, Livro V* (São Paulo: Companhia das Letras, 1999), 308.

27. Peter J. Paris, *The Spiritualities of the African Peoples: The Search for Common Moral Discourse* (Minneapolis: Fortress Press, 1995), 24.

relinquish outward signs of their indigenous and African spiritualities, they interpreted Christianity through their own cultural lenses, transforming it in the process.

Considering that a large number of indigenous peoples and African descendants in Latin America have after all embraced Christianity as their faith, understanding the makeup of Latin American Christianity becomes an important task. The study of religion from the perspective of an emerging Latin American Christianity requires that one pay attention to indigenous and African voices and agency that have been often suppressed in Eurocentric narratives. Those voices have always been there, but for centuries they have been silenced in textbooks and other sources.

THE BIRTH OF INDIGENOUS CHRISTIANITIES

In a recent Kaqchikel Maya celebration of ancestral authorities in Chuarrancho, Guatemala, an indigenous leader said, "It has been long, but we've recovered our voices. Now, we will continue to talk. We do not want to be more than others; we just want to be treated with equal respect. We hope that one day the authorities in this country will recognize that we have rights, we have culture, we have a philosophy, and that this country has many cultures, not just one."[28]

Some of the Kaqchikel Mayas participating in that ceremony were Christians. Intentionally or not, they have interpreted Christian identity through the lenses of their Mayan culture. Such an attitude goes beyond the idea of contextualizing a universal religious message to make it fit into a given culture. There is an epistemological turn here, and a significant change in the locus of enunciation.[29] This epistemological move is not without consequences. It subverts the Christianity transmitted by missionaries, giving birth to another sort of Christianity, one that can only be fully understood through indigenous cultural lenses. Paraphrasing historian Eduardo Hoornaert in his reference to Brazilian Christianity, one can say that Kaqchikel Christianity is likewise

28. Based on my recollection and notes of my participation in the ceremony, "Matyox Xixopa–Ejerciendo Nuestros Derechos: Autoridades Ancestrales," Chuarrancho, Guatemala, January 22, 2016.

29. Walter Mignolo, "Introduction," *Cultural Studies* 21, nos. 2–3 (2007): 158.

a *moreno* (dark-skinned) Christianity, emerging from the experience of black and brown peoples in Latin America.[30]

This same process has informed black religion in Latin America. I grew up in Salvador da Bahia, Brazil, a city that Umberto Eco has referred to as the "black Rome."[31] In Salvador, one finds, for instance, a lively black Catholicism. Every week, the Igreja Nossa Senhora do Rosário dos Pretos, an eighteenth-century Catholic church in the heart of the city, draws crowds of natives and tourists to an "inculturated mass,"[32] which combines elements of Afro-Brazilian traditional religions and popular Catholicism. This is an example of *moreno* Christianity.

Candomble,[33] an Afro-Brazilian religion formed by formerly enslaved Africans, in 1830, remains a strong force in the lives of many *baianos* (natives of the Bahia state). Even Pentecostals and Evangelicals in that context clearly incorporate elements that are characteristic of the Afro-Brazilian culture. Nevertheless, many Christians have learned to associate this lively spirituality with evil spirits. Such an attitude toward Afro-Brazilian and African religions is more fully understood when one traces it back to the initial encounters between European missionaries and African religions. According to John Mbiti, missionaries, both Catholics and Protestants, thought of their mission in Africa in terms of bringing God to a continent that in their view did not have a religion: "Part of the problem on their part was pure arrogance, racial prejudice, insufficient knowledge, misunderstanding and a narrow concept of anthropology and

30. Eduardo Hoornaert, *O Cristianismo Moreno do Brasil* (Petrópolis, Brazil: Vozes, 1991). In this book, Hoornaert was referring to the Brazilian case. I believe that his epithet, though, can be applied to other Christianities in Latin America.

31. Umberto Eco, *Foucault's Pendulum* (Orlando: Harvest, 1988), 169.

32. For more on inculturated Catholic mass, see John Burdick's study of the field of popular Christianity in Rio de Janeiro, chapter 2 in John Burdick, *Blessed Anastacia: Women, Race, and Popular Christianity in Brazil* (New York: Routledge, 1998), 51ff. As for the black devotion to Our Lady of the Rosary in Brazil, see Elizabeth W. Kiddy, *Blacks of the Rosary: Memory and History in Minas Gerais, Brazil* (University Park, PA: Pennsylvania University Press, 2005); and Carlos Ott, "A Irmandade de Nossa Senhora do Rosario dos Pretos do Pelourinho," *Afro*-Ásia 6, no. 7 (1968): 83–90.

33. Candomble is "a religion which teaches people a way to live in harmony with the energies of nature, which are manifested in the *Orixás*, the spirit emanations of the supreme divinity". It first emerged as "a religion of slaves and freed slaves," forming "an Afro-Brazilian synthesis of the African religious heritage brought by the slaves to Brazil." Raimundo C. Barreto Jr. and Devaka Premawardhana, "Protestantism and Candomblé in Bahia: From Intolerance to Dialogue (and Beyond)," in *The World's Religions after September 11*, vol. 3, ed. Arvind Sharma (Westport, CT: Praeger, 2009), 139, 141.

unwillingness to be challenged and enriched by other peoples and cultures."[34]

Diego Irarrazaval uses the expression "missionary colonialism" to speak about such arrogance.[35] Contrasting that attitude, though, another picture emerges when one looks through the lenses of the agency of Amerindians and enslaved Africans. If there were no indigenous agency—i.e., if indigenous and Afro-Brazilian peoples were not cultural agents—Latin American Christianity would simply mimic European Christianity. But that has not been the case. Latin American Christianity has its own distinct characteristics, which emerge out of the active interaction between the gospel—the story of Jesus—and Latin American cultures. In such contexts, although Jesus more than anything refers to a historical person and event that originally happened in the context of a strange and distant culture, Jesus gains new forms, shapes, names, and meanings when he interacts with memories and symbols particular to Latin American narratives, which become crucial for the understanding of Jesus in the region. In this example, one sees Latin American Christianity being born. It is not simply a foreign religion that is adapted to that particular context. It is a new Christianity, which did not exist before. But it is not only Latin American Christianity that needs to be named. The dominant Christianity that came to Latin America with the European conquistadores, explorers, and missionaries, which we, Latin Americans, were taught to treat in universal terms, also needs to be named. This is an important task.

THE LIBERATING ACT OF NAMING THE RELIGION OF THE COLONIZERS

If Christianity is always culturally shaped,[36] one must avoid referring to the Christianity Latin Americans encountered when Columbus arrived in the Caribbean in abstract terms, as merely "Christianity." Instead, it is important to name it. In this essay, I

34. John Mbiti, "Challenges Facing Religious Education and Research in Africa: The Case of Dialogue Between Christianity and African Religion," *Religion and Theology* 3, no. 2 (1996): 171.

35. Diego Irrarazaval, "Mission within Cultures and Religions," *Exchange* 30, no. 3 (2001): 230.

36. John Mbiti, "On the Article of John W. Kinney: A Comment," *Occasional Bulletin of Missionary Research* 3, no. 2 (1979): 68.

am calling it "colonial Christianity." Colonial Christianity developed universal aspirations as it became a central force in a new world system taking shape at the time of the conquest.[37] In spite of that, colonial Christianity was still culturally located. As such, it should not be treated in universal or abstract terms.

The exercise of naming colonial Christianity makes it possible for formerly colonized people to reject its deadly impact on their people and cultures on moral grounds, without having to relinquish their Christian identity. Chilean scholar Pablo Richard tells an anecdote that might be helpful for my argument here:

> When John-Paul II visited Peru, he received an open letter from various indigenous movements which contained the following passage: John-Paul II, we, Andean and American Indians, have decided to take advantage of your visit to return to you your Bible, since in five centuries it has not given us love, peace or justice. Please take back your Bible and give it back to our oppressors, because they need its moral teachings more than we do. Ever since the arrival of Christopher Columbus a culture, a language, religion and values, which belong to Europe, have been imposed on Latin America by force. The Bible came to us a part of the imposed colonial transformation. It was the ideological weapon of this colonialist assault. The Spanish sword which attacked and murdered the bodies of Indians by day at night became the cross which attacked the Indian soul.[38]

After telling this story, Richard argues for a more radical move. Instead of giving the Bible back to the colonizers, why don't we "make it our own"?[39] The Bible read through European lenses had indeed little to teach Andean indigenous peoples and could never be sharply delinked from the colonial morality of the Europeans who sought to Christianize them. But what if they read it through their own cultural lenses?

37. European modernity created the modern world system, turning itself into the center of that system and all other peoples and societies into its margins. Christianity was the European religion at the time of the conquest. As Dussel says, Christian Europe was the eschatological fulfillment of Christianity. As such, it had nothing to learn from other cultures. It had achieved its full realization. Dussel, *The Invention of the Americas*, 9, 24.

38. Pablo Richard, "1492: The Violence of God and the Future of Christianity," in *The Voice of the Victims, Concilium,* ed. Leonardo Boff and Virgil Elizondo (London: SCM, 1990), 58–67 (66).

39. Richard, "1492," 66.

Since the conquest, Latin Americans have had to deal with the contradictions of an imperialistic and colonialist evangelization.[40] Whereas the North American Protestant missions that arrived in the nineteenth century helped to break the monopoly of European colonial Catholicism, they offered their own version of colonial Christianity, functioning as the religious legitimizers of a neocolonial order.[41] Latin American Christianity is possible only through the agency of indigenous and African peoples. It has existed throughout the five centuries since the conquest, but its existence has either been made invisible or been depicted as a deviation from "true Christianity."

The five hundredth anniversary of the arrival of colonial Christianity in Latin America provided an occasion for a hitherto hidden darker-skinned Christianity to speak up. Latin American indigenous Christians were faced with the ambiguity of the first evangelization in Latin America and its lasting consequences for their people. The commemoration became a unique platform for the public display of the memories of Latin American pre-Columbian peoples.[42] The indigenous narratives shared with a larger audience in that context functioned, most of all, as reminders that indigenous peoples and their cultures remained alive in spite of the myths of their eradication. It is still common in some parts of Latin America to refer to indigenous peoples as having been wiped out. In 1992, indigenous peoples in Latin America took the opportunity of the commemoration to say, 'We are still here.'[43]

The persistence of indigenous peoples, cultures, and religions in Latin America is in itself a form of resistance. More than that, this persistence is an affirmation that the eclipse of the other enacted through

40. José Míguez Bonino quotes Lucio Gera as saying, "To annex a territory to the crown of Spain and to bring it to the altar of the Lord were one and the same thing; the cause of Jesus Christ and the cause of Spain were identical for that country which had just completed 'under the banner of the Catholic faith' the expulsion of the Moslems from its territory and the unification of the kingdom." Lucio Gera, "Apuntes para una Interpretation de la Iglesia Argentina," *Vispera* 15 (1970): 59ff, quoted in José Míguez Bonino, *Doing Theology in a Revolutionary Situation* (Minneapolis: Fortress Press, 2007), Kindle edition, Kindle Locations 143–45.

41. Bonino, *Doing Theology*, Kindle Locations 231–32.

42. Aiban Wagua, "Present Consequences of the European Invasion of America," in *The Voice of the Victims*, ed. Leonardo Boff and Virgil Elizondo (London: SCM, 1991), 47.

43. "Still there, always have been." With these words, Tony Castanha begins the preface of his book *The Myth of Indigenous Caribbean Extinction: Continuity and Reclamation in Borike* (Puerto Rico) (New York: Palgrave McMillan, 2011), xi-xvi, which uncovers the rich history and tradition of indigenous peoples in the lands we now know as Puerto Rico, one of the many areas in Latin America where the myth of indigenous extinction has been widely disseminated.

the process of conquest and colonization never entirely succeeded. As Wagua affirms, the retelling of "the marginalization, the violence, the genocide or ethnocide perpetrated against our indigenous communities of Abia Yala," as painful as it is, is also a remembrance of "our indomitable will."[44] Indigenous peoples and African descendants in Latin America have never given up their agency as moral, cultural, political, and religious subjects. Suffering and oppression have not deprived them of their will as a people. In fact, they continue to be killed and excluded in disproportionate ways in Latin America. But they are much more than victims. It is undeniable that genocide continues.[45] But so does resistance.

POPULAR RELIGION

Indigenous spirituality in Latin America has often taken the form of popular religion.[46] When observed from the perspective of the colonized and marginalized people, popular religion illustrates the active agency of indigenous and Afro-Latin American cultures as they create meaning in response to new and changing realities.[47]

Popular Catholicism is an important expression of popular religion in Latin America. The devotion, for instance, of Our Lady of Guadalupe, *La Morenita*, in Mexico, is well known. Our Lady of Guadalupe appeared to Juan Diego, a Nahuatl peasant, in 1531, on the hill of Tepeyac, present-day Mexico City. There was a shrine for the female Azteca deity Tonantzin in that location. In that event, Mary, a Christian symbol, is turned into a dark-skinned woman dressed in indigenous clothes. Indigenous spirituality is embodied through a Christian symbol. According to Judith Gleanson, "The Virgin of Guadalupe came to life in response to the putting down of her Nahuatl predecessor, Tonantzin, whom she continues in

44. Wagua, "Present Consequences," 49.

45. Pope Francis has recently warned against the threat of extermination of indigenous peoples in Brazil. "Além da ameaça: Indios no Brasil estão sendo eliminados," *Radio Vaticano*, July 7, 2016, http://br.radiovaticana.va/news/2016/07/07/além_da_ameaça_índios_no_brasil_estão_sendo_eliminados/1242585.

46. Popular religion includes popular Christianity but is also present outside of Christianity. As Miguel De La Torre and Edwin David Aponte state, "Through popular religion Latina/o peoples voice and act out their own theological and spiritual understandings of the Divine, themselves, and the world." Popular religion urges that the faith of the people be given proper attention. Miguel De La Torre and Edwin David Aponte, *Introducing Latino/a Theologies* (Maryknoll, NY: Orbis, 2001), 118.

47. Salazar, "The Invasion of Christianity," 40.

mysterious ways to embody."[48] On the hill where the Azteca mother goddess had been worshiped, a brown Catholic saint appeared to remind a Nahuatl convert that she remains the mother-goddess of her people.[49] The Catholic Virgin comes to the help of her child as an indigenous mother.[50] Commonly dismissed by early scholarship, popular religion has more recently caught greater scholarly attention as illustrative of "'the faith of the people' on their own terms."[51]

At the end of the day, religion and culture are dynamic. They change and adapt to face novel circumstances. It was a mistake to think that the power and violence of the colonizers would completely inhibit indigenous agency. Indigenous agency has not only resisted cultural genocide. It also continues to inform indigenous, African, and mestizo worldviews in the region. Although studies of *mestizaje* and syncretism are helpful to illuminate indigenous agency,[52] further language prioritizing agency from below is called for. Such a language must contribute to keep in check unequal power relations and highlight the diversity of local histories.

Instead of thinking of syncretism in terms of amalgamation, we are challenged to consider the different meanings of syncretic symbols and experiences. For instance, Afro-Brazilian religions forced to hide under Catholic symbols during the colonial era did not necessarily represent a melding of African traditional values and European Catholicism. In that unequal encounter, two different symbolic worlds occupied the same space, holding on, nevertheless, to distinctive meanings and values. Afro-Brazilian religions created sacred symbolic spaces where the "cumulative cultural cognizance and worldviews of enslaved Africans transported to the New World

48. Judith Gleanson, "Oya in the Company of the Saints," *Journal of the American Academy of Religion* 68, no. 2 (2000): 265.

49. See Robert Orsi, "She Came, She Saw, She Conquered," book review of *Goddess of the Americas: Writings on the Virgin of Guadalupe*, ed. Ana Castillo (New York: Riverhead, 1996), *Commonwealth* 124, no. 5 (1997): 24.

50. Dussel, *The Invention of the Americas*, 126.

51. De La Torre and Aponte, *Introducing Latino/a Theologies*, 119.

52. Virgilio P. Elizondo, *The Future Is Mestizo: Life Where Cultures Meet* (Boulder: University Press of Colorado, 2000); Tânia Lima, ed., *Sincretismo Religioso: O Ritual Afro-Brasileiro* (Recife: Editora Massangano, 1996). Also, Gustavo Benavides, "Syncretism and Legitimacy in Latin American Religion," in *Syncretism and Religion: A Reader*, ed. Anita Maria Leopold and Jeppe Sinding Jensen (London: Equinox, 2004), 194–216.

during the trans-Atlantic slave trade (1538–1888) remain operative," even when these persons could not overtly practice their faith.[53]

Lara Medina has used the Nahuatl word *nepantla* in an attempt to respond to such demands.[54] According to her, this word refers to the confusion and agony faced by Latin American indigenous peoples during the conquest. The world as the pre-Columbian peoples had known it was mortally wounded. A Christian order imposed by the Iberian conquistadores was in the process of full implementation. Indigenous peoples were caught in between worlds, being challenged to keep their indigenous identity alive while making sense of an overwhelming new reality. They creatively found a middle way, which, as Medina points out, went beyond overt resistance: "Indigenous peoples did not merely resist the imposition of Christianity but they responded to the foreign tradition by crafting their religiosity, developing unsanctioned traditions, reinforcing their community networks, and ultimately asserting their religious autonomy. They became Christian on their own terms and in the process Christianity was changed."[55]

According to Medina, the indigenous word *nepantla* described the trauma of living between ancient institutions and new, incomprehensible, ones brought by the colonizers. *Nepantla* is a space of discomfort, which does not allow for easy reconciliation of multiple worldviews without consideration of difference. Accordingly, reconciliation between Indigenous and Christian traditions demands the privileging of mother culture and the full respect of the indigenous.[56]

NEW THEOLOGICAL VOICES

Emerging Latin American Christianities have their own theological voices. Indigenous peoples, Afro-Latin Americans, and women are finding their own locus of enunciation as religious actors. One can see the emergence of these new theological actors in Latin America

53. Mikelle Smith Omari-Tunkara. "Candomblé," in *The Oxford Encyclopedia of African Thought*, ed. F. Abiola Irele and Biodun Jeyifo, Oxford African American Studies Center, http://www.oxfordaasc.com /article/opr/t301/e085, accessed June 24, 2015.

54. Lara Medina, "Nepantla Spirituality: Negotiating Multiple Religious Identities among U.S. Latinas," in De La Torre and Espinosa, *Rethinking Latino(a) Religion and Identity*, 248–66.

55. Ibid., 251.

56. Ibid., 250.

in light of Gustavo Gutierrez's the "irruption of the poor" in history.[57] Samuel Escobar has spoken in similar terms of popular Protestantism:

> My thesis is that popular Protestantism in Latin America is one of the most surprising manifestations of what theologian Gustavo Gutiérrez has called "the irruption of the poor" (1982: 108), and what missiologist Walbert Bühlmann has called "the coming of the Third Church" (1986: 6). It has to be understood within the frame of a new age in the history of Christianity, in which as Andrew Walls says, "its main base will be in the Southern continents, and where its dominant expression will be filtered through the culture of those continents" (1985: 221).[58]

Latin America is experiencing a revitalization of its religious life, along with a renewed awareness of its religious pluralism. Catholicism remains the dominant religion in the region. Pentecostalism, the main Protestant expression of popular religion, has emerged as an increasingly major player.

PLACE AND ROLE OF PENTECOSTALISM

Pentecostalism is the most visible face of Latin American Protestantism. Pentecostalism has, in fact, been claimed as a black religion in Brazil. Marco Davi de Oliveira, an Afro-Brazilian Baptist minister and theologian, has argued that Pentecostalism is the largest black religion in Brazil today.[59] Although his claim can be disputed, his point is that one will find more Afro-Brazilians in Pentecostal temples on any given Sunday than in any other place of worship. Another voice reclaiming the blackness of Brazilian Pentecostals is Hernani da Silva, a leader of the Brazilian Evangelical Black Movement (MNE, for Movimento Negro Evangelico) and a Pentecostal himself.[60] There

57. In his introduction to the fifteenth-anniversary revised edition of *A Theology of Liberation*, Gustavo Gutierrez acknowledged the limitations of the almost exclusively socioeconomic categories the first liberation theologians used to address oppression and injustice, and welcomed the contributions made by black, Hispanic, Amerindian, and feminist theologies to expand the views of liberation theologians. For him, "The world of the poor is a universe in which the socioeconomic aspect is basic but not all-inclusive." Gustavo Gutierrez, *A Theology of Liberation*, 15th anniv. ed. (Maryknoll, NY: Orbis, 1988), xxi.

58. Samuel Escobar, "Mission in Latin America: An Evangelical Perspective," *Missiology* 20, no. 2 (1992): 242.

59. Marco David de Oliveira, *A Religião Mais Negra do Brasil: Porque Mais de Oito Milhões de Negros São Pentecostais* (São Paulo: Mundo Cristão, 2004).

60. For an introduction to this movement, see John Burdick, "Why Is the Black Evangelical Movement Growing in Brazil?," *Journal of Latin American Studies* 37, no. 2 (2005): 311–32.

is a growing movement raising awareness among Afro-Brazilian Pentecostals of their *negritude*, or blackness.

This movement has had a positive impact on the existing difficult relationship between black Pentecostals/Evangelicals and the Brazilian Black Movement. Most black Evangelicals and Pentecostals tend to stay away from the Black Movement, because a significant number of their participants and leaders have connections with Afro-Brazilian religions. The majority of Brazilian Evangelicals and Pentecostals still demonize the Afro-Brazilian religions. Black Pentecostals participating in the Black Evangelical Movement, however, have been able to search for common ground with participants of Afro-Brazilian religions at least on the level of their *negritude*, creating spaces for political alliances in the struggle against oppression and racism. Black Pentecostals/Evangelicals such as Hernani da Silva, Marco Davi de Oliveira, and others are working to develop a "theology of African roots" that can help primarily Afro-Brazilian Christians to "articulate an anti-racist message in clear, theologically sophisticated biblical terms."[61]

On top of that, they are retelling the story of Brazilian Protestantism from an Afro-Brazilian perspective. For example, whereas most history books consider Scottish Presbyterian missionary Robert Reid Kalley as the founder of the first Portuguese-speaking Protestant congregation in Brazil (1855), Hernani da Silva gives credit to a lay black preacher, Agostinho Jose Pereira, who founded a Portuguese-speaking Protestant church in Recife in 1841.[62] By doing that, da Silva turns an unknown black evangelist and a black Protestant church into the cornerstone of Brazilian Protestantism. Through the lenses of the Evangelical Black Movement, the history of Brazilian Protestantism not only gains a new perspective, but also recovers lost or hidden memories of previously unheard black Protestant leaders, including women.[63] Evangelical and Pentecostal mobilization for racial justice is particularly timely, since hate crimes against members of Afro-Brazilian religions are on the rise.[64] Similar movements can be found in other parts of Latin America and the Caribbean.

61. Ibid., 325.

62. Hernani da Silva, *O Movimento Negro Evangélico: Um Mover do Espírito Santo* (São Paulo: Selo Editorial Negritude Crista, 2010), 9.

63. Ibid., 10.

64. Zoe Sullivan and Lydia Barros, "Followers of Afro-Brazilian Religions Feel under Attack," *Al Jazeera America*, September 13, 2014, http://america.aljazeera.com/articles/2014/9/13/prejudice-againstcandombleworshippersincreasesinbrazil.html.

CONCLUDING THOUGHTS

Survivors of the indigenous genocide and descendants of enslaved Africans have been active participants in renewed encounters and exchanges between gospel and culture in Latin America. Throughout the five centuries since the conquest, they have found creative strategies of survival and resistance. Their narratives not only unmask the face of colonial Christianity but also shape and form different streams of Latin American Christianity. They deserve particular attention from religious scholars interested in understanding Latin American religion in the context of the irruption of the poor.

Latin American Christianity emerges through the weaving together of the story of many peoples and communities. The effervescence of Latin American Christianity, thus, needs to be considered in the light of the revitalization of Indigenous and Afro-Latin American identities. A view from below, prioritizing indigenous and African voices, can promote fresher and healthier interfaith and intercultural relations in the region, which may contribute to the healing of the open wounds of a violent past that continue to haunt, in particular, brown and black Latin Americans.

PART IV

Church and Gender: Contributions from the Global North and South

7.

Church and Gender in Germany

UTA ANDRÉE

When I was invited to reflect about church and gender as a contribution from the Global North, I immediately thought about the unequal presence and role of women and men within German Protestant churches. Because of this focus, this will not be a representative reflection of the Global North—which is, in my opinion, a highly questionable term—but an attempt to describe the situation of a very specific reality of a powerful church in a secularized country. As I begin my reflection, I want to note that I find it interesting, as an individual from the Global North, to be asked to submit a contextual contribution, because usually when we think about contextual research, it is concerning specific topics of theologies from the Global South. This contextual perspective on Western backgrounds is a challenging but urgent shift.

One further preliminary remark in the form of a question that preoccupied me: How can I as a woman dare to give my ideas on questions that are related to men? Is it not audacious for a woman to seek answers to the question "Where are the men in our parish life?" My tentative answer is twofold: First, I think that if we could only conduct authentic research on matters and topics that we are directly concerned with, there would be no legitimacy for most research.[1] Furthermore, I even guess that a certain distance between the subject

1. I remember many liberation theologians starting their reflection with the avowal that even if their starting point is the reality of oppressed and marginalized people, they themselves do not belong to the group of marginalized and poor population of their own society. See the work of Leonardo Boff, Jon Sobrino and others.

and the scholar can be healthy. That is why I, as a woman, do not shy away in this article from addressing men. Perhaps this is so, because my final conclusion will pan out from a men-centered perspective on the question, bringing my conclusion to a different level.

I begin my paper with a section titled "Men: Who Are They?" where I will ask whether or not it is possible to talk about men as a collective group. This reflection is based on the many debates about whether masculinity is a biological, a social, an educational, or a historical concept—or a mixture of all these factors.[2] And as expected, I will come to the deconstructive conclusion that any definition of men as a collective must fail. In the next section, I offer some highlights about the proportions of men and women within the life of German Protestant churches. The repartition for men and women in different parts of church life seem to be gender specific, but other more invisible imbalances also play a major role. These are explored in the last section, and I conclude with three theses.

MEN: WHO ARE THEY?

One of the most popular German songs is "Männer" ("Men") by Herbert Grönemeyer.[3] Today this song is thirty-two years old, but still people from all generations know it by heart. I wonder what this song really says about men. People like it, and they seem to identify with the content in its literal and ironic sense. The truth and the irony are found in phrases like "Men take you in their arms. . . . Men cry secretly. . . . Men are so vulnerable" and "Men get thin hair, men are human beings too. . . . Men are just irreplaceable in this world."

Why was and is this song such a success? Why did men and women love it and sing it together? Why do they still sing this song together? Neither men nor women seem to feel as though women are rejected by the tough, macho lyrics ("Men buy women"). Similarly, men do not seem hurt by the ridiculous sentences about strange male habits ("Men are already drunk when they are still babies"). This song seems to take men seriously, taking into account all projections and expectations that men might be confronted with, both those things considered to be positive and those seen as negative: "Men are so

2. Raewyn Connell, *Der gemachte Mann: Konstruktion und Krise von Männlichkeiten* (Wiesbaden: Springer, 2015), 95–118.

3. Herbert Grönemeyer, "Männer," *Bochum*, EMI, 1984 (translation of quoted phrases into English by the author).

strong" and "Men are so vulnerable" or "Men cry secretly." As such, this song draws the boundaries into which men have to fit according to the expectations of the society ("Men have muscles"; "Men have a hard life, but they take it easy"). At the same time, this song instills a sense of humor as well as an understanding of potential spaces of vulnerability. Knowing that this song is a caricature, men and women love it and sing it.

This song makes one aware of the fact that it is impossible to describe men, but at the same time, it does what is impossible: the truth lies in the mixture of tenderness and pity and between seriousness and ease. Grönemeyer sings this song with full fervor and at the same time with a twinkle in his eye. This is probably the only adequate way of talking about men as a category. This is the only description that does not turn into something abstruse and untenable. And above all, this song sounds the question of when is a man a man.

Any other general description of men that does not embody the juxtaposition as this song does cannot be taken seriously—though we have many such descriptions. Or shall we call these descriptions "constructions"? I want to briefly mention some of these as they arise in Rainer Knieling's contribution on men and church, presented in 2010, as drawn from a scholarly survey on men's identity. Knieling states, "Achievements and success are important elements in the life of men,"[4] and "One important guiding theme for men's self-understanding is autonomy."[5] Examining the parental attitude toward each other in the church, he asserts: "I [as a man] don't want this kind of care. I need friends and support, but I don't want to be determined by or even be reduced to my neediness."[6] Attributing these three sentences to men's church relations and religious feelings provides a kind of gender construction, which does not do justice to men or women. Other examples from church pamphlets and small booklets could be added. Even if the opposite of the stereotype is emphasized, descriptions that refer to men become ridiculous. One example might be the masculinity courses that are spread throughout the United States and

4. Rainer Knieling, *Männer und Kirche: Konflikte, Missverständnisse, Annäherungen* (Göttingen: Vandenhoeck & Ruprecht, 2010), 81.

5. Ibid., 109.

6. Ibid., 100.

invoke programs like "Teaching Men to Be Emotionally Honest"[7] or "Five Habits of Highly Compassionate Men."[8]

We can assume that describing men is a risky enterprise and that it rarely comes to satisfying results. Our question, "Men: who are they?" seems to be the wrong approach.

The history of feminist and women's studies shows us that the concern surrounding women was just the opposite of what seems to happen in some attempts at men's studies ("men's faith is different,"[9] or "men as king, warrior, magician and lover," according to the four archetypes of C. G. Jung's philosophy[10]). Women's liberation was, and still is, also the liberation from stereotypes and clichés that squeeze them into a certain image and role. It really shocked me while preparing this article that men acquiesce in so many one-sided descriptions and assumptions about their feelings, longings, thinking, and even their "nature."

Describing male or female always means doing two tricky things: First, how is it possible to find common attributes in members of such a large group of diverse people (roughly 50 percent of the population)? Second, how is it possible to then compare this half of humanity with the other? A sentence that pretends to say something specific about men deprives 50 percent from fitting into the stated attribution. Additionally, stereotypes ostracize many of the very group they are attempting to define. Theories like the construction of "hegemonic masculinity," instead of giving an adequate description of men, design an oppressive picture, which has an impact on how men are seen and expected to behave.[11] Any of these constructions are disguised as description, but in fact, they have a (negative) effect on self-understanding and the self-estimation of men. Describing "men" or "masculinity" is a highly doubtful enterprise. Michael Meuser, from whom I learned a lot in this regard, asserts:

7. Andrew Reiner, "Teaching Men to Be Emotionally Honest," *New York Times*, April 4, 2016, www.nytimes.com/2016/04/10/education/edlife/teaching-men-to-be-emotionally-honest.html?_r=3.

8. Kozo Hattori, "Five Habits of Highly Compassionate Men," Stanford School of Medicine, Center for Compassion and Altruism Research and Education, September 29, 2014, ccare.stanford.edu/press_posts/5-habits-of-highly-compassionate-men/.

9. Title of a church magazine from April 2012. See Lothar Simmank, "Männer glauben anders," *Blick in die Kirche,* April 2012, 6.

10. Andreas Ebert, "Sonntagsblatt Thema: Männer." Evangelischer Presseverband für Bayern, Munich, January 2016, 4–8.

11. Connell, *Der gemachte Mann*, 129–35.

> Gender is a social category and the concern of any research can only be the relationship between male and female. We can focus on men and masculinity or on women and femaleness, but in both cases the study matter will be seen from a relational perspective. We cannot analyze male dominance without considering the relatedness of women's behavior view to the dominant position of men. Talking about a male way of communicating does only make sense comparing it to a (different) female way of communicating. The analysis of masculinity needs a comparative perspective, which takes into consideration the difference to women and vice versa.[12]

I highly appreciate that the World Council of Churches (WCC) and the World Communion of Reformed Churches (WCRC) in their recent gender training manual did not engage in a description or analysis of what is male or masculinity but found the starting point in a favorable partnership.[13]

MEN: WHERE ARE THEY?

> Women and children fill the church pews every Sunday. And as the boys approach puberty and are able to make decisions for themselves they also wander away from the church in droves, leaving the women to fill the pews. This begs the question "Where are the men in the church?" . . . There are possibly several factors that can explain the absence of men in the churches. Among these are possibly both the perception among men of the increasing irrelevance of religion in their lives, but also at another level a perception that the church is a "woman's place."[14]

Even though this observation from the WCC/WCRC gender training manual makes this claim at the global scale, it also fits particularly well into observations one could make about the German context.

12. Michael Meuser, "Modernisierte Männlichkeit?: Kontinuitäten, Herausforderungen und Wandel männlicher Lebenslagen," in *Mannsbilder: Kritische Männerforschung und Theologische Frauenforschung im Gespräch*, ed. Marie-Theres Wacker and Stefanie Rieger-Goertz (Berlin: Lit Verl., 2006), 24.

13. Patricia Sheerattan-Bisnauth and Philip Vinod Peacock, eds., *Created in God's Image: From Hegemony to Partnership, Church Manual on Men as Partners: Promoting Positive Masculinities* (Geneva: World Council of Churches and World Communion of Reformed Churches, November 2010), menengage.org/wp-content/uploads/2014/07/PositiveMasculinitiesGender-Manual_0.pdf. The subtitle of the published material, "A Church Manual on Men as Partners: Promoting Positive Masculinity," is quite misleading.

14. Ibid., 44.

This drives us to the question "Who are men, and why don't they go to church?" What is different about them?

We cannot deny that there is an imbalance in the presence of men and women in the churches. The worshipping community is more female than male. The diaconal and service workers of the church are more often staffed by women than by men. Yet, in contrast, the higher-ranking positions in churches are occupied by men. The presence of men is strong in leadership on every level, be it national, regional, or local. One example of this would be the eighteen men in the position of bishop or moderator of the German Protestant territorial churches (so-called *Landeskirchen*) out of a total of twenty such seats. On the national level, most of the most influential and highly ranked positions are occupied by men. This includes the director of mission organization, heads of diaconal companies, and advisory positions to the national and the regional governments.

The great majority of professors of theology are still men, but they teach a well-balanced auditorium of young men and women who want to become pastors, even though, on the pastoral level, men dominate the group. Statistics show that in German Protestant churches, out of 18,576 pastors, 32.1 percent are women, 60.8 percent of the part-time positions are occupied by women, and only 23.7 percent of the full-time positions are occupied by women.[15]

The church is one of the most important employers in Germany. In total, 229,668 people work for the church, of which 76.2 percent are female. This is part of the old story: women serve and men rule. The numbers dramatically show that women do not have the same access to higher positions. They are more likely to occupy part-time positions than men, and many of them (many more than men) work in areas of service with little influence on the organizational level or in positions that influence the "content" or constitution of the church.

A last sector that is interesting to evaluate is the voluntary work of men on a parish level. Even here, we find different tendencies of engagement and commitment between men and women. In the parishes, men are prominently involved in technical advice and in the committee work of the community. They preside over the committee for the graveyard, building and real estate, and finances, while

15. Evangelische Kirche in Deutschland, *Zahlen und Fakten zum kirchlichen Leben* (Hannover: EKD, 2015), 9.

the committees for the work with children and youth, the committee for visiting services, and the committee on liturgy and church music are often in the hands of women. Hence, a very traditional picture is drawn when it comes to the typical roles of men and women in ordinary parish life.

All this shows that church participation, particularly leadership, is still gender specific, whether one is officially acting in the church and in a position of responsibility or if one is among the consuming, the serving, or a part of the silent majority. In a simplistic way, we could presume that men do not bear up well in a position in which they are exposed to expostulations, moral appeals, and where they might be expected to take submissive attitudes to what is preached or announced.

Interestingly, there is debate about whether the reputation of the profession of a pastor and the reputation of the church could suffer from this development pejoratively called feminization.[16] Considering this claim, we have to keep in mind that such a discussion is taking place at a time in which the profession of pastor has only recently become accessible to women as well as to men but is still far from being accessed by as many women as it is by men. The feminization of the profession is largely considered a threat, but we have to ask what is the subject of this concern.

How do we now respond to this mix of facts and interpretations? Does this mix of facts and interpretations concern the essence of men, and do we go back to the question of what differs between men and women? In my opinion, to a great extent, the differences in the presence of men and women in the church must be explained historically. In Germany, we have a phrase that talks about the three *K*s, which claim to depict the life of women: *Kinder, Küche, Kirche* (children, kitchen, and church). Today, a woman's self-understanding does not match this claim, but we are still aware that women were confined to these fields in the past. And vice versa—men know that the church is one of the fields with which they are not expected to identify.

Perhaps the dissolution of women and the three *K*s was much more successful than the re-approximation of men to these three fields of life. Men still struggle to partake equally in the education and bringing up of their offspring. Even though many men want to share this

16. Friedrich Wilhelm Graf, *Kirchendämmerung: Wie die Kirchen unser Vertrauen verspielen* (Munich: Beck, 2011), 24. In official circles, Graf's thesis was, of course, strongly offensive, but on a more informal level, it gained a more positive response.

task with their wives, the working world often doesn't allow the application of new gender roles. Men still struggle to find access to household matters and unburden their wives from certain tasks, but for this, many still have to suffer mockery from their male peers.[17] The third field of the three *K*s—the church—undergoes the same presupposition that children and kitchen do. Church is something for women and belongs to their field of activity and responsibility. According to a survey on men from 1998, it is still strongly seen as the task of women to pray with the children, and religious education in general is considered women's responsibility.[18] Perhaps this is the field in which men have achieved less progress in their emancipation. These gender constructs are a heritage that we have to overcome; part of what we have to leave behind is the essentialist construction of a so-called masculinity and a so-called femaleness.[19]

IMBALANCES

If we take into account that any definitions of masculinity and femaleness are historically and socially routed, we can ask what is behind the absence of men in the churches, especially in the core activity of worship. It is related to their traditional absence, but as men rediscover their fervor for children and kitchen, we cannot relax on this historical explanation. Men do come back to the kitchens, they do come back to the playgrounds, but they do not come back to church.

This is the point where I want to leave the gender-specific perspective for a while, because it can mislead us by concentrating on men's absence from church—because, in Germany, in the main-

17. Interestingly, an article in a German church review talks about the male rediscovering of cooking on an elaborate level. The author calls men who perform their knowledge and abilities in kitchens as the gastro-sexual men. It is still something extraordinary, and we should not applaud if men reach out to classical women's fields and then earn their special merits with it. Real partnership means sharing of responsibilities in all fields of life. See Ebert, "Sonntagsblatt Thema: Männer," 46–48.

18. Rainer Volz, "Studie: Männer im Aufbruch; Männliche Identitäten, Rollenbilder und Geschlechterverhältnisse," in *Mannsbilder: Kritische Männerforschung und theologische Frauenforschung im Gespräch,* ed. Marie Therese Wacker and Stefanie Rieger Goertz (Berlin: Lit-Verlag, 2006), 43 and 55.

19. Raewyn Connell gives a very instructive overview on the history of masculinity in her book *Masculinities* and shows its constructedness and contextuality. Raewyn Connell, *Masculinities*, 2nd ed. (Berkeley: University of California Press, 2005). See Connell, *Der gemachte Mann*, 247–68.

line Protestant churches, many others are also missing. The church members survey from 2014 shows that only 22 percent of church members between ages fourteen and twenty-one feel "connected to the church."[20] Another 52 percent of this age group feel explicitly distanced from the church. The numbers seem to be more positive when it comes to the group of the twenty-two- to twenty-nine-year-old members (only 41 percent of them feel explicitly distanced, and 34 percent feel connected). The authors of the survey explain this shift through phenomena such as a strong religious mobility and a trial-and-error mentality toward spiritual experience within the adolescent group. I would say, unfortunately, these numbers, on a very practical level, have to do with the fact that people in their twenties initially remember that they are members of the church because the membership fee is taken from their salary. This leads many to leave the church as soon as they earn their own money. The reciprocal result is that the remaining people will reflect more on their membership and feel to a greater extent connected to the church because they chose to stay. From this point of view, the repartition of those who feel connected or distanced, contrarily to the first appearance, is not very reassuring. The numbers are stable until the age of sixty-five. Above that age, people feel significantly more connected to the church. And this picture is exactly what we see in Sunday services: the majority are retired people. And, coming back to our issue, there are usually more men in the church than younger people.

Another factor that has to be considered is the social affiliation of the members or worshippers. It is obvious that German Protestant churches lost ground in the so-called lower class and with those who have a lower educational level.[21] The church still is performing its services in a highly intellectual manner. The text load is tremendous, and it requires substantial knowledge to understand the preaching. In addition, dynamics and movement in services are usually very restricted. Only people who are accustomed to concentrating and listening for an extended period of time can enjoy this type of worship. Related to our question on the presence of men, we can act on the

20. The following data come from the church members survey from 2014: *Engagement und Indifference*, chapter 5.2., "Evangelische Kirche in Deutschland", in *Zahlen und Fakten zum kirchlichen Leben* (Hannover, 2015).

21. One study has been conducted in the southwest of Germany with a quite clear result: Evangelischer Oberkirchenrat. See *Evangelischer Oberkirchenrat der Evangelischen Landeskirche in Württemberg*, Bericht in der Sitzung der 14. Landessynode am Mittwoch 28.11.2014, zu Top 20: Beritch zur Milienstudie Baden und Württemberg.

assumption that there are many more men in worship and present in parish life than people from a lower educational background.

Given these imbalances, the church has to deal with these issues. The ministry of a pastor in the church has to take into account who is present and who should be invited and reached. Here lies perhaps the very truth of what Friedrich Graf called in a quite awkward way the "feminization" of the church.[22] In my opinion, he hits on something true about the self-understanding of the churches and of the church leadership in that it must draw its attention to the religious matters that the people are concerned with. The proclamation has to come to a spiritual intensity and authenticity that is often missing. And with this, the church loses its unique selling point. Instead of satisfying the expectations of a huge variety of social and political actors (or at a parish level of local institutions and influential circles), the church and the pastors should do what is their responsibility: preach, pray, and act according to the gospel. The fact that the church doesn't come to such an orientation has nothing to do with the number of women or men in responsible positions but with a self-understanding and a seriousness of responding to the call.

CONCLUSION

The presence of men and women on the different levels of church life cannot be ignored. Men still occupy the most important positions, yet they are less present in the worship life of the community. This social and educational heritage does not have qualitative but quantitative implications for the present situation.

Any attempt to explain the lack of men on the parish level that refers to the collective identity of men or to any kind of assumption like "men believe in a different way" is of little help. The description of "how men are" should turn into a description of how we can build a fruitful gender-balanced community according to Galatians 3:28.

Church has to be careful not to overlook other missing groups within the church by lamenting the absence of men. Poor preaching

22. See Graf, *Kirchendämmerung*. The title of Graf's book shows the tendency and the objective of his contribution: "Ecclesial Twilight: How Churches Gamble Our Confidence Away." His purpose was to call for more seriousness within the church, for an adequate talking about the holy God, for perceptible authentic faith in the pastoral work, for less moralism and more eloquent power in the proclamation of the gospel, for less paternalistic attitudes and more visionary uprising.

and fancy activities not only will keep men out of the church, but will also encourage women to stay away. Anyone—even those with a critical view of church—recognize the church as the place where things about life, death, and eternal life can be spoken about and experienced, whether the individuals participate or not, but being authentic is the first step to come to a new balance in any regard.

8.

Women and Academic Theological Education

A Reflection on the Experience of Female Students from the Faculdade Unida de Vitória-ES (Brazil)

CLAUDETE BEISE ULRICH

In this essay, I aim to offer a reflection on women and academic theological education based on the experience of female students from the Faculdade Unida de Vitória, in the state of Espírito Santo, Brazil. Academic theological education is an important step for women to achieve ecclesial agency. My reflection is based on narrative interviews conducted with female students concerning the impact of theological studies in their own life experiences. Academic theological training enhances the self-esteem of women, empowers them, and provides them with tools for reflection-action-reflection in their Christian communities or in other organizational spaces, and it is fundamental in the fight for gender equality as well. Furthermore, academic theological education, as well as education at all levels, is a human right of girls and women.

FACULDADE UNIDA DE VITÓRIA (UNIDA): ITS HISTORY IN A NUTSHELL

Faculdade Unida is the only accredited theological school in the state of Espírito Santo.[1] Its history is recent; it celebrates its 20th anniversary in 2017. It was born from the dream of three Presbyterian pastors: Wanderley Pereira da Rosa, Simonton César Araújo, and Alcimar Ribeiro de Paula. Those pastors aimed at creating a space for theological reflection featuring the following objectives: ecumenical commitment, well-grounded theology, courses that could be turned into practical tools for the daily life of students in their communities, and professors with diverse pastoral experiences, broadening the experiences addressed in the classroom. This educational endeavor was started in August 1997 with 30 students meeting in a church.

The baccalaureate program in theological studies was established in Brazil in 1999 through Directive 241/99 of the Ministry of Education and Culture (MEC). The first program of theological studies authorized by MEC in Brazil was that of Faculdades EST in São Leopoldo/RS. Only then was theology recognized as a field of studies in Brazilian academia.[2]

As a result, the dream of establishing a program in theology at the then-called Faculdade Teológica Unida (FTU) also arose. So the work to make the institution meet MEC requirements began. After some time preparing the necessary documents and building up a library and a computer lab, FTU received the MEC Assessment Committee in October 2005. This committee recommended the FTU accreditation and the authorization of the Baccalaureate Program in Theology, which was awarded the highest scores in all examined items. Directives 3,914 and 3,915 from November 14, 2005, signed by His Excellency the Minister of Education Fernando Haddad and published in the *Federal Official Gazette* on November 16, 2005, confirmed both the authorization and the accreditation.

1. The historical information on the Faculdade Unida was taken from its website, available at http://www.faculdadeunida.com.br/site/institucional/institucional-nossahistoria, accessed on June 20, 2016.

2. Lothar C. Hoch, "Primeiro curso de Teologia do Brasil autorizado pelo MEC," Portal Luteranos (Igreja Evangélica de Confissão Luterana no Brasil), http://www.luteranos.com.br/conteudo/primeiro-curso-de-teologia-do-brasil-autorizado-pelo-mec, accessed on June 20, 2016.

Directive MEC 38 on January 16, 2007, authorized the school to change its name from Faculdade Teológica Unida (FTU) to Faculdade Unida de Vitória (Unida).

The consolidation of the undergraduate program in theology took place in August 2009 through Directive MEC 1,173, which recognized the theology program.[3] December 18 of that same year marked the graduation of the first theology class recognized by MEC in the state of Espírito Santo.

Data from the 2010 Census by the Brazilian Institute for Geography and Statistics (IBGE) reveal that Espírito Santo is the state with the highest proportion of evangelicals in Brazil.[4] A report explains, "The survey showed that 33.1% of Espírito Santo natives are evangelicals, a proportion higher than the national average, which is 22.2%. In ten years, their number grew from 26.2 million to 42.3 million across the country."[5] Faced with this reality, Faculdade Unida, through its Theology Department, has taken on the task of training students so that they will be agents of transformation in their churches and their social contexts.

WOMEN: THE RIGHT TO ACADEMIC THEOLOGICAL EDUCATION

According to British historian Eric Hobsbawm, the twentieth century was marked by the most relevant social movement of the history of humankind: the movement for the emancipation of women, in

3. Note from the editors: The process of accreditation of higher-education programs by MEC in Brazil has two phases. First is the authorization of the program (when a credentialed higher-education institution is authorized to create a program), and second is the recognition of the program (which acknowledges that the program meets the necessary standards and validates its results).

4. Note from the editors: The word *evangélico* in Portuguese and Spanish is used as self-identification by most Protestants, from mainstream Protestant churches to Pentecostals. See Jose Miguez Bonino, *Faces of Latin American Protestantism*, trans. Eugene L. Stockwell (Grand Rapids: Eerdmans, 1995), viii. As David Stoll had noticed already in the early 1990s, a growing number of Latin Americans identify themselves as *Evangélicos*. See David Stoll, "Introduction: Rethinking Protestantism in Latin America," in *Rethinking Protestantism in Latin America*, ed. Virginia Garrard-Burnett and David Stoll (Philadelphia: Temple University Press, 1993), 2.

5. Rodrigo Araujo, "Proporção de evangélicos no Espírito Santo é maior do que no restante do país," *Gazeta*, June 29, 2012, http://gazetaonline.globo.com/_conteudo/2012/06/a_gazeta/minuto_a_minuto/1292361-proporcao-de-evangelicos-no-espirito-santo-e-maior-do-que-no-restante-do-pais.html.

which education played a fundamental role.[6] As I have stated elsewhere, the educational process represents an important interface for social mobility for women, and consequently for power in social relations, inasmuch as women have control over their lives and bodies, and plan their present and future. Accordingly, schooling has brought concrete gains for women, granting them entry into a variety of fields, which also results in access to better job positions and better salaries. Access to education is viewed here as an essential condition for changing women's social and cultural conditions. Despite the advances in education for women and the concrete gains from schooling, there are cultural, historical, social, and economic aspects that preserve the oppressive and discriminatory character that shows up in gender, ethnic, and class relations.[7]

As I have also noted,[8] the educational process—as seen from a feminist perspective—challenges what is taught about women and the way it is taught, taking into account social class, gender, generation, and ethnicity, among other demographic variables. In this regard, black women's movements have provided a great contribution, showing that very often their experiences are mistaken as simplistic, without proper discussion of the structuring of social relations and the impact of matters of race, ethnicity, class, and gender upon their lives.[9]

In addition to its political nature, feminism is also a humanist endeavor, as it seeks the liberation of women and men, breaking away from hierarchies, and establishing itself as a movement for autonomy. Men also need to be liberated "from the macho myth,

6. Eric Hobsbawm, *O novo século: Entrevista a Antonio Polito*, trans. Allan Cameron (Italian to English) and Cláudio Marcondes (English to Portuguese and comparison with the Italian ed.) (São Paulo: Companhia das Letras, 2000), 146–50: "There is no doubt women's emancipation was one of the greatest phenomena of the history of the 20th century. For the 21st century, the pending issue is defining what is left to be done. In reality, women's emancipation throughout the 20th century was limited to some regions of the world and some segments of the population. There are still vast parts of the globe in which this phenomenon has not taken place. . . . Greater women's emancipation will be one of the marks of the next century. Its most efficient tool will be the propagation of education throughout the planet, even in the most underdeveloped countries. Such revolution is spread by the knowledge that other people act in a way different than that was considered part of immutable laws of nature. From this viewpoint, women's emancipation has taken only its first step, as it has not affected most part of world's population."

7. Claudete Beise Ulrich, "Recuperando espaços de emancipação na história de vida de ex-alunas de escola comunitária luterana" (PhD diss., Faculdades EST, São Leopoldo, 2006), 21.

8. Ulrich, "Recuperando espaços de emancipação," 25.

9. Marie Jane Carvalho, "Qual cidadania desejamos?," in *As mulheres e a filosofia*, ed. Márcia Tiburi, Magali M. De Menezes, and Edla Eggert (São Leopoldo: Unisinos, 2002), 234.

which places them as false custodians of supreme power, strength and intelligence."[10] We cannot hold man, knowledge, and word as universal and abstract terms, as absolute and everlasting truths. In contrast, the feminist movement stresses that "there are not and there have never been generic men."[11] What exists is a classification of man and woman by gender within a certain context. According to Harding, when we do away with "the idea of an essential and universal man, the idea of his hidden companion also dies out." She continues, "There are myriad of women experiencing intricate and complex histories of class, race and culture,"[12] and they articulate these experiences together.

Claiming the right to education has been part of the feminist movement because it is an important factor for the social mobility of women, for the transformation of relations of oppression, and for the attainment of social power. As Deifelt points out, "only when women were granted full access to formal education they were also granted the right to vote, the right to property and the recognition of their work."[13] Thus, the right to education was one the main springboards for the feminist movement to take hold. Likewise, the access to academic theological studies is an important step for the ecclesial agency of women.[14]

ACADEMIC THEOLOGICAL EDUCATION AND WOMEN AT THE FACULDADE UNIDA DE VITÓRIA

This reflection on theological education and women at the Faculdade Unida de Vitória is based on a qualitative research carried out with female students through narrative interviews[15] and participant observation. The students provided narrative and free-form responses to the questions asked during the interviews. The research was conducted in late June

10. Maria Amélia de Almeida Teles, "Feminismo no Brasil: Trajetória e perspectivas," in *Gênero e teologia: Interpelações e perspectivas*, ed. SOTER (São Paulo: Loyola, Paulinas, 2004), 52.

11. Sandra Harding, "A instabilidade das categorias analíticas na teoria feminista," *Estudos Feministas* 1, no. 1 (1993): 9.

12. Ibid.

13. Wanda Deifelt, "Educação teológica para mulheres: um passo decisivo rumo à cidadania eclesial," in SOTER, *Gênero e teologia*, 269.

14. Ibid.

15. Camila Junqueira Muylaert et al., "Entrevistas narrativas: Um importante recurso em pesquisa qualitativa," *Revista da Escola de Enfermagem da USP* 48, esp. 2 (2014): 193–99, available at http://www.scielo.br/pdf/reeusp/v48nspe2/pt_0080-6234-reeusp-48-nspe2-00184.pdf.

2016. It is important to stress that at the end of the first semester—that is, June 2016—a total of 168 students were enrolled in the regular theology undergraduate program (morning and evening classes), of whom 41 were women and 127 were men. About 30 percent of all students from the theology undergraduate program at the Faculdade Unida (Unida) are women.

Women at Unida still make up a minority. Also, the theology undergraduate faculty has only one female professor.[16] During a library consultation with Unida librarian Marisete Bispo, we could see that only a few undergraduate final projects address specific issues concerning women in relation to hermeneutical or theological matters. Since 2009, there have been only eight papers dealing directly with issues concerning women or gender relations as it relates to theology or biblical hermeneutics, out of all 175 final theses in the theology baccalaureate program. There are papers addressing issues concerning gender relations and women, but they deal with them tangentially, and they are mainly in the area of pastoral counseling. It is necessary to conduct specific research involving male and female students and professors to know why there are so few bachelor theses in theology addressing gender relations, women, and feminist theology and hermeneutics.

We conducted eleven interviews with students from different classes, i.e., 25 percent of all female students. We applied a qualitative approach and opted for narrative interviews. Our choice of students was based on having a close relationship with them. Some of them were enrolled in the undergraduate courses I taught during the first semester of 2016, and others participated in the two research groups I coordinate: Religion, Gender and Violence: Human Rights, and the Rev. João Dias Araújo Chair of Public Theology and Religious Studies.

THE EXPERIENCE OF WOMEN AS A STARTING POINT

Feminist theology advances as its hermeneutical criterion not any sort of experience, but the particular experience of women who move from oppression and alienation to liberation and emancipation. According to Ruether:

16. I started working as a professor at the theology undergraduate program and at the graduate program of religious studies at the Faculdade Unida on August 1, 2015.

> Human experience is the starting point and the ending point of the hermeneutical circle. . . . The uniqueness of feminist theology lies not in its use of the criterion of experience but rather in its use of *women's* experience, which has been almost entirely shut out of theological reflection in the past. The use of women's experience in feminist theology, therefore, explodes as a critical force exposing classical theology, including its codified traditions as based on *male* experience rather than on universal human experience.[17]

What is unprecedented in feminist hermeneutics, as a theologically feminist approach, is that the experience of women becomes a source for creating theology,[18] which very much questions classical theology. If women's experience is a key concept for feminist theology, then we need to name such experience, since "all knowledge is contingent, bound to specific situations, localized in experiences, and temporal; it is not universal, and all experiences are not the interpretation of reality, rather, they are part of it."[19]

Ströher draws attention to the following fact:

> Just like any other type of knowledge, theology always caters to certain interests; theology is politically-bound, and precisely because of that it should give up the assumption of the so-called objectivity and neutrality, and admit its partiality, "become a partisan," as stated by Elisabeth S. Fiorenza (2004), showing who it speaks for and who it is made for.[20]

This is what feminist theology endeavors to do: name experiences, from specific and contextual realities of women, in the pursuit of the whole of life. Each woman, each culture, each organization produces its own experiences. Thus, each person, each woman, each body is a unique and a new place. Feminist hermeneutics and theology arises from the experience of the female body with transcendence, since one experiences the divine always corporeally.[21] Feminist theology, with the experience of women as its starting point, tries to avoid generalizations, and it insists on valuing particularity. These experiences are the events marking the daily life of women, forming the

17. Rosemary R. Ruether, *Sexism and God-Talk: Toward a Feminist Theology* (Boston: Beacon, 1993), 13.

18. Elaine Gleci Neuenfeldt. "Gênero e hermenêutica feminista: Dialogando com definições e buscando as implicações," *A palavra na vida*, no. 155/156 (2000).

19. Marga J. Stroher, "A história de uma história: O protagonismo das mulheres na teologia feminista," *História Unisinos* 9, no. 2 (2005): 122.

20. Ibid., 122.

21. Neuenfeldt, "Gênero e hermenêutica feminista," 49–50.

theoretical and practical starting point for feminism. Through this lens, issues deemed as personal and private are seen as public and political. Day-to-day life needs to be historicized and politicized;[22] therefore, it is in day-to-day life that the dimensions of "gender justice and corporeity become ethical and theological criteria."[23] Feminist theology points to the need for asking about daily experiences of women.

FEMALE STUDENTS FROM UNIDA TAKE THE FLOOR

To get the conversation started, the interviewed students first shared some of the facets of their life stories, their struggles, their wish to study, to go to college, the difficulties with working full-time during the day and studying at night. Ten interviewees are married with children, and only one is single. All the interviewed students were over thirty years of age. They have different occupations. Only one of them does not participate in any church. One did not mention the name of the ecclesial community she is part of. One participates in the Presbyterian Church of Brazil (IPB). Three interviewees participate in Assemblies of God churches. Two of them participate in Baptist churches. Three participate in Free Pentecostal churches. All of them mentioned their dreams and their joy of being enrolled in a college-level program.

Interviewee B said, "I live in Vila Velha; I am thirty-four, married with a sixteen-year-old daughter. I have always dreamed of going to college, and I managed to do it through the educational-loan programs implemented by the federal government, when my daughter became more independent." Based on the narrative of this interviewee, it is clear that a number of poor women have been able to go to college thanks to loan programs implemented by the federal government in the past decade. Also, we noticed most interviewed women went back to school after their children had grown, becoming more independent. One of them had already completed another undergraduate program and also a graduate program.

22. Branca Moreira Pitanguy Alves, *O que é feminismo?* (São Paulo: Brasiliense, 2003), 8. She writes, "By stating that sex is political, as it also happens in the midst of power relations, feminism breaks away from traditional political models which ascribe neutrality to individual spaces and define as political only the 'objective' public sphere."

23. Stroher, "A história de uma história," 122.

When asked about what motivated them to study theology, one student said she wanted "to acquire more knowledge of biblical themes and [chose theological studies] because the theology program was in the field of humanities." (Interviewee B). Another mentioned her fascination with the Bible, and how she enjoyed teaching in the church:

> First, the fascination for the sacred scriptures and the wish to understand better a book that is so old and so much respected by so many people. Then, the fact that I like to teach in the church made me want to learn more to help people who also like to study the Bible, help them understand the scriptures. I have always felt there was something else, more than what was taught at the Sunday Bible school and preaching from the pulpit. It was "something else" that I wanted to understand and obtain. Finally, I want to improve my relationship with the God of the Bible, with the desire to know him better. (Interviewee A)

While Interviewee A reached out to obtain knowledge in order to understand more, to satisfy a desire to know "more than what was taught at the Sunday Bible School and the preaching from the pulpit," Interviewee D described her motivation in terms of her professional goals: "I am involved in preaching ministry and hold leadership position in the church. Studying [theology] for me meant the fulfillment of a dream, and I also did it to improve my qualification." Interviewee D saw that even though she was a preacher and held a position in the church, she needed better qualifications. Concomitantly, she is fulfilling her dream of studying theology. This is fundamental: women seek to make their dreams come true. They leave their houses and want more than what is offered to them.

Interviewees also said that it is important to acquire academic theological knowledge. Interview B described going beyond confessional boundaries, relating with the other, affirming the importance of knowledge—"the academic knowledge acquired on matters I previously had learned only from a confessional perspective." Interviewee A pointed out the importance of interdisciplinary dialogue: "I found out it is possible to have a dialogue between theology and other sciences: sociology, psychology, philosophy, anthropology, and others." Theology is an academic discipline in dialogue with other disciplines. It is not isolated, it needs to challenge and be challenged by other sciences, so it will be a democratic and socially responsible discipline. Therefore, theology is a science that cannot be viewed in a singular form. It spans a long history; it has many faces. There is not one single theology; there are plural theologies. Interviewee A said, "I also enjoyed learning about the diverse existing theologies, such as feminist theology, black theology, gay theology, liberation theology. In short, I appreciate knowing the many theological approaches and concepts which enrich the sacred scripture even more."

Different theologies propose new historical subjects who wish to be incorporated into theological reflection: women, African descendants, and LGBTQI people, among others. Interviewee A said that by studying theology, "she was in search of the transcendent, and it turned out that she improved her relationship with her neighbor." By studying different theologies, she opened up to people around her, and she found an understanding of life in its wholeness: "Through academic theology, I learned to value life more—all types of life. And the best way to relate with the transcendent is to respect our neighbors." Another matter that has fascinated students is "understanding the Bible in contexts in which there is a dialogue with sociology, philosophy, anthropology. It is also finding out that theology itself is open" (Interviewee G). Interviewee L said her goal is to "learn what is not talked about in the churches, broaden my vision, break paradigms, know the other."

Therefore, both the dialogue between theology and other sciences and the understanding that the Bible cannot be read in a fundamentalist way have been an important discovery for women. Such discovery makes them doubt texts rendered as truths that cannot be challenged.

However, they find it hard to conflate theory and practice. They expressed that one of the difficulties is applying the knowledge acquired in school at the local church level (a narrative shared by all interviewees). Interviewee A said, "The biggest difficulty was related to the myths, because up until then, I had been taught to read the Bible literally. Consequently, it was hard to understand the historical-critical method, which deconstructs so many deeply ingrained prejudices and fundamentalist doctrines. It is really difficult to apply all that knowledge in the community where I live." The interviews showed the difficulty of blending academic studies and community life. Most interviewed students hail from free communities or traditional communities that do not ordain women and are based on fundamentalist readings of the Bible.

The eleven interviewees expressed that they had felt shy and embarrassed when they started college. Interviewee J said, "In the beginning, I was very embarrassed (shy), afraid of asking questions, clearing my doubts, and asking for help when I had difficulties." That same student delivered a public address in July 2016 at the Symposium for Religious Studies. This is a big change in her life history. Interviewee A pointed out a difference between the relationship with schoolmates and professors, and the importance of the arrival of a female professor at the college:

> My relationship with my schoolmates was great. I made great friends. We helped each other and discussed some issues to clear possible doubts. But I used to feel a little embarrassed and shy around the professors. I didn't ask many questions, because I was afraid of being criticized or being laughed at. But that was a block I had; it had nothing to do with the professors, they are great. I think it's because of the way I was raised. We were not allowed to ask questions, especially as a woman. The situation changed when a female professor arrived at the college. I felt more comfortable to interact.

Interviewee A, a student in her last year of the theology baccalaureate program, reaches the conclusion that she did not ask questions because she was afraid of being criticized or being laughed at, as a result of "the way I was raised." Women were not allowed to ask questions. As a student, she needed to accept things the way they were taught, and that was exacerbated by her experience of being a woman—until she felt encouraged and strengthened by the arrival of a female professor at the school. Interviewee A stresses in her narrative the importance of female professors in the field of theology. Female professors bring other emphases and questions into the process of making theology.

The interviewees were also asked about the ordination of women in their churches. Most of them said their churches do not ordain women as pastors. For two of the interviewees, ordaining women is an issue that has never been addressed. The participating interviewees from Baptist churches replied practically with the same reasoning:

> The Brazilian Baptist Convention is very conservative concerning this issue. I have sought information, and apparently there is a woman who was ordained not long ago, and some others were ordained by local churches autonomously, bypassing the pastors' council. The way I see

> it, there is a long path ahead. Ordaining women as pastors is a complex issue, full of taboos, and prejudices in Baptist circles, even for some women. I believe we will get there, but we have to fight and persevere. (Interviewee A)

Despite the taboos and prejudices these women have seen in their Baptist communities, there are local Baptist communities that ordain women. Because they are organizationally congregational and therefore autonomous, congregations have been able to ordain women as pastors. The interviewees made it clear that they hope one day the ordination of women as pastors will be a reality in Baptist circles. Nevertheless, they are also aware it will be a long process, requiring fight and perseverance.

In their turn, students from the Assemblies of God said some churches ordain women as deacons and missionaries. Students from freestanding Pentecostal churches said they ordain women. The Presbyterian Church of Brazil (IPB) does not ordain women. According to the students, the arguments presented by their churches for not ordaining women are grounded on a fundamentalist reading of the Bible. Interviewee I gave the following reason: "because it follows an interpretative instruction that there was no explicit election of women among the leadership of Christ or Paul's followers, or even in the Old Testament." Interviewee C answered that her church doesn't ordain women "because the Church thinks it doesn't have a biblical basis." It is clear in the answers that ordaining women for the different ministries of the church is still a topic to be discussed thoroughly by women and by different churches. Academic theology might offer leverage for deepening the discussion about ordaining women. We still need to fight for the rights of women to different positions in church activities. Women have yet to achieve equal rights in their churches.

As regards the importance of ordaining women to different church ministries, the students said they considered it "normal, as the criterion should not be based on gender, but on capacity and proper training" (Interviewee B). One important outcome for their academic training was finding out that "in the Bible there are accounts of great female leaders" (Interviewee A). Interviewee A continues her narrative by saying:

> We are fully capable of taking up pastorate. What we first need to do is to fight—peacefully but decisively—this whole macho idea that women are born solely for being mothers, wives, and for household work. Also, the idea that women serve only for supporting the church through prayers and paying visits must be done away with. We need to *empower* women and show that we do not want to be better than men or take up their space; all we want is equality, and I think that is not asking too much.

To achieve the right of ordination, we need to break paradigms that affirm that women are born solely to be "mothers, wives, and for household work," and empower women. No one wants to replace another person. It is just a struggle for equal rights in the church. The interviewees also point out that ordaining women would bring growth to the church; that is, this change offers another way for the church to organize itself, especially in a more human and heartfelt way as they express themselves. The ordination of women is an achievement in a context—the church—to which women also have a right. Breaking paradigms is of fundamental importance.

The theology student who is also an ordained missionary narrated the following:

> I think it is important to break paradigms, because in my church I feel undervalued, for even though I am an ordained missionary, I am not invited to sit at the pulpit, and I don't have the same opportunities to express myself in the services. I am referred to only as a sister; my ordination as a missionary is not respected. (Narrator D)

In other words, despite being ordained—as a missionary, in this case—this woman is not seen as equal. The missionary ministry is not viewed with the same regard as the pastoral ministry, which in this case belongs to men. In complaining that she is not seen as an ordained missionary, but simply as a sister, she expresses a concern that her ministry is not valued as it should be. Women must fight for being valued the same way as men, especially when performing the same role.

THE IMPORTANCE OF STUDYING THEOLOGY: FEMALE STUDENTS HAVE THEIR SAY

When asked why it is important for women to study theology, the students pointed out the importance of "acquiring theological knowledge, because this is the only way they can perform their roles in their communities with higher quality and also grow professionally" (Interviewee B), and because it may be the only way toward being ordained to the pastorate. The study of theology "enables other ways of interpretation based on biblical and textual exegesis. Theological knowledge is important for women" (Interviewee I). Another interviewee expressed the importance this way: "to have knowledge, to free ourselves from a number of fundamentalisms, to perform the ministry with leadership" (Interviewee H). Interviewee E said it is important "to break down barriers put up by biblical content concerning women." The female students make it clear they want to go beyond caring for the church, and they want to achieve equal rights and duties in their churches. Having their say as women is essential! Theology is made of words. Words have life; they have stories made of blood, crying, joy, and hope. Women want to have the right to have their say. They also said knowledge sets people free. One student said:

> First, knowledge sets us free. We are set free from negative constructs which have always been imposed upon us. Second, having academic training is very important for the development of our ministry. To be better qualified for ordination and to overthrow negative representations of women that still exist, and are based on Bible reading (Interviewee G).

Thus, knowledge sets people free and academic training is fundamental for ministry development.

The female students seek qualification for the ministry so as to overthrow negative representations of women based on a fundamentalist reading of the Bible. Interviewee D makes it clear: "Women need to study in order to propose fundamental changes armed with specific knowledge, so female ministry will be more respected." Having theological knowledge also means earning respect in their communities.

They go further in their argumentation by saying, "Women can study and know any academic discipline. In spite of being Christian, they need to prepare themselves with knowledge to perform their roles well" (Interviewee C). Interviewee C also pointed out "the lack of women teaching theology," offering the example that "for now there is only one female professor in the theology undergraduate program." The presence of female theology professors is also a fundamental step for empowering female theology students. They need to be aware that "theological knowledge will bring them recognition from institutions . . . and they might get to 'speak' with as much authority as 'men.'" Interviewee A said the following:

> It is very important that women study theology, especially academic theology. That may be a form of empowerment; that was what happened with me. Quoting Serena Nocetti, it is important "for valuing and recognizing differences," to break down resistance to female leadership and prove that women's voices can contribute greatly to the good of society.

The academic endeavor of theological studies is viewed as a fundamental step for empowering women, for providing them with autonomy in both thinking and acting. The students are aware that academic studies and knowledge acquisition will boost their self-esteem and will prepare them better for performing their work in the church. Also, they will have more arguments with which to fight for egalitarian ordination to all church ministries.

According to Ströher,

> Women cannot and do not want to be just included or attached to the building of knowledge and the organization of society, but to be recognized as social and political subjects, as ethical subjects of knowledge. In theology, women also want to be recognized and qualified as the subject of knowledge and theological development, that is, to have their theological citizenship recognized, as put by Ivone Gebara.[24]

Achieving theological citizenship is one the biggest goals of feminist theology of liberation. For women, that means being qualified through theological learning and practice, and being recognized as ethical subjects of knowledge and of theological development. The theology students who gave their narratives made that clear in their different levels of reflection.

24. Stroher, "A história de uma história," 119.

They seek knowledge to be recognized as historical subjects who are developing theological knowledge while they seek qualification to perform their activities better in their work environments, and consequently to obtain recognition as full citizens.

CONCLUSION

Feminist theology and gender analysis are crosscutting themes in the theology program at the Faculdade Unida; that is, they cut across various courses and are also dealt with in extension courses and research groups, in which female students participate actively. We have noticed that academic theological knowledge is highly valued by female students, as it is viewed as a fundamental passport for recognition in their churches of origin. We observed that there has been an increase in the interest in discussions on the role of women in the church, of women's ordination, feminist theology, violence against women, justice in gender relations, and the relationship between theology and other sciences. The students also have difficulties coupling theology studies with practice in their communities. There is a reflection on theory and practice and the need of historical patience to change conflictive gender relations in the communities, especially as regards the recognition of ministries undertaken by women and those they still want to achieve.

They also make it clear that the struggles are collective, not individual struggles, and because of that, it is necessary to empower women, value them, challenge them, and provide them with tools for the struggle for gender equality, in theological studies, in the work in the churches, and also in society as a whole. Faculdade de Teologia Unida, as an academic, critical, ecumenical, plural school that is open to interfaith dialogue, has been a meeting space for women from different religious traditions as well as for women with no religion. Such fact has been very important in the debate about theological knowledge and the space for women in theological learning and practice.

Women receiving theological education will be able to discuss theology on an equal footing with men and also fight for their egalitarian citizenship within churches as well. Theological education is an important step to overcome the patriarchy so pervasive in Christian churches.

The very fact that women are studying theology snubs patriarchal power, which has long denied women theological education and kept them from reaching the upper echelons of the church. When women study theology, they create contact with plural theologies, with the theology of liberation, feminist theology, black theology, indigenous theology, queer theology, integral mission—that is, with contextual theologies. Thus, through their academic studies, the knowledge of theology is enhanced. It is in a respectful, ethical, and democratic sense of community that we learn to know, act, live, and exist together.[25] It is in this intense process of learning in different dimensions that the development of the field of theology is placed, and its goal is to build egalitarian, ethical, and democratic relationships.

Therefore, teaching theology to women expands the knowledge and practice of theology itself, making it more plural, fuller, more ecumenical, more critical; breaking paradigms of a patriarchal church tradition; raising suspicions; and in this way, enabling processes of deconstruction and new biblical and theological constructions, in which both women and men can set themselves, in a new and more holistic way, as human beings in the context of evolving relationships. Furthermore, theological education qualifies and enables women theologically to act in an ethical and responsible way, be it in their Christian communities or in other organizational spaces. Academic theological studies enable women to have their own say in regard to their own experience with the divine. Speaking of transcendence is always human speaking. Women's speech about their experiences with transcendence enriches human experiences, making them more beautiful, deeper, multiple, diversified, subject to criticism and questions, thus building more egalitarian relationships of gender, race/ethnicity, age, and social classes; overcoming dichotomies; and aiming to build new family, community, ecclesial, and social possibilities, interwoven with care for all creation.

25. Jacques Delors, coord., "Os quatro pilares da educação," in *Educação: Um tesouro a descobrir* (São Paulo: Cortezo, 1997), 89–102.

PART V

World Christianity and Migration

9.

A New Frontier

Intercultural Communication and the Urgency of a Migratory Epistemology

YVETTE JOY HARRIS-SMITH

In Christianity, we move through cultural contexts often. Whenever we recite scripture or sing hymns penned long ago, listen to sermons or read the Bible privately or aloud, we are moving through cultural contexts. The study of World Christianity is interested in the myriad of expressions of the Christian faith as seen across several continents. It is interested in the cultural contexts through which people express their belief in God.[1] Similarly, the field of public religion is interested in the expressions of religious beliefs through behaviors that "have a direct bearing on public order."[2] The common thread that connects these fields is their interest in expressions of faith, and particularly here, the Christian faith, which occur through the communicative process. Communication is influenced by culture, and culture is shared when communication occurs. Therefore, it is only fitting that World Christianity, public religion, and the church universal engage intercultural communication. By engaging intercultural communication, scholars, ministers, and laypersons alike can learn how to communicate more effectively with Christians, who are culturally

1. Dale Irvin, "World Christianity: An Introduction," *Journal of World Christianity* 1, no. 1 (2008): 1–2.

2. "Public Religion," in *Encyclopedia of Religion and Society*, ed. William H. Swatos Jr., http://hirr.hartsem.edu/ency/PublicR.htm, accessed July 1, 2016.

different from one another; develop an authentic respect for one another; and learn to love humankind more faithfully, the way God intended.

This chapter has several aims. The first is to highlight briefly the new frontier, and the second is to connect shifts in migration to the need for and importance of intercultural communication. Third, the chapter will make two or three practical suggestions for how the church and the field of world Christianity can engage intercultural communication. Finally, it will introduce a working understanding of a migratory epistemology. This chapter serves as a clarion call to Christians, local churches, seminaries, and the collective body of Christ worldwide (regardless of location) that change is upon us. Action is required—not later, but now.

THE NEW FRONTIER

Globalization has helped usher the world to a seat on the front line as we approach a new frontier.[3] This place offers both opportunity and challenge. The opportunity is the unlimited potential we have with a society that is connected, physically and technologically. Transportation and new media afford humanity the opportunity to learn and share as never before. Yet one of the challenges remains the rapid pace at which we encounter change. In addition to shifting demographics, which bring new people and resources to a particular area, the impact of this wave of globalization also alters the environment permanently. These changes affect Christian faith and praxis. Failure to address this new frontier may result in stagnant, stale, and perfunctory faith and praxis. Some might say Christianity has already reached this place. Yet hope remains.

Intercultural communication provides a starting point to engage this new frontier. This goes beyond knowledge and passion, pleasantries and rhetoric; this requires skill. That skill, for some, may need to be developed; for others, it may need to be practiced regularly. It may mean being uncomfortable, but it also means not being the center (of the communicative process). Through honest and ethical engagement in intercultural communication, we can learn about one

3. John F. Kennedy used this phrase while he was the Democratic presidential candidate in the 1960s.

another and, while in that process, discover and perhaps rediscover things about our individual and collective selves.

MIGRATION AND INTERCULTURAL COMMUNICATION

There have been at least three waves of global migration. The first lasted well into the sixteenth century, the second one involved the colonization of Africa, Asia, and America up into middle of the twentieth century, and by all accounts we are still in the third wave.[4] This third wave has been referred to by some, particularly in the United States, as the "browning of America."[5] This refers to the change in migration trends particularly to the United States from places like Asia, Latin America and Africa.

"Migration is not a new phenomenon"[6] in human history. Part of the human story is migration, and it affects culture, the communicative process, and religion. In addition, the speed at which these movements of people are occurring now is forcing all to stop and take notice—and the church should as well. This is a specific feature of globalization in its present form.[7]

The Christian community has seen major growth in certain parts of the world. For example, on the continent of Africa a century ago, there were approximately 11 million Christians, but since 2010, the number of African Christians exceeds 490 million.[8] Over half of the world's Christian population lives in Africa, Asia, Latin America, and the Pacific. Jared Alcantara explains, "Statistically speaking, Africa and Latin America are now the Christian heartlands. Instead of Wittenburg and Geneva, think São Paulo and Jakarta. The majority of the world's Christians live in the eastern and southern hemispheres."[9]

4. Judith M. Martin and Thomas K. Nakayama, *Intercultural Communication in Contexts* (New York: McGraw-Hill, 2013), 316.

5. Peter C. Phan, "The Experience of Migration as Source of Intercultural Theology," in *Contemporary Issues of Migration and Theology*, ed. Elaine Padilla and Peter C. Phan (New York: Palgrave Macmillan, 2013), 181.

6. G. T. Cruz, "Between Identity and Security: Theological Implications of Migration in the Context of Globalization," *Theological Studies* 69, no. 2 (2008): 358.

7. Ibid.

8. Jared Alcantara, *Crossover Preaching: Intercultural-Improvisational Homiletics in Conversation with Gardner C. Taylor* (Downers Grove, IL: IVP Academic, 2015), 18.

9. Ibid., 22.

Similarly, immigration trends to the United States have also shifted over the past half century. For example, during the 1960s, over 49 percent of immigrants to the United States came from Europe, Canada, and Oceania (Australia, New Zealand).[10] However, records from 2013 reveal that over 86 percent of immigrants to the United States hail from Africa, Asia, and Latin America.[11] Thus, "the world that most Christians occupy today is markedly different from the one Western Christians occupied in the early twentieth century."[12] We must also not forget what these changes mean on the local level. The makeup of churches and the communities in which they are located, at least in the United States, are shifting, too. And this is just one of the many ripple effects of migration and globalization on the church.

With migration shifts and immigration increasing in certain parts of the world, learning how to effectively communicate becomes important both for those who migrate and for those who are residents of the host country. Therefore, intercultural communication skills are needed by both the migrant and the host. Emmanuel Ayee says, "Intercultural communication has been taking place since the dawn of recorded human history."[13] Intercultural communication relates to messages sent and received between persons or groups where there are cultural differences that can affect the interpretation of those messages.[14] More simply, intercultural communication looks at the interaction between people who are different from one another.

There are two particular perspectives in intercultural communication. The first type looks at the interaction between people who are different from one another,[15] and the other type focuses on similarities and differences.[16] Overemphasizing differences or similarities leads to problems and ignores the nuances of a culture, whether implicit or explicit. There must be a balance between appreciating the similarities and respecting the differences among cultures. Culture is not a

10. Ibid.

11. Ibid.

12. Ibid., 18.

13. Emmanuel Ayee, "Christian Perspective on Intercultural Communication," *Pro Rege* 35, no. 3 (June 2007): 1.

14. Larry Samovar, Richard Porter, and Edwin McDaniel, *Communication between Cultures* (Boston: Wadsworth Cengage Learning, 2009), 12.

15. Larry Samovar and Richard Porter, *Communication between Cultures*, (Boston: Wadsworth Cengage, Learning, 2004), 15.

16. Judith M. Martin, Thomas K. Nakayama, and L. A. Flores, *Readings in Intercultural Communication* (New York: McGraw-Hill, 2002), 65.

finished product but rather has a "canon" that makes it distinguishable from other cultures.

The world stage presents us with situations that affect us all—eventually. These include changes in migration and immigration, climate changes, political unrest, violence, varying levels of food and water supply, challenging educational systems, and shifting economic markets. We share a planet with billions of people, so these issues have repercussions for all. However, as we begin to engage intercultural communication, we must be careful not to "study culture and intercultural communication from a theoretical, or abstract and technical perspective and to ignore the fact that we are dealing with human beings with personalities, feelings, histories, struggles, hopes, and dreams."[17]

THE CHURCH AND INTERCULTURAL COMMUNICATION

The reality is that "if the church in the United States bears even a remote resemblance to the overall population, it will be an intercultural church with an intercultural witness to an intercultural society."[18] This new frontier means change. This new frontier means that preaching and teaching cannot be focused on what is comfortable for solely the person who teaches or preaches, but rather must be concerned with the ways in which the people for whom the message or services are intended can access what is being shared. Many of the world's cultures are oral, and even where there is literacy, orality is the dominant mode of communication and way of making meaning. We must rethink, then, our overemphasis on the written word and literacy as prerequisites for communicating and engaging the gospel of Christ.

The church must intentionally include people, especially Christians—Christians who may be migrants, on the margins of society. The church must be sensitive to the migrant and other visitors among us. The church must become aware of its assumptions regarding race, class, gender, culture, and theology. The church needs to invest in consciously learning communicative strategies and effective pedagogies that will help the church be salt and light for the earth.

17. Ayee, "Christian Perspective on Intercultural Communication," 3.
18. Alcantara, *Crossover Preaching*, 27.

So what might this look like? There are three ways that churches can begin to engage in intercultural communication. First, churches should collaborate to support the learning of another language. Through learning another language, one also learns some of the nuances within a culture. In addition, offering a sermon or Bible studies in the language to which others are accustomed—even if that means using an interpreter—is another way to show love and open dialogue. Another idea worthy of consideration is to have joint services across denominations and cultures. Providing an opportunity for people to pray, worship, and fellowship together is powerful. Planning the service would require openness to other styles of worship and not just what is culturally comfortable to the planners. Third, if people can begin to meet one another where they are and understand the ways in which others communicate, perhaps then they can begin to address concerns that affect the communities to which they belong. These suggestions are, of course, contextual. The point is that every congregation should be doing something to enhance its ability to communicate interculturally. Through the development of intercultural communication skills we extend hospitality to one another.

The Bible is an intercultural document of intercultural communication and relationships. In the Bible, religion and culture are seen permeating and shaping the way persons understand their purpose in life. Likewise, according to the biblical text, our communication with God and with humankind is challenged by our fallen nature. Yet this is the gospel that Christ preached. Emmanuel Ayee articulates this, saying, "The Christian gospel is radical in its claims and scope; therefore, it demands radical, transformed, and continually reforming lifestyles that reflect values of the kingdom."[19] Learning to communicate interculturally and developing cultural intelligence helps us live out continually reforming lifestyles—especially in this present time.

TOWARD A MIGRATORY EPISTEMOLOGY

In a context where the dominant perspective is often Western, Eurocentric, and male, it is important to name concepts, thoughts, and ideas that centralize specific viewpoints. To not name or define leaves the presumption, possibly, that preference is given to the majority

19. Ayee, "Christian Perspective on Intercultural Communication," 8.

understanding of a concept or idea. Naming creates space and specifies what or whose perspective is being highlighted. Paulo Freire says, "To exist, humanly, is to *name* the world, to change it. . . . Human beings are not built in silence, but in word, in work, in action-reflection."[20] Freire also says that naming is not the right of only a privileged few but the right of everyone. My goal here is to name and define the term *migratory epistemology* and by doing so give it voice and legitimacy, in both academia and the church. Thus, a migratory epistemology grants epistemological privilege to the migrant experience.

A migratory epistemology understands that the human story involves movement and change in order to survive. It means that the primary way people make meaning is through their lived experience of physically moving out of their own cultural context or a context with which they are most familiar—whether voluntary or involuntary, but with emphasis on the latter. The existential predicament of the immigrant, particularly the involuntary migrant, is often characterized by violent uprootedness, economic poverty, anxiety about the future, and loss of national identity, political freedom, and personal dignity—the existing betwixt and between, particularly of external (or transnational) migrants.[21]

We need to be more compassionate and become not just conscious but painfully aware of our ethnocentricity as a culture and as Christians. While our perception is shaped by our culture's worldview, we should remember that it is not the measuring stick for all cultures. Within the next two generations, Alcantara explains, "Christians born *in* the Global South or with ethnic and cultural ties *to* the Global South will be a major force in the preservation, reshaping and renewal of the US church and its mission."[22] Therefore, it is imperative that we develop an increased sense of global awareness and cultural sensitivity. Through intercultural dialogue, we can deepen theological insight, which can result in a broader understanding of the mission of the church at home and abroad—wherever that may be for the reader. Through intercultural communication and dialogue, we can increase the likelihood of having a "successful" and effective intercultural experience while learning about another culture and also one's self.

20. Paulo Freire, *Pedagogy of the Oppressed* (New York: Continuum, 2000), 87.
21. Phan, "The Experience of Migration," 182–83.
22. Alcantara, *Crossover Preaching*, 27.

The church—and the discipline of World Christianity, for that matter—is on a new frontier. This new frontier requires that we grant epistemological privilege to the migrant experience. Globalization, demographic changes, and the myriad of concerns affecting the world confirm that things are different. However, the church cannot be silent. The church cannot stand by and hope for the best. As human culture continues to evolve, affected by migration, so too will Christianity. Intercultural communication and dialogue can help both the academy and the church in navigating this new and intimidating terrain.

10.

"Who You Are Does Not Matter in Europe!"

African Diaspora Christianities and the Ethical Politics of Wasting Bodies and Unwanted Immigration in Fortress Europe

AFE ADOGAME

On May 20, 2015, Nicolas Haque anchored the story of sixteen-year-old Senegalese Abdou as he prepared his perilous journey to Europe.[1] This was part of a prolonged Al Jazeera TV documentary *Desperate Journeys,* chronicling a series of woes, misery, and catastrophe in which hundreds of thousands of African and other immigrants, hopeless but with sanguine expectations, are fleeing economic hardship, poverty, natural disasters, ethnic clashes, political oppression, and unwarranted civil strife partly orchestrated by failing governments. By raising a loan of over $3,000 to facilitate the journey organized by individuals in the migration industry, including people smugglers or human traffickers, Abdou's parents perceived their son's voyage to Europe as the only option left for salvaging family life and survival. On the fateful day that Abdou prepared to leave home into the uncertain sojourn, his father gave him his final words of advice and blessing with a rather brisk emotion: "Throw your passport into the sea. Who you are doesn't matter in Europe. You are going there

1. For a full video transcript, http://www.aljazeera.com/news/2015/05/migrant-journey-begins-150520080857232.html. Nicolas Haque, "Desperate Journeys: Senegal Migrant Seeks Better Life in Europe," *Al Jazeera*, September 19, 2016, http://video.aljazeera.com/channels/eng/videos/senegal-migrant-seeks-better-life-in-europe/4246430493001.

to work. Have faith in God. We love you." With these brief admonitions amid flowing tears of his parents, Abdou set out on his journey rather undauntedly. The parent's counsel, no doubt, evokes some controversy emanating from sheer ignorance of life and work in Europe, his father's contentious disavowal of identity claims and dignity, an unbridled faith in God in the face of illegality and amorality, and the licentious display of desperation laced with an equivocal tone of love.

Hardly a week goes by now without a breaking news story of migrants, refugees, asylum seekers from Africa or Asia drowned or rescued while trying to arrive at the European shores. While it was reported that over 170,000 successfully landed on the Italian shores in 2014 alone, at least 2,500 Africans are reported to have drowned on the Mediterranean Sea between January and April of 2015. In actual fact, the numbers involved in the ongoing tragedy are staggering, because no one really knows how many people have drowned in the sea or died under harsh desert conditions. Within one week, 1,141 deaths were recorded.[2]

Historically, the Mediterranean landscape has represented the theater of encounters between peoples, cultures, and systems, where Europe meets Africa, and East meets West. During the initial decades of the twenty-first century, we increasingly witness in the Mediterranean a new encounter, both profound and dramatic, in the form of people on the move. Thus, the Mediterranean Sea has come to represent one major frontline on the battlefield of irregular migration, where many poor, youthful, vulnerable, and desperate migrants, including women and children, launch onto the path of tragic death on the high sea in their struggle between survival and death. In most recent times, most migrants and refugees are fleeing from Libya, Eritrea, Ethiopia, Somalia, Nigeria, Ghana, Mali, and Senegal.

2. See, for example, Joe Mills, "More than 400 People Drown in Mediterranean Sea as Ship Carrying African Migrants from Libya to Italy Capsizes," *International Business Times*, April 14, 2015, http://www.ibtimes.co.uk/more-400-people-drown-mediterranean-sea-ship-carrying-african-migrants-libya-italy-capsizes-1496416; Tom Kington, "Another 41 African Migrants Drown Making Perilous Crossing to Italy," *Los Angeles Times*, April, 16, 2015, http://www.latimes.com/world/europe/la-fg-italy-migrants-drowned-20150416-story.html; and Patrick Kingsley, Alessandra Bonomolo, and Stephanie Kirchgaessner, "700 Migrants Feared Dead in Mediterranean Shipwreck," *Guardian*, April 19, 2015, http://www.theguardian.com/world/2015/apr/19/700-migrants-feared-dead-mediterranean-shipwreck-worst-yet.

I do not suggest that all immigrants are implicated in this gory picture, as that will mean simplifying the complex trajectories of African migration. Nor do African immigrants experience this precarious state only in the exodus from the African shores. Such contradictions are evident in internal migration within the continent itself. It is not Europe alone that needs immigrants but does not want them.[3] The recurring politics of Afrophobia, xenophobic violence, and hate-related incidents in South Africa in April 2015 and earlier in 2008 vividly underscore the quandary immigrants now face within the theater of international migration.[4]

At the same time, a majority of Africans who migrate within the continent and to Europe are regular, skilled, legal, documented migrants arriving mostly through the airports and recruited into the labor force as nurses, doctors, engineers, IT specialists, athletes, or as students, diplomats, and artists, but also as tourists. For the purpose of family reunion, many Africans have migrated to Europe. Most recently, some Africans have been given missional tasks and have migrated or are sent by their home churches to Europe as missionaries.[5] However, we cannot deny that the African immigrant populations and African-led churches comprise those who also made it to Europe through irregular means. Migrants' travel can be clandestine through the travails of crossing the desert, sneaking in with boats and canoes, or hiding in trucks to beat the eagle-eyed surveillance of border police patrols and immigration officials. Other migrants have traveled by air and sea using other people's travel documents or fake travel documents to exploit the ignorance of immigration entrepreneurs.

The causes and courses of the new migration are legion—economic, social, political, religious, historical, technological, and more. The outcomes of a migration decision are often positive but too fre-

3. Andrew F. Walls, "Mission and Migration: The Diaspora Factor in Christian History," *Journal of African Christian Thought* 5, no. 2 (December 2002): 10; and Afe Adogame, *The African Christian Diaspora: New Currents and Emerging Trends in World Christianity* (London: Bloomsbury Academic, 2013), 182.

4. See Jean-Jacques Cornish, "South Africa: Xenophobic Attacks Erupt in South Africa's Limpopo Province," *AllAfrica*, March 5, 2015, http://allafrica.com/stories/201503051136.html; Jeff Wicks, "KZN Xenophobic Violence Spreads to KwaMashu," *News24*, April 13, 2015, http://www.news24.com/SouthAfrica/News/KZN-xenophobic-violence-spreads-to-KwaMashu-20150413; and Bongani Hans, "King's Anti-foreigner Speech Causes Alarm," *Independent Online*, March 23, 2015, http://www.iol.co.za/news/politics/king-s-anti-foreigner-speech-causes-alarm-1.1835602#.VSzaLPCROYM.

5. Adogame, *The African Christian Diaspora*, 169–89.

quently disturbing and sometimes tragic. Paul Zeleza vividly demonstrates how the dynamics and directions of global mobility and African participation in international migration, particularly in Western Europe and North America, have become more pronounced, notwithstanding the imposition of stringent immigration controls by these countries.[6] The adoption of restrictive immigration policies and regional policy harmonization has partially impeded the flow of legal immigration and asylum flows but also indirectly transformed illegal immigration.

The preferred new analytic frameworks for understanding and contextualizing international migratory trends and processes are migration systems theory and the transnational theory.[7] Both theories, encapsulating several levels of analysis, account for the direction and texture of international migration, and the complex dynamics. The basic principle of the migration systems theory is that any migratory movement can be seen as a result of interacting and intertwined macro–, meso–, and micro-structures.[8] Crucial to our understanding of regular and irregular migration are the macro-structures, that is, the political economy of the world market, interstate relationships, and the laws, structures, and practices established by the states of sending and receiving countries to control migration settlement; the micro-structures, those embracing the networks, practices, and beliefs of the migrants themselves; and the intermediate meso-structures, or certain individuals, groups, or institutions that take up a mediating role between migrants and political or economic institutions. The "migration industry," including recruitment organizations, lawyers, agents, smugglers, NGOs, charitable bodies, and other intermediaries that emerge, can be both helpers and exploiters of migrants. A further consideration of a new, emerging migrant population whose networks, activities, and life patterns encompass and transcend their home and host societies has produced a new body of theory on "transnationalism" and "transnational communities."[9] The transnational theory in this regard captures migrants, their lives,

6. Paul Zeleza, "Contemporary African Migrations in a Global Context," *African Issues* 30, no. 1 (2002): 13.

7. Adogame, *The African Christian Diaspora*, 6.

8. Stephen Castles and Mark Miller, *The Age of Migration: International Population Movements in the Modern World*, 3rd ed. (New York: Guilford, 1993), 27–28.

9. Linda Basch, Nina Glick-Schiller, and Cristina Blanc-Szanton, eds., *Nations Unbound: Transnational Projects, Postcolonial Predicaments, and Deterritorialized Nation-States* (New York: Gordon and Breach, 1994).

experiences, and consciousness as cutting across national boundaries and brings two (or more) societies onto a single social field. Alejandro Portes defines transnational activities as those that take place on a recurrent basis across national borders and that require a regular and significant commitment of time by participants.[10]

The morality and politics of migration are among the most contested issues globally. However, the ethics of international migration is a relatively recent field of study in the robust literature on migration.[11] A burgeoning in the discourse on migration and ethics was witnessed in the 1970s, parallel to the globalization of migration and the increase in irregular migration during the period. Since the 1980s, following the pioneering works by Walzer and Carens,[12] there has been an impressive development in ethical thinking in relation to international migration. Carens illuminates one of the most pressing issues of our time:[13] immigration poses practical problems for Western democracies and also challenges the ways in which people in democracies think about citizenship and belonging, about rights and privileges, and about freedom and equality.

The discourse about the ethics and morality of migration engenders a realistic perspective that dwells on what is possible in the face of existing realities and an idealistic approach that requires policy makers to assess current reality in light of a nation's highest ideals.[14] The investigation of ethics applied to migration concerns three areas: the right to migrate, the treatment of migrants, and the norms for a peaceful coexistence in societies that are increasingly pluralistic.[15] While borders are fixed lines of geography and sovereignty, they also connote ethical values. Immigration and admission do raise fundamental ethical questions. This is particularly the case at a time when

10. Alejandro Portes, "Towards a New World: The Origins and Effects of Transnational Activities," *Ethnic and Racial Studies* 22, no. 2 (1999): 464.

11. Ricard Zapata-Barrero and Antoine Pécoud, "New Perspectives on the Ethics of International Migration," *American Behavioral Scientist* 56, no. 9 (2012): 1159–64; R. Zapata-Barrero, "Theorizing State Behaviour in International Migrations: An Evaluative Ethical Framework," *Social Research* 77 (2010): 325–52; Christine Straehle and Patti T. Lenard, "The Ethics of Migration: Introduction," *Journal of International Political Theory* 8, nos. 1–2 (2012): 118–20.

12. M. Walzer, *Spheres of Justice: A Defence of Pluralism and Equality* (Oxford: Robertson, 1983); J. Carens, "Aliens and Citizens: The Case for Open Borders," *Review of Politics* 49 (1987): 251–73.

13. Joseph H. Carens, *The Ethics of Migration* (Oxford: Oxford University Press), 2013.

14. Ilse van Liempt and Veronica Bilger, eds., *The Ethics of Migration Research Methodology: Dealing with Vulnerable Immigrants* (Sussex: Sussex Academic Press, 2009).

15. Graziano Battistella, "The Contributions of Ethics to the Management of Migration," *Ciberteologia: Journal of Theology and Culture* 37, year 8 (2012).

restrictive migration policies lead to outcomes that are ethically or morally questionable.[16]

The ethical discourse of migration is closely related to the theology of migration. Theologies of migration are emerging from and built around the *longue dureé* of migration:[17] the home of origin as a point of departure, the transitory journey to El Dorado, the arrival at temporary and final destinations, the circumstances shaping their lived experiences of adaptation or resistance to integration, and even the imagined, illusory thoughts of return migration. William O'Neill draws biblical insights underlying the ethics of migration, focusing on three themes: the primacy of the love command, justice as covenant fidelity, and the virtue of hospitality.[18] He translates and interprets these themes for citizens of faith in a religiously pluralist polity. According to Donald Senior, "The Christian gospel unfolds against the backdrop of exile and redemption—of Israel in Egypt and the infant Jesus in Egypt. Sharing this history of migration, the people of God, then and now, are called to particular care for the most vulnerable members of society, especially the immigrants."[19] Christian hospitality to "strangers and aliens" shaped the earliest understanding of disciples as fellow "citizens with the saints" in the "household of God" (Eph 2:19). Hospitality is offered not only to kin and kind, but also to those whose only claim is vulnerability and need (Matt 8:11; 22:1–14; Luke 14:12–24). For citizens of faith, then, the urgency of basic human rights establishes the relative priority of migrants' rights as the touchstone of policy.[20]

The unwarranted waste of human bodies, mostly African immigrants desperate to cross the sea to Europe, marks an unprecedented watershed in the history and politics of ir/regular migration to Europe. Most appalling is the somewhat international stolidity, lassitude, and apathy of policy makers and several stakeholders which contributed to many ignominies—an indifference that has perhaps encouraged the self-martyrdom and devaluing of human bodies on

16. O. Parker and J. Brassett, "Contingent Borders, Ambiguous Ethics: Migrants in (International) Political Theory," *International Studies Quarterly* 49 (2005): 233–53.

17. Adogame, *The African Christian Diaspora*, 15.

18. W. O'Neill, "'No Longer Strangers' (Ephesians 2:19): The Ethics of Migration," *Word and World* 29, no. 3, (2009): 227–33.

19. D. Senior, "Beloved Aliens and Exiles," in *A Promised Land, a Perilous Journey: Theological Perspectives on Migration,* ed. Daniel G. Groody and Gioacchino Campese (Notre Dame, IN: University of Notre Dame Press, 2009), 23.

20. O'Neill, "'No Longer Strangers,'" 231.

the Mediterranean Sea. African national governments, the African Union (AU),[21] the New Partnership for Africa's Development (NEPAD), African religious institutions, the European Union (EU), European national governments, European churches, and African-led churches in Europe in greater or lesser degrees have conspired in a feat of political and socio-religious inaction, negligence, and indifference that seem to exacerbate the celerity of wasting human bodies in both desert lands and seas. Speaking from Saint Peter's Square, Pope Francis, an outspoken advocate for greater European-wide participation in rescue efforts, reiterated his call for action during mass on a Sunday after learning of the latest disaster. He said: "They are men and women like us—our brothers seeking a better life, starving, persecuted, wounded, exploited, victims of war."[22] Besides the Vatican's voice, what is the role and position of the church in all these scenarios? It is scandalous that African and European churches are not seen to make a significant public outcry and condemn this disaster nor call for rescue efforts.

The rest of the chapter will tease out whether, how, and to what extent African-led churches in Europe are engaging in (or not) the politics of wasting bodies and unwanted migration but responding to the ethical dilemma that shapes the EU immigration policies vis-à-vis their social relevance in Europe.

The historiography of the new African Christian diaspora is located within recent trajectories of international migration, a dynamic process in which Africans are largely implicated as both actors and benefactors. They are not just passive recipients but active participants.

The literature of African-led churches in Europe has burgeoned since the 1980s.[23] However, scholars have not given much attention to the ethics and politics of African migration in Europe. How do churches in Africa and Africa-led churches in Europe encourage or support and discourage regular and or irregular migration? In what ways does ir/regular migration have an impact on African Christian-

21. It is beyond any imagination that the African Union waited for the loss of over 2,500 lives before discussing the issues of migration and xenophobia at their recent summit in June 2015. See Jean-Jacques Cornish, "Migration and Xenophobia Top AU Agenda at Summit," *Eyewitness News*, June 11, 2015, http://ewn.co.za/2015/06/11/Migration-and-xenophobia-on-the-agenda-for-African-Executive-Council-meeting.

22. See Kingsley et al., "700 Migrants Feared Dead."

23. For an extensive historiography of African-led churches in Europe and North America, see Adogame, *The African Christian Diaspora*, 2013.

ities? How do African-led churches respond to the dehumanization, the unethical posture and policies of EU toward African migrants? How do the religious communities engage in the discourses of identity, inclusion/exclusion, and citizenship against the backlash of harsh anti-immigrant debates within the dwindling welfare economies of EU states? What methodological issues and ethical questions arise in research of irregular migration in Europe? We need a critical assessment and analysis of EU policies on irregular migration and how these may affect the place and status of African-led churches in Europe.

African Christian communities in diaspora present a robust religious demography as they continue to mushroom across Europe. The explanations for their emergence, expansion, and visibility are quintessential in understanding their spiritual worldviews and emerging theologies. As most of these religious communities are relatively new in Europe, having started within the last three decades, their evolving theologies emerge out of ongoing contestation between resilience and change. The very fluidity, insecurity, and vulnerability of irregular and transit immigration affect the life, demography, and mobility of African-led churches in Europe. The status of migrants is always in limbo and susceptible to abuse, exploitation, xenophobia, deportation, incarceration, clandestine existence, and "doing the jobs that many Europeans would normally not do." Right-wing politics heightens the vulnerability of immigrants. The gruesome experiences shape the spirituality and theology of African migrants in Europe. Prior to examining some of the ways in which the ethics and politics of migration have an impact on African-led churches in Europe and how they respond, it is important to give a little taste of the EU immigration policies and the ethical dilemma they embody.

EU IMMIGRATION POLICIES: AN ETHICAL DILEMMA

During the formative years of the EU in the 1950s and 1960s, immigrants were primarily an extra workforce in most western European countries. Countries like France, Germany, and the Netherlands used a permissive migration policy motivated by the need for extra labor.[24] By the late 1960s and 1970s, immigration was increasingly becoming

24. See Jef Huysmans, "The European Union and the Securitization of Migration," *Journal of Common Market Studies* 38, no. 5 (2000): 751–77.

a subject of public concern, thus marking a radical shift from the permissive immigration policy to a control-oriented, restrictive policy. Political rhetoric increasingly linked migration to the destabilization of public order. Restrained immigration was beginning to take root all over western Europe at the end of 1973, when labor recruiting was halted abruptly in the face of increasing social tensions and fear of economic recession. In fact, the fortressization of European immigration policy is linked to the 1973 economic recession.

A significant Europeanization of migration policy took off in the 1980s, when policy coordination became institutionalized in European interstate cooperation, the European Union. Since 1993, with the ratification of the Treaty of Maastricht, the European Community took a new turn, the EU. The Schengen Accord, which came into being in 1995, was a definite attempt to harmonize their immigration procedures and regulate flows of people. The EU set out the elements for a common EU immigration policy at the 1999 European Council in Tampere. Its adoption was confirmed by the Hague program in 2004. In the last three decades, EU member states moved toward further cooperation at the supranational level and introduced increasing numbers of regulations at the EU level on migration-related matters. The Europeanization of migration laws and policies is tied to wider social, political, economic, and strategic dynamics. Thus, the European integration process is implicated in the development of restrictive migration policies and the social construction of migration as a security question.[25]

Over the past two decades, the EU not only developed a joint and coherent approach to migration but also increasingly integrated source and transit countries in its neighborhood and beyond its efforts. This policy is sometimes dubbed the internationalization or externalization of the EU's migration policy.[26] The EU and respective national governments are struggling to define attitudes toward and policies concerning immigrants and immigration for the twenty-first century. This national, continental, and global debate revolves surreptitiously around the economic impact and legal status of individuals or groups of immigrants more than the very welfare and well-being of the migrants. EU immigration policies and strategies are hardly static or fixed. They mutate depending on the prevailing

25. Ibid.

26. Franck Düvell and Bastian Vollmer, *Irregular Migration in and from the Neighbourhood of the EU: A Comparison of Morocco, Turkey and Ukraine* (European Commission, Clandestino, September 2009), 5.

sociopolitical problems, national-security questions, and most importantly, economic needs and emergencies, especially the quest for sustained high-skilled labor from foreign countries to complement Europe's aging, dwindling workforce. As refugees are integral to international migration processes, legal rules on refugees constitute a significant part in the regulation of international migration.

Thus, the EU is vigorously protecting its external borders, notably against unwanted and irregular immigration. Considerable efforts are made and significant funds invested to enforce this goal.[27] Fences are erected, as in the Spanish enclaves of Ceuta and Melilla. Blue borders are patrolled by air and sea by coast guards and navies, as in Spain, Italy, Malta, and Greece. These operations are enforced by national forces but increasingly coordinated by the EU's border agency, Frontex.[28] This focus on the external borders comes despite the fact that irregular migrants overwhelmingly enter EU territory legally and then overstay or work in breach of employment regulation.[29] Thus, the meaning attached to the security of external borders goes beyond the material. Indeed, it involves political principles, the integrity of borders, symbols, the sovereignty of the state, and emotions, specifically, fears about uncontrolled population movements.[30]

Some European national governments, such as the United Kingdom, seem to suggest that the best way to deal with the proliferation of irregular, unwanted migrants is to ignore their travails on the new front line of migration, not to do anything by way of rescue for the increasing loss of lives on the seas and desert nor to accept any refugee quota, so as to serve as a natural and acceptable way to discourage immigration. Thus, Britain has been reluctant in supporting a sustained EU search-and-rescue operation to prevent further mass drownings of migrants and refugees in the Mediterranean, claiming that it would contribute to more people dying needlessly on Europe's doorstep and that it will simply encourage more people to attempt the dangerous sea crossing.[31] Ironically, the UK government

27. Düvell and Vollmer, "Irregular Migration," 5.

28. See Frontex, "Interceptions at EU Land and Sea Borders during 2008," http://www.europarl.europa.eu/document/activities/cont/201008/20100805ATT79751/20100805ATT79751EN.pdf.

29. Franck Düvell, "Paths into Irregularity: The Legal and Political Construction of Irregular Migration," *European Journal of Migration and Law* 13 (2011): 275–95.

30. Düvell and Vollmer, "Irregular Migration," 5.

31. See Alan Travis, "UK Axes Support for Mediterranean Migrant Rescue Operation," *Guardian*, October 27, 2014.

has stated, "We do not support planned search and rescue operations in the Mediterranean," because they have "an unintended 'pull factor,' encouraging more migrants to attempt the dangerous sea crossing and thereby leading to more tragic and unnecessary deaths. The government believes the most effective way to prevent refugees and migrants attempting this dangerous crossing is to focus our attention on countries of origin and transit, as well as taking steps to fight the people smugglers who willfully put lives at risk by packing migrants into unseaworthy boats."[32] The British refusal came to light as the official Italian search-and-rescue operation, Mare Nostrum, was due to come to an end after contributing for over twelve months to the rescue of an estimated 150,000 people since the Lampedusa tragedies in which five hundred migrants died in October 2013. Despite these efforts, more than 2,500 people are known to have drowned or gone missing in the Mediterranean in 2014 alone.

Africa appears to be the continent that matters most to EU policy makers working on migration. The prevailing perspective of the EU concerning African migration is still focused mainly on security and prevention. The politicization of immigration has attained an alarming level in which immigrants and asylum seekers are portrayed as a challenge to the protection of national identity and welfare provisions. Thus, one main focus of the European Commission and of European Council policies and meetings has been to counter the entry of illegal migrants through the EU's southern and eastern borders. The security shift in EU migration policy contradicts the so-called global approach to migration. Also witnessed is the externalization of border controls, in which countries close to European coastlines (Morocco, Algeria, Tunisia, Libya, and Turkey) have been encouraged to cooperate on specific security issues, including border management and readmission agreements. The adoption of uniform, rigid EU immigration laws has turned the coasts of southern Italy and Spain into important points of entry into continental Europe, albeit the securitization of migration and externalization of border controls. One consequence is that it is increasingly transforming and translating Europe into a "fortress."

32. Lady Anelay, former Foreign Office minister, spelling out British policy in the House of Lords. See ibid.

ETHICAL POLITICS OF MIGRATION AND AFRICAN-LED CHURCHES IN EUROPE

The uncertainty just described no doubt has implications for immigrants and the migratory process, but also for the religious communities such as African-led churches that are dominated by both regular and irregular migrants. It is within these ecologies of migration that we better understand the relevance and resilience of religion within African immigrant/diaspora communities. These developments raise the ethics and theology of migration in the unethical posture of the EU toward the vulnerable regular/irregular and transit immigrants, their sometimes inhuman treatment at the hands of security operatives and immigration personnel, and the maltreatment and exploitation at the hands of people smugglers, sex traffickers, and all those who profit from the booming migration industry in human bodies of men, women, and children. The attitude of EU countries has included silence, leaving immigrants to drown and die; debates over how to rescue them; and the ways they attack the people smugglers and give migrants temporary shelter.

The "august" visit of British prime minister David Cameron to the Redeemed Christian Church of God (RCCG) Festival of Life event in April 2015, on the eve of UK parliamentary elections, best illustrates the ambivalent stance of Tory politicians on immigration. Cameron seems to have become a temporary pastor-prophet while giving a disguised manifesto speech at the event. Cameron enthused, and I will quote generously here:

> I want to thank you, Pastor Agu, and I'd like to thank Pastor Adeboye, too; thank you, Daddy G.O. It is an honour to be here, and I'm proud of this festival, which started as a camp just off the Lagos expressway and set the world alight. It is now a permanent fixture here in London, and I'm delighted it's getting bigger, and it's getting better every year. Now, I have to say I don't envy the organisers of tonight; it must be like the feeding of the five thousand, except I can see you, you are forty-five thousand. You must be relieved that it's just spiritual food on the menu tonight.
>
> Now, I remember when my good friend Boris Johnson came here to the Festival of Life a few years ago; he made some comments on the subject of aspiration. He said he believed in aspiration, and he looked out into this huge crowd, and he said he knew someone would now be out there who would follow in his footsteps—someone who would one day

become mayor of this great city of London. Well, I would go further. I believe in aspiration; I believe the only limit to someone's potential is their own ambition and talent, and I look out into this crowd, and I can see someone who will hold my role and become prime minister of this great country. . . .

Now, for me, tonight is about one thing. It's about family. You're here with your own family: parents and children, siblings and cousins, aunts and uncles. You're united with your spiritual family—old friends, dear friends, people you've known for many years—and together we are all part of one family. As Jesus said with his arms outstretched to his disciples, "Here are my Mother and my brothers, for whoever does the will of my Father in heaven is my brother, my sister and my Mother," and that is what we are. As God's children, we are all one big family.

Now, when I was a child, I had a very specific image of what a church was. I thought to be a church, it had to be an old grey building with a slate roof and a big spire, that it had to have pews and a pulpit, and a graveyard where the naughty boys would play hide-and-seek. But I was wrong, and you proved that. You proved that church is people, church is a family, and it doesn't matter what the roof is made of, because with your energy, your devotion, your love of Jesus Christ, you raised that roof every time. Now, your dedication to family—your family in blood and your family in humanity—it goes way beyond this room. I think of how many ways you love your neighbour—with care for those who are sick and lonely, with mentoring for teenagers who think they have no hope, with fund-raising for hospices, for looked-after children, for those suffering unimaginable trauma overseas. Like Jesus turning water into wine, you turn loneliness into companionship, you turn deprivation into comfort, and you turn lost lives into lives with purpose.

For years, I have tried to explain to people what the Big Society is. Some people were determined not to understand it. Well, I should have brought them here to the Festival of Life, because this is the Big Society in action, and it's as vibrant and as loud and as powerful as ever. Now, just think how great our country Britain could be if we built on that, if we had an even bigger Big Society where even more people shared your family values—values of prudence, of hard work, of looking out for those who fall on hard times. With these values, we can achieve the Britain we all want to live in—where the oppressed are cared for, where the lonely are befriended, where it's not where you come from but it's the content of your character that really matters.

Tonight, let us be proud that this is a Christian country where we stand for the freedom to practice your faith and where we stand up for Christians and all those who are persecuted anywhere in our world; they are family, too. A year ago this week, 276 Nigerian schoolgirls were cruelly snatched by Boko Haram. I am a father of two young daughters,

> Florence and Nancy, and I have an understanding of what it's like to lose a child in tragic circumstances. So my prayer tonight to light yours is that those girls will be found soon and there will be peace in Nigeria.
>
> So thank you once again for having me here tonight with you. Thank you once again to the great Pastor Daddy G.O. Thank you to Pastor Agu and your team. Thank you for what you do; thank you for making the Festival of Life such a great British tradition. So let us tonight join with our brothers and sisters here. Let us pledge to make this Big Society bigger. Let us pledge to make our great country better. Let us make this Festival of Life even better, even louder, and even prouder next year. Thank you and good night.[33]

I would need another essay to unpack the themes and threads that such a speech contains, yet it is ironic that the prime minister was speaking to a mixed audience of over 45,000 worshippers, many of whom are probably irregular/undocumented migrants. How is it that the same man who spoke very passionately about building a "Big Family" and "Big Society" including migrants, refugees in Britain is the same one whose government prefers that immigrants drown on the sea with reckless abandon? He leads a government that refuses to take in refugees in the EU's temporary measure to provide shelter for immigrants/refugees rescued on the Mediterranean Sea. Is it a coincidence that Cameron visited an African church event on the eve of the UK parliamentary elections?

The general overseer of RCCG, Enoch Adeboye, who was attending the event from Nigeria, seized the opportunity to offer prayers for the prime minister. He prayed:

> Will you please stretch your hands to our prime minister and together pray that the Almighty God will give him wisdom, the wisdom of Solomon. God will give him the courage of David, so that in his days and in our days, Great Britain will be great again. Let's pray together. Pray that God will grant him divine wisdom, courage, strength, and special anointing from heaven, so that in his days and in our days, Great Britain will be great again, that the entire glory of this nation will be fully restored, that there be revival in this land. So Father Almighty, we want to thank you for our prime minister. Your word says that we are to pray for those who are in authority. So in obedience, Lord, to your commandment, we pray that you will give our prime minister divine wisdom, divine enablement, and divine courage, so that he will rule

33. For a full transcript of Prime Minister Cameron's speech at the RCCG, Festival of Life, London, see https://www.youtube.com/watch?v=uz6P_ruQL9A.

> this nation aright, that during his time and during our own days, Great Britain will be great again. Father, you are the burden bearer; help him to carry his burdens. Please bless him, bless his family, and Lord God Almighty, bless the United Kingdom. In Jesus' mighty name we have prayed. Amen.[34]

Tactically, neither the prime minister nor the general overseer made any mention of the elections that were a few days ahead. One might guess that Cameron obviously recognized this religious community as a voting constituency at a time of uncertainty about his reelection as prime minister. The fact that he won the election could be reinterpreted by some church members as an answer to prayers rendered during the visit. Much more striking is the fact that the prime minister's visit is indicative of the potentially civic relevance that African-led churches have come to assume in the United Kingdom. Some churches are playing a civic role to cushion hardships, frustration, and uncertainties faced by immigrants against the backdrop of public narratives of identity and belonging. The physical, emotional, and psychological trauma that many African immigrants undergo under dastardly circumstances explains why African-led churches have assumed an abode of security and community. It is within these scenarios of uncertainty, insecurity, shattered hopes, and forlorn dreams of migrants that the church appears to fill a vacuum.

The role and place of African-led churches as spiritual vacuum fillers, as spaces for socialization, and as engines for social, religious (spiritual), and capital formation are noteworthy. African-led churches in Europe, in a limited sense, help to cushion pains and strains of unemployment by serving both as employers and as channels of information for job opportunities in both formal and informal economic subsectors of the society. Some are involved in the provision of spiritual and social services, thus transforming church vicinities into both religious (spiritual) and social centers, where religious rituals and extrareligious activities take place contemporaneously.

Both regular and irregular migrants employ religious resources and appropriate religious rituals through the different stages of the migration process. The role of religious/spiritual specialists such as Christian pastors and prophets underscores the centrality of prophecy, divination, and spiritual armament in preparatory stages of the journey. Prospective migrants and their families patronize sacred or religious

34. Ibid.

sites, shrines, prayer camps, and religious events to fortify against the machinations of witches, sorcerers, the evil eye, and envious relatives and friends. The religious impulse and experiences encountered in the preparation and takeoff stages of the potential immigrant or traveler has consequences for the journey itself, but also implications for latter stages of the immigration process and settlement. Ogbu Kalu explains:

> The immigrant condition is riddled with hope, hardship, broken dreams, and measures of success. Immigrant Christianity serves as a balm in the entire process, ranging from why and how the immigrants came to their new countries, to how they cope in the new homeland. The journey begins with prayers in Pentecostal churches and prayer camps for travel visas, to prayers in immigrant churches for everyday survival needs such as working permits, employment, and money for rent, mortgage, health insurance, and other bills. There is also the added pressure to accumulate money and goods to transfer home.[35]

In sum, the lived experiences of African Christian immigrants and refugees shape their spiritual/religious lives, as do the theologies constructed from both those experiences and from the reservoir of indigenous religious worldviews they retain in their new homes. The ways in which the immigrant experience shapes religious lives and in which immigrants' spiritualities speak to and condition their day-to-day experiences and expressions are illuminated by their narratives partly woven between and betwixt themes of survival and security, adaptation and mobility. Such narratives are verbal contestations of a growing fortressization of Europe, which is characterized by the adoption of stringent, restrictive immigration policies. Immigrants' actions are to be understood in terms of their own goals—strategies established first in order to survive and after that to adapt (or not adapt) to the new social milieu. There is a certain link between theology of hope and theology of empowerment in the diaspora.

35. Ogbu Kalu, *African Pentecostalism: An Introduction* (Cambridge: Cambridge University Press 2008), 282.

Bibliography

Adogame, Afe. *The African Christian Diaspora: New Currents and Emerging Trends in World Christianity*. London: Bloomsbury Academic, 2013.

Alcántara, Jared E. *Crossover Preaching: Intercultural-Improvisational Homiletics in Conversation with Gardner C. Taylor*. Downers Grove, IL: IVP Academic, 2015.

Althaus-Reid, Marcella. *Indecent Theology: Theological Perversions in Sex, Gender and Politics*. London: Routledge, 2000.

_____. *The Queer God*. London: Routledge, 2003.

_____. "El Tocado (Le Toucher): Sexual Irregularities in the Translation of God (the Word) in Jesus." In *Derrida and Religion: Other Testaments*, edited by Yvonne Sherwood and Kevin Hart. New York: Routledge, 2004.

Alves, Branca Moreira Pitanguy. *O que é feminismo?* São Paulo: Brasiliense, 2003.

Alves, Rubem. *A Theology of Human Hope*. Washington, DC: Corpus, 1969.

_____. "Towards a Theology of Liberation: An Exploration of the Encounter between the Languages of Humanistic Messianism and Messianic Humanism." PhD diss., Princeton Theological Seminary, May 1968.

Anselmo, Santo. *Proslogion seu Alloquium de Dei existentia*. Covilhã, Portugal: Universidade da Beira Interior, 2008.

Anzaldúa, Gloria. *Borderlands/La Frontera*. San Francisco: Aunt Lute, 1987.

Araujo, Rodrigo. "Proporção de evangélicos no Espírito Santo é maior do que no restante do país." *Gazeta*, June 29, 2012, http://gazetaonline.globo.com/_conteudo/2012/06/a_gazeta/minuto_a_minuto/1292361-proporcao-de-evangelicos-no-espirito-santo-e-maior-do-que-no-restante-do-pais.html.

Armstrong, Karen. *The Battle for God*. New York: Knopf, 2000.

Ascroft, Bill. "Threshold Theology." In *Colonial Contexts and Postcolonial Theologies: Storyweaving in the Asia-Pacific*, edited by Mark E. Brett and Jione Havea, 3–22. New York: Palgrave Macmillan, 2014.

Assmann, Hugo. *Opresión–Liberación: Desafío a los cristianos*. Montevideo: Tierra Nueva, 1971.

Ayee, Emmanuel. "Christian Perspective on Intercultural Communication." *Pro Rege* 35, no. 4 (June 2007): 1–9, doi:http://digitalcollections.dordt.edu/pro_rege.

Barreto, Raimundo C., and Devaka Premawardhana. "The Church and Society Movement and the Roots of Public Theology in Brazilian Protestantism." *International Journal of Public Theology* 6, no. 1 (2012): 70–98.

_____. "Protestantism and Candomblé in Bahia: From Intolerance to Dialogue (and Beyond)." In *The World's Religions after September 11*, vol. 3, edited by Arvind Sharma, 137–51. Westport, CT: Praeger, 2009.

Barth, Karl. "Revelação, Igreja, Teologia." In *Dádiva e Louvor: Artigos Selecionados*. São Leopoldo: Sinodal, 1986.

Basch, Linda, Nina Glick-Schiller, and Cristina Blanc-Szanton, eds. *Nations Unbound: Transnational Projects, Postcolonial Predicaments, and Deterritorialized Nation-States*. New York: Gordon and Breach, 1994.

Battistella, Graziano. "The Contributions of Ethics to the Management of Migration." *Ciberteologia: Journal of Theology and Culture* 37, year 8 (2012).

Beasley, Chris. "Problematizing Contemporary Men/Masculinities Theorizing: The Contribution of Raewyn Connell and Conceptual-Terminological Tensions Today." *British Journal of Sociology* 63, no. 4 (2012): 747–65.

Benavides, Gustavo. "Syncretism and Legitimacy in Latin American Religion." In *Syncretism and Religion: A Reader*, edited by Anita Maria Leopold and Jeppe Sinding Jensen, 194–216. London: Equinox, 2004.

Benedict XVI. *General Audience*. Vatican City, 2010.

Bevans, Stephen B. *Models of Contextual Theology*. Rev. and expanded ed. Maryknoll, NY: Orbis, 2002.

Bittencourt Filho, José. "Por uma eclesiologia militante: ISAL como nascedouro de uma nova eclesiologia para a América Latina. Dissertação." Master's thesis, Instituto Metodista de Ensino Superior, 1988.

Boesak, Allan A. "Theodicy: 'De Lawd Knowed How It Was'; Black Theology and Black Suffering." In *The Cambridge Companion to Black Theology*, edited by Dwight N. Hopkins and Edward P. Antonio, 156–68. New York: Cambridge University Press, 2012.

Boff, Leonardo. *Eclesiogênese: As comunidades eclesiais de base reinventam a Igreja*. Petrópolis, Brazil: Editora Vozes, 1977.

_____. *Igreja, carisma e poder: Ensaios de eclesiologia militante.* Petrópolis, Brazil: Vozes, 1981.

_____. *Jesus Cristo libertador: Ensaio de cristologia crítica para o nosso tempo.* Petrópolis, Brazil: Editôra Vozes, 1972.

Bonhöffer, Dietrich. *Letters and Papers from Prison.* Edited by Eberhard Bethge. London: Folio Society, 2000.

Bonino, José Miguez. *Rostos do Protestantismo Latino-Americano.* São Leopoldo: Sinodal, 2003.

Bouchey, L. Francis, and Lewis A. Tambs. *A New Inter-American Policy for the Eighties*. Committee of Santa Fe. Washington, DC: Council for Inter-American Security, 1981.

Burdick, John. *Blessed Anastacia: Women, Race, and Popular Christianity in Brazil.* New York: Routledge, 1998.

_____. "Why Is the Black Evangelical Movement Growing in Brazil?" *Journal of Latin American Studies* 37, no. 2 (2005): 311–32.

Carens, Joseph H. "Aliens and Citizens: The Case for Open Borders." *Review of Politics* 49 (1987): 251–73.

_____. *The Ethics of Migration*. Oxford: Oxford University Press, 2013.

Carvalho, Marie Jane. "Qual cidadania desejamos?" In *As mulheres e a filosofia*, edited by Márcia Tiburi, Magali M. De Menezes, and Edla Eggert. São Leopoldo: Unisinos, 2002.

Casanova, Jose. *Public Religions in the Modern World.* Chicago: University of Chicago Press, 1994.

_____. "Rethinking Public Religions." In *Rethinking Religion and World Affairs*, edited by Timothy Samuel Shah, Alfred Stepan, and Monica Duffy Toft. Oxford: Oxford University Press, 2012.

Castanha, Tony. *The Myth of Indigenous Caribbean Extinction: Continuity and Reclamation in Borike (Puerto Rico).* New York: Palgrave Macmillan, 2011.

Castillo, Ana, ed. *Goddess of the Americas: Writings on the Virgin of Guadalupe.* New York: Riverhead, 1996.

Castles, Stephen, and Mark Miller. *The Age of Migration: International Population Movements in the Modern World.* 3rd ed. New York: Guilford, 1993.

CEDI. *Identidade Negra e Religiao.* Rio de Janeiro: Edicoes Liberdade, 1986.

Cervantes-Ortiz, Leopoldo. *Serie de sueños: La teología ludo-erótico-poética de Rubem Alves.* Quito, Ecuador: Consejo Latinoamericano de Iglesias, 2003.

Chacón, Jonathan Pimentel. *Modelos de Dios en las teologías latinoamericanas.* Heredia, Costa Rica: Universidad Nacional de Costa Rica, 2008.

Clarke, Sathianathan. "World Christianity and Postcolonial Mission: A Path Forward for the Twenty-First Century." *Theology Today* 71, no. 2 (2014): 192–206.

Cobban, Helena. *The Palestinian Liberation Organisation: People, Power and Politics.* Cambridge: Cambridge University Press, 1984.

Congregação para a Doutrina da Fé. *Declaração "Dominus Iesus" sobre a unicidade e a universalidade salvífica de Jesus Cristo e da Igreja.* http://www.vatican.va/roman_curia/congregations/cfaith/documents/rc_con_cfaith_doc_20000806_dominus-iesus_po.html.

Connell, Raewyn. *Der gemachte Mann: Konstruktion und Krise von Männlichkeiten.* Wiesbaden: Springer, 2015.

_____. *Masculinities.* 2nd ed. Berkeley: University of California Press, 2005.

Cook, Guillermo. "Introduction: Brief History of the Maya Peoples." In *Crosscurrents in Indigenous Spirituality: Interface of Maya, Catholic and Protestant Worldviews*, edited by Guillermo Cook, 1–33. Leiden: Brill, 1997.

Cornish, Jean-Jacques. "Desperate Journeys: Senegal Migrant Seeks Better Life in Europe." *Al Jazeera,* April 13, 2016. http://video.aljazeera.com/channels/eng/videos/senegal-migrant-seeks-better-life-in-europe/4246430493001.

_____. "Migration and Xenophobia Top AU Agenda at Summit." *Eyewitness News,* June 11, 2015, http://ewn.co.za/2015/06/11/Migration-and-xenophobia-on-the-agenda-for-African-Executive-Council-meeting.

_____. "South Africa: Xenophobic Attacks Erupt in South Africa's Limpopo Province." *AllAfrica,* March 5, 2015, http://allafrica.com/stories/201503051136.html.

"Cottesloe Declaration (1960)." NG Church in South Africa's Archives website, http://kerkargief.co.za/doks/bely/DF_Cottesloe.pdf.

Cruz, G. T. "Between Identity and Security: Theological Implications of Migration in the Context of Globalization." *Theological Studies* 69, no. 2 (2008): 357–75.

Cunha, Magali do Nascimento. *A Explosão Gospel: Um olhar das ciências humanas sobre o cenário evangélico contemporâneo no Brasil.* Rio de Janeiro: Mauad, 2007.

Dario Antiseri, Giovanni R. *História da Filosofia: Patrística e Escolástica.* São Paulo: Paulus, 2005.

Da Silva, Hernani. *O Movimento Negro Evangelico: Um Mover do Espirito Santo.* São Paulo: Selo Editorial Negritude Cristã, 2010.

De Castro Maia, Moacir Rodrigo. "Uma Nova Interpretação da Chegada de Escravos Africanos à América Portuguesa (Minas Gerais, século XVIII)." *Anais do XXVI Simpósio Nacional de História (ANPUH)*, São Paulo, July 2011, http://www.snh2011.anpuh.org/resources/anais/14/1308192610_ARQUIVO_TextocompletoANPUHjunho2011.pdf.

De Gruchy, John W. *The Church Struggle in South Africa.* Minneapolis: Fortress Press, 2005.

De la Torre, Miguel, and Edwin David Aponte. *Introducing Latino/a Theologies.* Maryknoll, NY: Orbis, 2001.

De Oliveira, Marco David. *A Religião Mais Negra do Brasil: Porque Mais de Oito Milhões de Negros São Pentecostais.* São Paulo: Mundo Cristão, 2004.

de Vos, Pierre. "Chief Justice on 'Fornication' and 'Sanctity of the Family.'" *Constitutionally Speaking*, May 28, 2014, http://constitutionallyspeaking.co.za/chief-justice-on-fornication-and-sanctity-of-the-family/.

Deifelt, Wanda. "Educação teológica para mulheres: um passo decisivo rumo à cidadania eclesial." In *Gênero e teologia: Interpretações e perspectivas*, ed. SOTER, 265–282. São Paulo: Loyola, Paulinas, 2004.

Delors, Jacques, coord. "Os quatro pilares da educação." In *Educação: Um tesouro a descobrir*, report to UNESCO of the International Commission on Education for the Twenty-First Century, 89–102. São Paulo: Cortezo.

Dias, Zwinglio Motta. "O Movimento Ecumênico: História e Significado." *Numen* 1, no. 1 (1998): 127–63.

Duquoc, Christian. *A Teologia no Exílio: O Desafio da Sobrevivência da Teologia na Cultura Contemporânea.* Petrópolis: Vozes, 2006.

Dussel, Enrique. *1492: El encubrimiento del otro (Hacia el origen del "mito de la modernidad").* Bogotá: Ediciones Antropos, 1992.

_____. *The Invention of the Americas: Eclipse of 'the Other' and the Myth of Modernity*. New York: Continuum, 1995.

Düvell, Franck. "Paths into Irregularity. The Legal and Political Construction of Irregular Migration." *European Journal of Migration and Law* 13 (2011): 275–95.

Düvell, Franck, and Bastian Vollmer. *Irregular Migration in and from the Neighbourhood of the EU: A Comparison of Morocco, Turkey and Ukraine.* European Commission and Clandestino, September 2009.

Eco, Umberto. *Foucault's Pendulum*. Orlando, FL: Harvest, 1988.

Elizondo, Virgilio P. *The Future is Mestizo: Life Where Cultures Meet*. Boulder: University Press of Colorado, 2000.

Ellacuría, Ignacio, and Jon Sobrino, eds. *Mysterium liberationis: Conceptos fundamentales de la Teologíade la Liberación.* Madrid: Editorial Trotta, 1990.

Elon, Amos. *Jerusalem: Battlegrounds of Memory*. New York: Kodansha International, 1995.

Elphick, Richard. *The Equality of Believers: Protestant Missionaries and the Racial Politics of South Africa*. Charlottesville: University of Virginia Press, 2012.

Elphick, Richard, and Rodney Davenport. *Christianity in South Africa: A Political, Social, and Cultural History*. Berkeley: University of California Press, 1997.

Escobar, Samuel. "Mission in Latin America: An Evangelical Perspective," *Missiology* 20, no. 2 (1992): 241–53.

_____. *The New Global Mission: The Gospel from Everywhere to Everyone.* Downers Grove, IL: InterVarsity, 2003.

Evangelische Kirche in Deutschland, ed. *Zahlen und Fakten zum kirchlichen Leben.* Hannover, 2015.

Evangelische Landeskirche in Württemberg, Evangelischer Oberkirchenrat, "TOP 20: Bericht zur Milieustudie Baden und Württemberg." 14 Synod, November 28, 2012, http://www.veranstaltungen.elk-wue.de/fileadmin/mediapool/elkwue/dokumente/landessynode/12_herbsttagung/berichte-reden/TOP20_Bericht_OKR_Hempelmann.pdf.

Evangelischer Presseverband für Bayern. *Sonntagsblatt Thema: Manner*, January 2016.

Faculdade Unida. "Breve Histórico da Faculdade Unida." At http://www.faculdadeunida.com.br/site/institucional/institucional-nossahistoria, accessed on June 20, 2016.

Fanon, Franz. *The Wretched of the Earth*. New York: Grove, 1965.

Ferguson, Nail. *Civilization: The West and the Rest.* New York: Penguin, 2011.

FitzGerald, Frances. "The National Liberation Front." Chapter 4 in *Fire in the Lake: The Vietnamese and the Americans in Vietnam.* Boston: Little, Brown, 1972.

Flannery, Austin P., ed. *Vatican Council II: The Basic Sixteen Documents; Constitutions, Decrees, Declarations.* Northport, NY: Costello, 1996.

Forrester, Duncan B. Preface to *Decolonizing the Body of Christ: Theology and Theory After Empire?*, edited by David Joy and Joseph Duggan, xi–xii. New York: Palgrave Macmillan, 2012.

Forte, Bruno. *Teologia em Diálogo.* São Paulo: Loyola, 2002.

Frahm-Arp, Maria. "The Political Rhetoric in Sermons and Select Social Media in Three Pentecostal Charismatic Evangelical Churches Leading up to the 2014 South African Election." *Journal for the Study of Religion* 28, no. 1 (January 2015).

Freire, Paulo. *Educação como prática da liberdade.* Rio de Janeiro: Paz e Terra, 1967.

_____. *Pedagogia do oprimido.* 7th ed. Rio de Janeiro: Paz e Terra, 1979.

_____. *Pedagogía del oprimido.* Montevideo: Tierra Nueva, 1970.

_____. *Pedagogy of the Oppressed.* New York: Continuum, 2000.

Freyre, Gilberto. *Casa-Grande y Senzala: Introducción a la Historia de la Sociedad Patriarcal en el Brasil.* Prólogo y Cronologia Darcy Ribeiro. Caracas: Biblioteca Ayacucho, 1977.

Frontex. General Report 2009. http://www.europarl.europa.eu/document/activities/cont/201008/20100805ATT79751/20100805ATT79751EN.pdf.

Fukuyama, Francis. *The End of History and the Last Man.* New York: Free Press, 1992.

Gebara, Ivone. *O que é teologia feminista.* São Paulo: Brasiliense, 2007.

Gera, Lucio. "Apuntes para una Interpretation de la Iglesia Argentina." *Vispera,* 15 (1970): 59ff.

Gibson, Douglas. "In Defiant Support of Rainbowism." *Independent Online,* January 12, 2016, http://www.iol.co.za/the-star/in-defiant-support-of-rainbowism-1969925.

Gleanson, Judith. "Oya in the Company of the Saints," *Journal of the American Academy of Religion* 68, no. 2 (2000): 265–92.

Glendon, Mary Ann. *A World Made New: Eleanor Roosevelt and the Universal Declaration of Human Rights.* New York: Random House, 2001.

González, Justo L., and Ondina E. González. *Christianity in Latin America: A History*. New York: Cambridge University Press, 2008. Kindle edition.

Graf, Friedrich Wilhelm. *Kirchendämmerung: Wie die Kirchen unser Vertrauen verspielen*. Munich: Beck, 2011.

Granberg-Michaelson, Wesley. *From Times Square to Timbuktu: The Post-Christian West Meets the Non-Western Church*. Grand Rapids: Eerdmans, 2013.

Grönemeyer, Herbert. "Männe." *Bochum*. EMI, 1984.

Grooves, Stephen. "Analysis: The Judgment at the End of the Nkandla Road." *Daily Maverick*, March 31, 2016, http://www.dailymaverick.co.za/article/2016-03-31-analysis-the-judgment-at-the-end-of-the-nkandla-road/#.V3y3AKLQPZN.

Gutiérrez, Gustavo. *Las Casas: In Search of the Poor of Jesus Christ*. Maryknoll, NY: Orbis, 1993.

_____. "The Meaning and Scope of Medellín." *The Density of the Present: Selected Writings*. Maryknoll, NY: Orbis, 1999.

_____. *Teología de la liberación: Perspectivas*. Salamanca: Sígueme, 1973.

_____. *A Theology of Liberation*. 15th anniv. ed. Maryknoll, NY: Orbis, 1988.

Habermas, Jürgen. *The Structural Transformation of the Public Sphere: An Inquiry into a Category of Bourgeois Society*. Cambridge: Polity, 1989.

Haight, Roger. *A Dinâmica da Teologia*. São Paulo: Paulinas, 2004.

Hanks, William F. *Converting Words: Maya in the Age of the Cross*. Berkeley: University of California Press, 2010. Kindle edition.

Hans, Bongani. "King's Anti-foreigner Speech Causes Alarm." *Independent Online*. March 23, 2015, www.iol.co.za/news/politics/king-s-anti-foreigner-speech-causes-alarm-1.1835602#.VSzaLPCROYM.

Harding, Sandra. "A instabilidade das categorias analíticas na teoria feminista." *Estudos Feministas* 1, no. 1 (1993).

Hartley, George. "The Curandeira of the Conquest: Gloria Anzaldúa's Decolonial Remedy,"*Aztlán: A Journal of Chicano Studies* 35, no. 1 (2010): 135–61.

Hattori, Kozo. "Five Habits of Highly Compassionate Men." Stanford School of Medicine, Center for Compassion and Altruism Research and Education, September 29, 2014, ccare.stanford.edu/press_posts/5-habits-of-highly-compassionate-men/.

Heim, Mark. "The Next Ecumenical Movement." *Christian Century* 113, no. 24 (1996): 780–83.

Hennelly, Alfred T. *Liberation Theology: A Documentary History*. Maryknoll, NY: Orbis, 1992.

Hinkelammert, Franz. *El grito del sujeto: Del teatro-mundo del evangelio de Juan al perro-mundo de la globalización*. San José, Costa Rica: DEI, 1998.

Hobsbawm, Eric. *Age of Extremes: The Short Twentieth Century, 1914–1991*. London: Michael Joseph, 1994.

_____. *O novo século: Entrevista a Antonio Polito*. Translated from Italian into English by Allan Cameron. Translated from English into Portuguese and compared with Italian edition by Cláudio Marcondes. São Paulo: Companhia das Letras, 2000.

Hoch, Lothar C. "Primeiro curso de Teologia do Brasil autorizado pelo MEC." Portal Luteranos, December 1, 2000, http://www.luteranos.com.br/conteudo/primeiro-curso-de-teologia-do-brasil-autorizado-pelo-mec.

Hofer, Markus. "Glauben Männer anders?" In *Mannsbilder: Kritische Männerforschung und theologische Frauenforschung im Gespräch*, edited by Marie Therese Wacker and Stefanie Rieger Goertz. Berlin: Lit, 2006.

Hoornaert, Eduardo. *O Cristianismo Moreno do Brasil*. Petrópolis: Vozes, 1991.

Horne, Alistair. *A Savage War of Peace: Algeria 1954–1962*. New York: Penguin, 1987.

Houston, Walter J. *Contending for Justice: Ideologies and Theologies of Social Justice in the Old Testament*. London: T & T Clark, 2006.

Hume, David. *The Natural History of Religion*. London: A. & C. Black, 1956.

Huysmans, Jef. "The European Union and the Securitization of Migration." *Journal of Common Market Studies* 38, no. 5 (2000): 751–77.

Irrarazaval, Diego. "Mission within Cultures and Religions." *Exchange* 30, no. 3 (2001): 229–34.

Irvin, Dale. "What Is World Christianity?" In *World Christianity: Perspectives and Insights*, edited by Jonathan Y. Tan and Anh Q. Tran, 3–26. Maryknoll, NY: Orbis, 2016.

_____. "World Christianity: An Introduction." *Journal of World Christianity* 1, no. 1 (2008): 1–2.

Joh, Wonhee Anne. *Heart of the Cross: A Postcolonial Christology*. Louisville, KY: Westminster John Knox, 2006.

Kalu, Ogbu. *African Pentecostalism: An Introduction*. Cambridge: Cambridge University Press, 2008.

Karle, Isolde. *"Da ist nicht mehr Mann noch Frau . . .": Theologie jenseits der Geschlechterdifferenz*. Gütersloh: Gütersloher, 2006.

Keller, Catherine, Michael Nausner, and Mayra Rivera. *Postcolonial Theologies: Divinity and Empire.* St. Louis, MO: Chalice, 2004.

Kgatlhane, Ntlanta. "National Interfaith Council Welcomes President Zuma's Apology." *SABC News,* April 11, 2016, http://www.sabc.co.za/news/a/da582a804c5dac8d866ff79ffda8f5e4/National-Interfaith-Council-welcomes-President-Zumas-apology-20160411.

Khaleeli, Homa. "'A Frenzy of Hatred': How to Understand Brexit Racism." *Guardian*, June 29, 2016, http://www.theguardian.com/politics/2016/jun/29/frenzy-hatred-brexit-racism-abuse-referendum-celebratory-lasting-damage.

Kiddy, Elizabeth W. *Blacks of the Rosary: Memory and History in Minas Gerais, Brazil*. University Park: Pennsylvania University Press, 2005.

King, Martin Luther Jr. "A Christmas Sermon on Peace." In *A Testament of Hope: The Essential Writings and Speeches of Martin Luther King, Jr.*, edited by James M. Washington, 253–58. New York: HarperCollins, 1991.

Kingsley, Patrick, Alessandra Bonomolo, and Stephanie Kirchgaessner. "700 Migrants Feared Dead in Mediterranean Shipwreck." *Guardian*, April 19, 2015, http://www.theguardian.com/world/2015/apr/19/700-migrants-feared-dead-mediterranean-shipwreck-worst-yet.

Kington, Tom. "Another 41 African Migrants Drown Making Perilous Crossing to Italy." *Los Angeles Times*, April, 16, 2015, http://www.latimes.com/world/europe/la-fg-italy-migrants-drowned-20150416-story.html.

Kinnamon, Michael. *Can a Renewal Movement be Renewed? Questions for the Future of Ecumenism*. Grand Rapids: Eerdmans, 2014.

Kinney, John W. "The Theology of John Mbiti: His Sources, Norms, and Methods." *Occasional Bulletin of Missionary Research* 3, no. 2 (1979): 65–67.

Kirchenamt der Evangelischen Kirche in Deutschland (EKD). *Engagement und Indifferenz: Kirchenmitgliedschaft als soziale Praxis.* EKD-Erhebung über Kirchenmitgliedschaft. Hannover, March 2014, www.ekd.de/download/ekd_v_kmu2014.pdf.

Kistner, Wolfram. *Outside the Camp: A Collection of Writings*. Johannesburg: South African Council of Churches, 1988.

Knieling, Rainer. *Männer und Kirche: Konflikte, Missverständnisse, Annäherungen.* Göttingen: Vandenhoeck & Ruprecht, 2010.

Koschorke, K. "New Maps of the History of World Christianity: Current Challenges and Future Perspectives." *Theology Today* 71, no. 2 (2014): 178–91.

Lara, Silvia H., ed. *Ordenações Filipinas, Livro V*. São Paulo: Companhia das Letras, 1999.

Lenchak, Timothy. "The Bible and Intercultural Communication." *Missiology: An International Review* 22, no. 4 (1994): 457–67.

Levinas, Emmanuel. *Totalidade e Infinito*: Lisbon: Edições 70, 2000.

Lima, Tânia, ed. *Sincretismo Religioso: O Ritual Afro-Brasileiro*. Recife: Editora Massangano, 1996.

Lind, Dara. "1,600 Migrants Have Drowned in the Mediterranean This Year: Europe Refuses to Fix the Crisis." *Vox World*, April 20, 2015, http://www.vox.com/2015/4/20/8457719/mediterranean-migrant-shipwreck.

Lowry, Michael. *The War of Gods: Religion and Politics in Latin America*. London: Verso, 1996.

Mackay, John. *Ecumenics: The Science of the Church Universal*. Englewood Cliffs, NJ: Prentice-Hall, 1964.

Makgoba, Thabo. "Mr Prez, Please Step Aside." *CityPress*, March 27, 2016, http://citypress.news24.com/Voices/mr-prezplease-step-aside-20160325.

Makhaye, Chris. "Church Lauds Zuma as Honorary Pastor." *Independent Online*, May 6, 2007, http://www.iol.co.za/news/politics/church-lauds-zuma-as-honorary-pastor-351656.

Marcuse, Herbert. *An Essay on Liberation*. Boston: Beacon, 1969.

Martí, José. "Carta a Manuel Mercado." In *Obras escogidas*. Havana: Editora Política, 1982.

_____. *Inside the Monster: Writings on the United States and American Imperialism*. New York: Monthly Review Press, 1975.

Martin, Judith M., and Thomas K. Nakayama. "Understanding Intercultural Transitions." In *Intercultural Communication in Contexts*, 315-56. 6th ed. New York: McGraw-Hill, 2013.

Martin, Judith M., K. Thomas Nakayama, and L. A. Flores. *Readings in Intercultural Communication*. New York: McGraw-Hill, 2002.

Marty, Martin E. "Public Religion." In *Encyclopedia of Religion and Social Science*, ed. William H. Swatos Jr. Hartford, CT: Hartford Institute for Religion Research, Hartford Seminary, http://hirr.hartsem.edu/ency/PublicR.htm, accessed July 9, 2016.

Mbiti, John. "Challenges Facing Religious Education and Research in Africa: The Case of Dialogue between Christianity and African Religion." *Religion and Theology* 3, no. 2 (1996): 170–79.

_____. "On the Article of John W. Kinney: A Comment," *Occasional Bulletin of Missionary Research* 3, no. 2 (1979): 68.

McGrath, Alister. *A Revolução Protestante*. Brasília: Palavra, 2012.

Medina, Lara. "Nepantla Spirituality: Negotiating Multiple Religious Identities Among U.S. Latinas," in *Rethinking Latino(a) Religion and Identity*, edited by Miguel A. de La Torre and Gaston Espinosa, 248–66. Cleveland, OH: Pilgrim, 2006.

Medina, Nestor. *Mestizaje: (Re)Mapping Race, Culture and Faith in Latina/o Catholicism*. Maryknoll, NY: Orbis, 2009.

Metz, Johannes Baptist. *Zur Theologie der Welt*. Mainz: Matthias-Grúnewald, 1968.

Meuser, Michael. "Modernisierte Männlichkeit? Kontinuitäten, Herausforderungen und Wandel männlicher Lebenslagen." In *Mannsbilder: Kritische Männerforschung und theologische Frauenforschung im Gespräch*, edited by Marie Therese Wacker and Stefanie Rieger Goertz. Berlin: Lit, 2006.

Mignolo, Walter. *The Darker Side of the Renaissance: Literacy, Territoriality, and Colonization*. Ann Arbor: University of Michigan Press, 1995.

_____. "Introduction." *Cultural Studies* 21, nos. 2–3 (2007): 155–67.

_____. *Local Histories/Global Designs: Coloniality, Subaltern Knowledges, and Border Thinking*. Princeton Studies in Culture/Power/History. Princeton, NJ: Princeton University Press, 2000. Kindle edition.

Miguez Bonino, Jose. *Doing Theology in a Revolutionary Situation*. Minneapolis: Fortress Press, 2007. Kindle edition.

Milbank, John. *Teologia e Teoria social*. São Paulo: Loyola, 1995.

Mills, Joe. "More than 400 People Drown in Mediterranean Sea as Ship Carrying African Migrants from Libya to Italy Capsizes." *International Business Times*, April 14, 2015, http://www.ibtimes.co.uk/more-400-people-drown-mediterranean-sea-ship-carrying-african-migrants-libya-italy-capsizes-1496416.

Moltmann, Jürgen. *Experiences in Theology: Ways and Forms of Christian Theology*. Minneapolis: Fortress Press, 2000.

_____. *Theologie der Hoffnung*. Munich: Chr. Kaiser, 1966.

Montes, Adolfo G. *Fundamentación de la Fe*. Salamanca: Secretariado Trinitário, 1994.

Moreau, A. Scott, Evvy Hay Campbell, and Susan Greer. *Effective Intercultural Communication: A Christian Perspective*. Grand Rapids, MI: Baker Academic, 2014.

Müller, Retief. *African Pilgrimage Ritual Travel in South Africa's Christianity of Zion*. Burlington, VT: Ashgate, 2011.

Muylaert, Camila Junqueira, et. al. "Entrevistas narrativas: Um importante recurso em pesquisa qualitativa." *Revista da Escola de Enfermagem da USP* 48, esp. 2 (2014): 193–99, available at http://www.scielo.br/pdf/reeusp/v48nspe2/pt_0080-6234-reeusp-48-nspe2-00184.pdf.

Neely, Alan P. "Protestant Antecedents of the Latin American Theology of Liberation." PhD diss., American University, 1977.

Neuenfeldt, Elaine Gleci. "Gênero e hermenêutica feminista: Dialogando com definições e buscando as implicações." *A palavra na vida*, nos. 155/156 (2000).

Olamint Films. "The Prime Minister of Great Britain RT Hon David Cameron at RCCG Festival of Life London April 25." YouTube, https://www.youtube.com/watch?v=Nt-hB1ROjjg.

Omari-Tunkara, Mikelle Smith. "Candomblé." In *The Oxford Encyclopedia of African Thought*, edited by F. Abiola Irele and Biodun Jeyifo. Oxford African American Studies Center, http://www.oxfordaasc.com/article/opr/t301/e085, accessed June 24, 2015.

O'Neill, W. "'No Longer Strangers' (Ephesians 2:19): The Ethics of Migration." *Word and World* 29, no. 3 (2009): 227–33.

Ott, Carlos. "A Irmandade de Nossa Senhora do Rosario dos Pretos do Pelourinho." *Afro-Ásia* 6, no. 7 (1968): 83–90.

Paris, Peter J. *The Spiritualities of the African Peoples: The Search for Common Moral Discourse*. Minneapolis: Fortress Press, 1995.

Parker, Owen, and James Brassett. "Contingent Borders, Ambiguous Ethics: Migrants in (International) Political Theory." *International Studies Quarterly* 49 (2005): 233–53.

Pham, Paulus Y. *Towards an Ecumenical Paradigm for Christian Mission: David Bosch's Missionary Vision*. Rome: Gregorian & Biblical Press, 2010.

Phan, Peter C. "The Experience of Migration as Source of Intercultural Theology." Chapter 9 in *Contemporary Issues of Migration and Theology*, 179-99. New York: Palgrave Macmillan, 2013.

_____. *In Our Own Tongues: Perspectives from Asia on Mission and Inculturation*. Maryknoll, NY: Orbis, 2003. Kindle edition.

Pixley, Jorge V. *Exodo, una lectura evangélica y popular.* Mexico City: Casa Unida de Publicaciones, 1983.

Pixley, Jorge V., and Jean-Pierre Bastian, eds. *Praxis cristiana y producción teológica.* Salamanca: Ediciones Sígueme, 1979.

Pixley, Jorge V., et al. *Por un mundo otro: Alternativas al mercado global.* Quito, Ecuador: Consejo Latinoamericano de Iglesias, 2003.

Plou, Dafne Sabanes. *Caminhos de Unidade.* Itinerário do Diálogo Ecumênico na América Latina. São Leopoldo: Sinodal; Quito: Clai, 2002.

Porfirio Miranda, José. *Marx y la Biblia.* Salamanca: Ediciones Sígueme, 1972.

Portes, Alejandro. "Towards a New World: The Origins and Effects of Transnational Activities." *Ethnic and Racial Studies* 22, no. 2 (1999).

Pui-lan, Kwok. *Postcolonial Imagination and Feminist Theology.* Louisville, KY: Westminster John Knox, 2005.

Pui-lan, Kwok, Don H. Compier, and Joerg Rieger, eds. *Empire and the Christian Tradition: New Readings of Classical Theologians.* Minneapolis: Fortress Press, 2007.

Pulikottil, Paulson. "One God, One Spirit, Two Memories: A Postcolonial Reading of the Encounter between Western Pentecostalism and Native Pentecostalism in Kerala." In *The Spirit in the World: Emerging Pentecostal Theologies in Global Contexts*, edited by Veli-Matti Karkkainen, 69–88. Grand Rapids: Eerdmans, 2009.

Rathbone, Mark. "Religious Leaders Say President Zuma Has Lost All Morality to Govern." *Cii Broadcasting*, April 7, 2016, http://www.ciibroadcasting.com/2016/04/07/religious-leaders-say-president-zuma-has-lost-all-morality-to-govern/.

_____. "The Road to South African Freedom: Programme of the South African Communist Party." *African Communist* 2, no. 2 (January–March 1963).

_____. "Sphere Sovereignty and Irreducibility: The Ambiguous Use of Abraham Kuyper's Ideas during the Time of Apartheid in South Africa." *Koers* 80, no. 1 (January 2015): 1–8, doi:10.4102/koers.v80i1.2208.

Reiner, Andrew. "Teaching Men to Be Emotionally Honest." *New York Times*, April 4, 2016, www.nytimes.com/2016/04/10/education/edlife/teaching-men-to-be-emotionally-honest.html?_r=3.

Ribeiro, Claudio de Oliveira, and Magali do Nascimento Cunha. *Reflexões sobre ecumenismo e paz.* São Paulo: Fonte Editorial, 2013.

Ribeiro, Osvaldo L. "Da Indefensável Posição Protestante." *Ouviroevento*, June 20, 2008, http://www.ouviroevento.pro.br/teologicofilosoficos/da_indefensavel.htm.

Richard, Pablo. "1492: The Violence of God and the Future of Christianity." In *The Voice of the Victims, Concilium*, edited by Leonardo Boff and Virgil Elizondo, 58–67. London: SCM, 1990.

Rieger, Joerg. *Christ and Empire: From Paul to Postcolonial Times*. Minneapolis: Fortress Press, 2007.

Ricoeur, Paul. *Percurso do Reconhecimento*. São Paulo: Loyola, 2006.

Ritschl, Dietrich, and Martin Hailer. *Fundamentos da Teologia Cristã*. São Leopoldo: Sinodal/EST, 2012.

Rivera, Mayra. *The Touch of Transcendence: A Postcolonial Theology of God*. Louisville, KY: Westminster John Knox, 2007.

Rivera-Pagán, Luis N. "Doing Pastoral Theology in a Post-Colonial Context: Some Observations from the Caribbean." *Journal of Pastoral Theology* 17, no. 2 (Fall 2007): 1–28.

Robertson, Roland. "Globalization and the Future of 'Traditional Religion," In *God and Globalization: Theological Ethics and the Spheres of Life*, edited by Max L. Stackhouse and Peter J. Paris, 53–68. New York: Trinity Press International, 2000.

Romero, Oscar. *Voice of the Voiceless: The Four Pastoral Letters and Other Statements*. Introductory essays by Ignacio Martín-Baró and Jon Sobrino. Maryknoll, NY: Orbis, 1998.

Ruether, Rosemary R. *Sexismo e religião: Rumo a uma teologia feminista*. Translated by Walter Altamann and Luís Marcos Sander. São Leopoldo: Sinodal, 1993.

Salazar, Vitalino Similox. "The Invasion of Christianity into the World of the Mayas." In *Crosscurrents in Indigenous Spirituality: Interface of Maya, Catholic and Protestant Worldviews*, edited by Guillermo Cook, 35–48. Leiden: Brill, 1997.

Samovar, Larry A., Richard E. Porter, and Edwin R. McDaniel. *Communication between Cultures*. Belmont, CA: Thompson/Wadsworth, 2007.

Sanneh, Lamin. *Whose Religion Is Christianity?* Grand Rapids: Eerdmans, 2003.

Santa Ana, Julio de. "The Ecumenical Movement at the Crossroads." *Student World* 1 (2003): 11–23.

_____. *Ecumenismo e Libertação: Reflexão sobre a relação entre unidade cristã e o Reino de Deus*. Petrópolis: Vozes, 1987.

Scott, James C. *Domination and the Arts of Resistance: Hidden Transcripts.* Ann Arbor, MI: Yale University Press, 1990.

Segovia, Fernando. "Mapping the Postcolonial Optic in Biblical Criticism: Meaning and Scope." In *Postcolonial Biblical Criticism: Interdisciplinary Intersections*, edited by Stephen D. Moore and Fernando Segovia. London: T & T Clark, 2005.

Segundo, Juan Luis. *Liberación de la teología.* Buenos Aires: Ediciones Carlos Lohlé, 1975.

_____. *O Dogma que Liberta*: Fé, *Revelação e Magistério Dogmático.* São Paulo: Paulinas, 1991.

_____. *Teologia Aberta para o Leigo Adulto.* São Paulo: Loyola, 1976.

_____. *Teología de la liberación: Respuesta al Cardenal Ratzinger.* Madrid: Ediciones Cristiandad, 1985.

Senior, Donald. "Beloved Aliens and Exiles." In *A Promised Land, a Perilous Journey: Theological Perspectives on Migration*, edited by Daniel G. Groody and Gioacchino Campese. Notre Dame, IN: University of Notre Dame Press, 2009.

Severino Croatto, José. *Exodus, a Hermeneutics of Freedom.* Maryknoll, NY: Orbis, 1981.

Shaull, Richard. *Hombre, ideología y revolución en América Latina,* Montevideo: ISAL, 1965.

Sheerattan-Bisnauth, Patricia, and Philip Vinod Peacock, eds. *Created in God's Image: From Hegemony to Partnership; Church Manual on Men as Partners: Promoting Positive Masculinities.* Geneva: World Council of Churches, World Communion of Reformed Churches, 2010, menengage.org/wp-content/uploads/2014/07/PositiveMasculinitiesGender-Manual_0.pdf.

Sheers, Owen. *The Dust Diaries.* London: Faber & Faber, 2005.

Silva Gotay, Samuel. *El pensamiento cristiano revolucionario en América Latina: Implicaciones de la teología de la liberación para la sociología de la religión.* Salamanca: Ediciones Sígueme, 1981.

Simmank, Lothar. "Männer glauben anders." *Blick in die Kirche*, April 2012, p. 6.

Smit, Dirkie. *Essays in Public Theology: Collected Essays 1* (Stellenbosch: African Sun Media, 2007).

Sobrino, Jon. *La fe en Jesucristo: Ensayo desde las víctimas.* San Salvador: UCA, 1999.

_____. *Jesucristo liberador: Lectura histórico teológica de Jesús de Nazaret.* San Salvador: UCA, 1991.

Sölle, Dorothee. *Politische Theologie: Auseinandersetzung mit Rudolf Bultmann.* Stuttgart: Kreuz-Verlag, 1971.

Sozialwissenschaftliches Institut der Evangelischen Kirche in Deutschland (EKD). *Männer in Kirche und Gemeinde.* November 8, 2013, https://www.si-ekd.de/download/Maenner_in_Kirche_Gemeinde.pdf.

Straehle, Christine, and Patti T. Lenard. "The Ethics of Migration: Introduction." *Journal of International Political Theory* 8, nos. 1–2 (2012): 118–20.

Stroher, Marga J. "A história de uma história: O protagonismo das mulheres na teologia feminista." *História Unisinos* 9, no. 2 (2005).

Tan, Jonathan Y., and Anh Q. Tran, eds. *World Christianity: Perspectives and Insights.* Maryknoll, NY: Orbis, 2016.

Taylor, Mark L. "Duas Palestras Sobre Teologia Publica." In *Religiao e Sociedade (Pos)Secular*, edited by Wanderley Pereira da Rosa and Osvaldo Luiz Ribeiro. Santo Andre, Brazil: Edotira Unida, 2014.

Teles, Maria Amélia de Almeida. "Feminismo no Brasil: Trajetória e perspectivas." In *Gênero e teologia: Interpelações e perspectivas perspectivas*, ed. SOTER. São Paulo: Loyola, Paulinas, 2004.

Temple, William. *The Church Looks Forward.* New York: Macmillan, 1944.

Tomkins, Stephen. *David Livingstone: The Unexplored Story.* Oxford: Lion, 2013.

Travis, Alan. "UK Axes Support for Mediterranean Migrant Rescue Operation." *Guardian*, October 27, 2014.

Ulrich, Claudete Beise. "Recuperando espaços de emancipação na história de vida de ex-alunas de escola comunitária luterana." PhD diss. Available at http://dspace.est.edu.br:8080/xmlui/handle/BR-SlFE/25. São Leopoldo: Faculdades EST, 2006.

Valentin, Benjamin. *Mapping Public Theology: Beyond Culture, Identity, and Difference.* Harrisburg, PA: Trinity Press International, 2002.

van Liempt, Ilse, and Veronica Bilger, eds. *The Ethics of Migration Research Methodology: Dealing with Vulnerable Immigrants.* Sussex: Sussex Academic, 2009.

Vasquez, Manuel. "Rethinking Mestizaje." In *Rethinking Latino(a) Religion and Identity*, edited by Miguel de La Torre and Gaston Espinosa, 129–57. Cleveland: Pilgrim, 2006).

Vigil, José María, ed. *Bajar de la Cruz a los Pobres: Cristología de la Liberación.* Mexico City: Ediciones Dabar, 2007.

Vilanova, Evangelista. *Para Compreender a Teologia*. São Paulo: Paulinas, 1998.

Volz, Rainer. "Studie: Männer im Aufbruch. Männliche Identitäten, Rollenbilder und Geschlechterverhältnisse." In *Mannsbilder: Kritische Männerforschung und theologische Frauenforschung im Gespräch*, edited by Marie Therese Wacker and Stefanie Rieger Goertz. Berlin: Lit, 2006.

Wagua, Aiban. "Present Consequences of the European Invasion of America." In *The Voice of the Victims*, edited by Leonardo Boff and Virgil Elizondo, 47–56. London: SCM, 1991.

Walls, Andrew F. *The Cross-Cultural Process in Christian History: Studies in the Transmission and Appropriation of Faith*. Maryknoll, NY: Orbis, 2002.

_____. "Mission and Migration: The Diaspora Factor in Christian History." *Journal of African Christian Thought* 5, no. 2 (December 2002).

_____. *The Missionary Movement in Christian History: Studies in the Transmission of Faith*. Maryknoll, NY: Orbis, 1996.

Walzer, Michael. *Spheres of Justice: A Defence of Pluralism and Equality*. Oxford: Robertson, 1983.

Whiteman, Darrell L. "Contextualization: The Theory, the Gap, and the Challenge." *International Bulletin of Missionary Research* 21, no. 1 (1997): 2–7.

Wicks, Jeff. "KZN Xenophobic Violence Spreads to KwaMashu." *News24*, April 13, 2015, www.news24.com/SouthAfrica/News/KZN-xenophobic-violence-spreads-to-KwaMashu-20150413.

Wilfred, Felix. "Christianity between Decline and Resurgence." In *Christianity in Crisis?*, edited by Jon Sobrino and Felix Wilfred. *Concilium* 3. London: SCM, 2005.

Witte, John. *The Reformation of Rights: Law, Religion and Human Rights in Early Modern Calvinism*. Cambridge: Cambridge University Press, 2007.

Wood, Matthew R. "Public Religions and Civil Society: The Case of London Methodism." *Fieldwork in Religion* 1, no. 3 (2005): 235–51.

Zapata-Barrero, Ricard. "Theorizing State Behaviour in International Migrations: An Evaluative Ethical Framework." *Social Research* 77 (2010): 325–52.

Zapata-Barrero, Ricard, and Antoine Pécoud. "New Perspectives on the Ethics of International Migration." *American Behavioral Scientist* 56, no. 9 (2012): 1159–64.

"ZCC_Response_Constitutional_Judgement.pdf," Google Docs, accessed July 6, 2016.

Zeleza, Paul. "Contemporary African Migrations in a Global Context." *African Issues* 30, no. 1 (2002).

Index